THE LUFTWAFFE: A History

PEN & SWORD MILITARY CLASSICS

We hope you enjoy your Pen and Sword Military Classic. The series is designed to give readers quality military history at affordable prices. Below is a list of the titles that are planned for 2003. Pen and Sword Classics are available from all good bookshops. If you would like to keep in touch with further developments in the series, including information on the Classics club, then please contact Pen and Sword at the address below.

2003 List

Series No.		
	JANUARY	
1	The Bowmen of England	*Donald Featherstone*
2	The Life & Death of the Afrika Korps	*Ronald Lewin*
3	The Old Front Line	*John Masefield*
4	Wellington & Napoleon	*Robin Neillands*
	FEBRUARY	
5	Beggars in Red	*John Strawson*
6	The Luftwaffe: A History	*John Killen*
7	Siege: Malta 1940-1943	*Ernle Bradford*
	MARCH	
8	Hitler as Military Commander	*John Strawson*
9	Nelson's Battles	*Oliver Warner*
10	The Western Front 1914-1918	*John Terraine*
	APRIL	
11	The Killing Ground	*Tim Travers*
12	The War Walk	*Nigel Jones*
	MAY	
13	Dictionary of the First World War	*Pope & Wheal*
14	1918: The Last Act	*Barrie Pitt*
	JUNE	
15	Hitler's Last Offensive	*Peter Elstob*
16	Naval Battles of World War Two	*Geoffrey Bennett*
	JULY	
17	Omdurman	*Philip Ziegler*
18	Strike Hard, Strike Sure	*Ralph Barker*
	AUGUST	
19	The Black Angels	*Rupert Butler*
20	The Black Ship	*Dudley Pope*
	SEPTEMBER	
21	The Fight for the Malvinas	*Martin Middlebrook*
22	The Narrow Margin	*Wood & Dempster*
	OCTOBER	
23	Vimy	*Pierre Berton*
24	Warfare in the Age of Bonaparte	*Michael Glover*
	NOVEMBER	
25	Dictionary of the Second World War	*Pope & Wheal*
26	Not Ordinary Men	*John Colvin*

PEN AND SWORD BOOKS LTD

47 Church Street • Barnsley • South Yorkshire • S70 2AS

Tel: 01226 734555 • 734222

E-mail: enquiries@pen-and-sword.co.uk • **Website:** www.pen-and-sword.co.uk

JOHN KILLEN

THE LUFTWAFFE:
A History

PEN & SWORD MILITARY CLASSICS

First published in Great Britain in 1967 by Frederick Muller Ltd
Published in 2003, in this format, by
PEN & SWORD MILITARY CLASSICS
an imprint of
Pen & Sword Books Limited
47, Church Street
Barnsley
S. Yorkshire
S70 2AS

The publishers have made every effort to trace the author, his estate and his agent without success and they would be interested to hear from anyone who is able to provide them with this information.

ISBN 0 85052 925 5

A CIP record for this book is
available from the British Library

Printed in England by
CPI UK

CONTENTS

ILLUSTRATIONS

FOREWORD

by Marshal of the Royal Air Force, Sir John Slessor, G.C.B., D.S.O., M.C.

THE Germans are exceedingly efficient men of war—temperamentally, tactically and technically, and on land, at sea and in the air—as we know to our bitter cost in two world wars. Fortunately for us there have been fatal flaws in their system for higher strategic direction in both wars, but especially the second. Field Marshal Smuts, in a moment of relaxed rumination, once said to me, "You know—it's the greatest mistake to imagine that it's great victories that win wars. On the contrary—it's the great blunders. We ought to put up a statue in Trafalgar Square to Hitler for having been such a fool as to attack Russia."

Readers of this book may reflect that in the air war Hitler was indeed our secret weapon—ably abetted by Hermann Goering. After our near-fatal blindness and prevarication in the locust years before 1939, it would have gone ill with us had not the efforts of the RAF been supplemented by the colossal blunders of the egregious Reichsmarschall and his crazy master. One's heart almost bleeds for the senior commanders of the Luftwaffe—many of them very capable Generals as well as brave fighting men—subject as they were to the follies and misjudgements of the man who had been a fine fighter leader in the First World War but was such an unbelievably incompetent Commander-in-Chief in the second.

It was as well for us that the basic German concept of war was still rooted in Army tradition. The battle of Britain might have been a very different story had the Nazis followed up and developed the astonishingly advanced techniques of "strategic" air warfare initiated by the old Imperial Air Force in their attacks on Britain a quarter of a century earlier. The personnel of the Luftwaffe were brave and determined; the scientific and technical backing was excellent; the organisation, with its emphasis on mobility and flexibility, was basically sound. Its tactics as the spearhead of Blitzkrieg in France in 1940 and in Russia in 1941 were devastatingly effective; this sort of thing wins battles : it does not in itself win wars.

The Luftwaffe had too much to contend with—and not only, in the end, a World in Arms. From Goering's first fatal decision to switch from attacks on our radar stations during the Battle of Britain, to Hitler's God-sent inspiration to transform the ME 262 jet fighter into a bomber four years later, it was constantly thwarted and frustrated by almost unbelievable ineptitude at the highest levels.

All this is well described in Mr. Killen's most readable book, which should certainly find a place on the shelves of all senior officers of the Nato Air Forces.

J. C. SLESSOR

CHAPTER I

AIRCRAFT AND ACES: 1914-1916

ON a bright August morning in 1915 a young German airman dived his single-seater scout monoplane out of the summer clouds over the Western Front. The English biplane beneath him swerved away at once, but too late; the single fixed machine-gun of the Fokker monoplane stammered briefly, stopped, then stammered again. The acrid scent of cordite fumes in his nostrils, the German pilot turned in his seat, watching with surprise as the enemy machine faltered in the air. Slowly at first, then rapidly gaining speed, it drifted lazily towards the earth below. Leutnant Max Immelmann, the German pilot, saw the biplane land heavily in a field, and knew then that he had gained his first victory. Later, he would have many other victories, and still later become known as the Eagle of Lille, but Immelmann would never equal his first achievement as a fighting airman. On that day in 1915 he unwittingly fulfilled the true purpose of a German fighter aircraft for the first time.

When the assassination of Archduke Franz Ferdinand of Austria and his consort in Sarajevo on 28th June, 1914, precipitated Europe into the wholesale slaughter that was to last for four long and weary years, Germany, in common with her opponents, was totally unprepared for war in the air. Eleven years after Orville and Wilbur Wright had made history at Kitty Hawk the aeroplane still remained something of a novelty to the narrow military mind. It was considered to be of little use except perhaps in a reconnaissance or observation role, secondary even to the splendid cavalry that would play such an unimportant part in this modern war.

Nevertheless, an Austrian, Igo Etrich, had already provided the basis for the future Imperial German Air Force. In 1908, he designed an attractive monoplane which became known as the Taube—or Dove—because of its graceful sweeping form and the remarkable resemblance it bore to a bird in flight. After various early flying successes, including an altitude record of

20,000 ft., Etrich sold the rights of his monoplane to the German Government, who handed the design to the Rumpler factory at Berlin-Litchtenberg for development. The twenty Taubes produced by the Rumpler concern proved to be such outstanding aircraft that eventually a number of other factories began manufacturing the little monoplanes, and by 1914 more than half of the total aeroplanes assigned for use with the German armies were of that type.

When von Kluck's forces surged across Belgium and north-east France during the night of 4th August, 1914, Germany could muster some thirty-eight airships and about eight hundred assorted aeroplanes, all unarmed, and including the cumbersome L.V.G., Albatros and D.F.W. two-seater biplanes, which were later to prove so slow and unwieldy in action. These air units were distributed along the front in batches of six aircraft, known as Feldfliegerabteilungen, and were reserved for use in a reconnaissance or photography role, as had been anticipated. The Feldfliegerabteilungen were organised within the German Army on a basis of one to each Army H.Q., and also one to each Army Corps. Various experiments to provide a successful aircraft armament continued to be ignored by the German High Command, who simply failed to envisage the aeroplane as a fighting weapon. The carrying of pistols or rifles into the air thus became a normal practice during the first year of war.

The two-seater heavy biplanes, carrying a pilot and observer, and known as "B" machines, were the aircraft commonly used for reconnaissance purposes during 1914. Later, when these mounted a Parabellum machine-gun for rearward defence, they were designated as "C" machines. The little single-seater "A" machines, mostly Taube monoplanes, were particularly suitable for reconnaissance when advantage was taken of their fast, high-flying qualities, and Max Immelmann flew over Paris in a Rumpler model in the autumn of 1914 and dropped a note on the city calling upon the people to surrender. Strange as it may seem, history records that on both sides a well-aimed rifle bullet would occasionally find a target—Oberleutnant Reinhold Jahnow, Germany's first pilot to be killed in action, fell on 12th August, 1914—but in those early days of military aviation casualties in the air were the exception rather than the rule.

Then, in 1915, the Fokker E.1 monoplane appeared over the Western Front, and immediately the fighter aircraft was born. As used by Max Immelmann, Oswald Boelcke, and later a number of other famous German airmen, the small 80-h.p. Eindecker monoplane designed by a young Dutch engineer named Anthony Fokker created a milestone in the history of aviation. Of surprisingly conventional appearance, but with an excellent performance, the true secret of the Fokker monoplane's amazing success lay in its armament, which completely revolutionised aerial fighting and achieved within the space of a few weeks unlimited supremacy for the German air forces in the field.

After examining a captured French Morane monoplane fitted with a primitive form of interrupter gear invented by an engineer named Eugene Gilbert, and used with some success by the pilot of the Morane, Roland Garros, Fokker designed a greatly improved mechanism which enabled a rigid forward-firing machine-gun to fire through the arc of an aeroplane air-screw without the bullets striking the blades. For the first time, a pilot could aim his aircraft directly at the enemy, using it as a steady gun platform; consequently the unsuspecting Allied reconnaissance biplanes with their clumsy rearward-firing Lewis guns were bound to suffer increasing losses. The peaceful early months of the war in the air had abruptly ended, and the un-armed Taubes and Aviatiks of 1914 were already fading away into the mists of time.

The new single-seater Fokker monoplanes were carefully allotted to only the most experienced German pilots, and origin-ally distributed on a basis of two fighters to each existing Fliegerabteilungen for protection of the slow two-seater obser-vation biplanes. However, the Aviation Staff Officer of the 6th Army, Major Stempel, quickly saw that the monoplanes could be used to better purpose if they were formed into definite fighter units, and, on his own initiative, commenced a reorgani-sation of the machines in his own area. At about the same time that Major Stempel ordered the formation of three units of fighter monoplanes at Douai, General Ludendorff decided that the air forces had now grown to such an extent that it was time for them to break away from the Army; this eventually led, with the Kaiser's approval, to the establishment of the Deutschen

Luftstreitkrafte, or German Air Force, with General von Hoeppner placed in command. Slowly but surely, military aviation was coming into its own.

The three single-seater fighter units, or Kampfeinsitzerkommandos, organised by Major Stempel, immediately began to prove their worth in action, and two Fokker monoplane pilots, Max Immelmann and Oswald Boelcke, began the steady rise to fame later to earn them Germany's highest award for valour, the *Ordre Pour le Mérite*, while operating from Douai. During the long winter of 1915 and the spring of 1916, they and the other Eindecker pilots waged a bitter and unceasing war against the depleted Allied observation aircraft; yet the persistently offensive policy of the Royal Flying Corps continued to carry its machines relentlessly into the enemy skies, regardless of the odds that faced them. In the early months of 1916 two new British aircraft, the De Havilland 2 scout and the F.E.2b two-seater fighter, appeared on the Western Front to challenge the German air supremacy. Both were pusher-engined machines, fitted with free forward-firing Lewis guns, a partial answer to the yet unsolved mystery of Anthony Fokker's interrupter mechanism. A little French sesquiplane scout, the Nieuport 17, came into action about the same time, and in the hands of such outstanding airmen as Albert Ball and Georges Guynemer fought, outflew, and gradually destroyed the Fokker menace. With it, in the summer of 1916, passed Max Immelmann, the Eagle of Lille, the monoplane he was flying shaken to pieces by a faulty engine.

On the morning of 1st July, 1916, the incredible weight of shellfire that had pounded the German trenches for a full week reached a climax of fire and steel, raining down death and destruction at a rate hitherto unequalled in war. As the British infantry went over the top, wave after wave, and the German machine-guns broke the brief silence with their heavy repeating clamour, the Royal Flying Corps rose to find an unchallenged sky. Ten thousand feet below, the running khaki figures struggled forward until they fell like corn before the scythe, their voices drowned for ever by the merciless hammering of the guns; but that first day of the tragic Somme offensive remained unforgettably quiet and serene for the men who fought in the air.

It could not last, of course. Oswald Boelcke, the young Saxon schoolmaster's son who had achieved such success with the Fokker monoplane over Verdun, had already suggested the formation of new units, to be known as Jagdstaffeln, elite squadrons whose only purpose would be to invite combat and regain the initiative from the Allies. Boelcke was much more than an outstanding fighter pilot; he was also a brilliant strategist, whose tactics for waging a successful air war would later prove as sound in the Battle of Britain as they did during the weary struggle of the Somme. After an inspection of the South-eastern Front, he returned to Douai to find that his suggestions had been fully approved by the High Command, and he was ordered to supervise the formation of two fighting squadrons. Jagdstaffel 1, commanded by a Hauptmann Zander, came into being on 23rd August, 1916, and a week later Jagdstaffel 2, under Boelcke, was formed at Lagaicourt. The man who had fought at the side of Max Immelmann lost no time in turning his pupils into expert fighter pilots; Werner Voss, Erwin Boehme, and young Leutnant Manfred von Richthofen were three of the novices who listened to the wisdom of Boelcke and later found glory because they remembered it. Two new types of single-seater biplane fighter aircraft were introduced almost simultaneously to the new Jagdstaffeln, or Jasta, as they were often known. The Halberstadt D.II, the first German biplane to be fitted with twin synchronised machine-guns, was destined to be brilliantly but only temporarily successful. Faster than the D.H.2 it opposed, it was nevertheless not easy to control, and required the skilful hands of an experienced pilot, yet at the same time it did much to regain Germain air supremacy in the autumn of 1916. The Albatros D.I was faster and more manoeuvrable than any Allied aircraft in service at the time. Fitted with the same armament as the Halberstadt, the Albatros was a much more attractive design, with a streamlined fuselage remarkable for the period, a rounded airscrew spinner, and powered by a 160 h.p. Mercedes engine. In later versions, which were the backbone of the German fighter forces until 1918, the struts were altered to the famous Vee layout already in use on the French Nieuport 17, and to be seen a year later on the Pfalz D.III.

On 17th September Boelcke led Jasta 2 into action for the

first time. With him in the formation was Manfred von Richthofen, then twenty-two years of age. The son of a Prussian aristocrat, he had transferred from the Uhlans to the Air Force in the first year of war, and a chance encounter with Boelcke, who was impressed by his boyish enthusiasm, quickly led to his transfer from the Russian theatre of operations to the Western Front. The slow two-seater aircraft that Jasta 2 met that day proved to be hopelessly inadequate to face the new Albatros scouts, and the brilliant strategy of Oswald Boelcke, so often imparted to his willing pupils, sent six F.E.2b and two B.E.2c machines to the shell-torn earth below. Richthofen destroyed an F.E2b manned by Second Lieutenant Morris and Lieutenant Rees, his first victory in a battle which was destined to be the prelude to bitter fighting between Jasta 2 and the Royal Flying Corps.

As the warm September days slid by the new Jagdstaffeln gained experience in a baptism of fire that might well have consumed them, and during October the air fighting continued without respite for either side until by the 17th of that month Boelcke had shot down thirty-five enemy aircraft. Then, on 28th October, Jasta 2 suffered a tragic loss when Germany's most outstanding fighter pilot, the idol of a nation, was killed. That ill-fated afternoon, Oswald Boelcke led his formation into battle against some D.H.2s of No. 24 Squadron, Royal Flying Corps. Together with Erwin Boehme, who was flying alongside him, Boelcke dived in pursuit of one British machine, then abruptly banked away when another D.H.2, hammered by Richthofen's guns, hurtled across his line of sight. Boehme's aircraft swerved, then touched Boelcke's black Albatros, which staggered away with the interplane struts and upper wing collapsed and breaking asunder. Slowly but surely it fell into a spin, and plunged headlong to earth near Bapaume. So passed Oswald Boelcke, the man responsible for turning a collection of men and machines into efficient fighting squadrons, and then outlining the tactics that would regain Germany the air supremacy that her defensive policy so badly needed. His instructions—the famous dicta of Boelcke—were the most valuable legacy any airman could leave to his successors, and perhaps his greatest achievement was the way in which they so unfailingly stood the test of time.

By Imperial decree, Jasta 2 was named Jasta Boelcke after the death of its leader. Leutnant Stephen Kirmaier assumed command of the Jagdstaffel, but was killed in action within a month; Hauptmann Waltz was his successor. While the air battles raged unceasingly over the Somme during the winter of 1916-1917, the whole German Air Force was undergoing a complete reorganisation, which eventually led to the distribution of all the existing Feldfliegerabteilungen into definite fighter, bomber, reconnaissance or photography units. Thus, as the fighting squadrons, or Jagdstaffeln, increased in numbers, at the same time battle flights, known as Schutzstaffeln, and bombing units, designated Bombenstaffeln, came into existence.

Meanwhile, the Royal Flying Corps offensive continued unabated, despite rising casualties and the vital need for faster single-seater aircraft. On 23rd November, Major Lanoe George Hawker, holder of the Victoria Cross and a contemporary of Oswald Boelcke, fell to the guns of Manfred von Richthofen; he was the eleventh victim of the man soon to be Germany's leading air ace. The indomitable spirit of the Allied airmen at that time was typified by Captain Albert Ball, already recognised along the front as one of the most outstanding British fighter pilots. He had taken part in twenty-three battles within the space of a fortnight, and was utterly exhausted when he reluctantly agreed to return to England for a rest, only a few weeks before the useless struggle for the Somme finally died away in the November of 1916.

The year closed with the hopeful introduction of a new British single-seater fighter biplane, the Sopwith Pup, which not only featured a synchronised forward-firing Vickers machine-gun but also had a performance that easily matched the speed and manoeuvrability of the Albatros D.III scouts then opposing the Royal Flying Corps. Nevertheless, neither the Pup nor the latest French scout, the Spad, which had also made an appearance, were the decisive air weapons the Allies needed, and many months would pass before the adversaries of the German Air Force were in a position to meet it on equal terms.

The German Naval Air Service came into being in 1912 as an essential part of the Imperial Navy, and a year later was divided into an airship section, known as the Marine Luftschiffabteilung, and an aeroplane and seaplane section, designated the Marine Fliegerabteilung. Due to the great interest and enthusiasm that the huge Zeppelin dirigibles mistakenly engendered in the German people before the war, the Naval Air Service in 1914 possessed only about twenty aeroplanes and a few seaplanes, and the Marine Fliegerabteilung continued to be neglected as a fighting service until 1917, when the remarkable Hansa-Brandenburg seaplanes designed by Ernst Heinkel were introduced, proving highly successful in many an air action over the North Sea.

Germany commenced her airship offensive against England in 1915, with a number of scattered bombing attacks on the coastal and rural areas. These early onslaughts, mostly made by naval dirigibles, were largely ineffective, but as the raids increased, it became obvious to the British War Office that the situation called for an immediate reorganisation of the sadly insufficient ground and air defences. To this end, anti-aircraft guns and night-flying aircraft appeared for the protection of London near the end of the year, and these, particularly the aeroplanes, eventually mastered the huge and awe-inspiring Zeppelins acclaimed by Germany as instruments of wholesale destruction.

However, in 1915 the airships remained a definite threat to an uncertain London. The latest type of Zeppelin in use at that time had an internal keel gangway, three gondolas mounting a number of machine-guns, balanced monoplane rudders and elevators, and was powered by four heavy Maybach engines. On the night of 8th-9th September, 1915, the L.13, commanded by Kapitanleutnant Heinrich Mathy, perhaps the most resolute officer in the Luftschiffabteilung, bombed London and caused widespread damage, at the same time inflicting a number of civilian casualties. After three Zeppelins had again reached the capital in the October, Britain strengthened her home front defences, but both naval and military airships continued to attack London with some success until the late summer of 1916, when the first German airship to fall on English soil was shot down.

The Shutte-Lanz wooden-framed dirigible SL.11 was cruising over the London area on the night of 2nd-3rd September, 1916, heedless of the searchlights that probed the sky all around her, when Lieutenant W. Leefe Robinson, flying a B.E.2c biplane, dived to the attack. As he sped along the vast length of the airship he fired two drums of alternate Brock and Pomeroy explosive and incendiary ammunition into her, without any noticeable effect, and then emptied a third drum into one spot at the rear of the dirigible. Immediately, the ill-fated SL.11 erupted into a roaring mass of flame that turned the night sky brighter than any day, then tilted and plunged blazing to earth at Cuffley, in Middlesex, with the loss of all sixteen members of her crew.

The destruction of the Shutte-Lanz airship proved to be the beginning of the end for the Zeppelins. Later in September, two more of the great lighter-than-air craft were shot down, and then on the night of 1st-2nd October, the L.31, commanded by the famous Heinrich Mathy, was attacked by Second Lieutenant W. J. Tempest, who was based at North Weald. Undeterred by the heavy machine-gun fire directed at him from the airship's gondolas, Tempest dived towards the Zeppelin, raking her with burst after burst of the devastating Brock and Pomeroy ammunition. "As I was firing," he reported afterwards, "I noticed her begin to go red inside like an enormous Chinese lantern. She shot up about two hundred feet, paused, and came roaring down straight on to me before I had time to get out of the way. I nose-dived for all I was worth, with the Zeppelin tearing after me . . . I put my machine into a spin and just managed to corkscrew out of the way as she shot past me, roaring like a furnace." The Zeppelin fell at Potters Bar, and the life of Kapitanleutnant Heinrich Mathy was ended.

During the last airship raid of 1916 eight Zeppelins reached England. One, the L.34, was shot down into the sea near Hartlepool by Second Lieutenant I. V. Pyott; another, the L.21, was hit by anti-aircraft fire and eventually fell to pieces in the air while attempting to struggle back to her home base. Thus by the end of the year the airship offensive was almost ended, although Fregatten-Kapitan Peter Strasser, the man who had done much to organise the raids on London and the provinces, could look back on a not inconsiderable achievement. Anti-aircraft guns and aeroplanes urgently needed in France had been compelled to remain in England for defence of the home front, and during the airship attacks the transport of vital raw materials and munitions had been reduced almost to a standstill. However, the actual bombing results had never really justified the expenditure on such large and vulnerable aircraft.

The Super Zeppelins, monster dirigibles powered by six engines, were the ultimate development of the airships specifically designed to attack London. When these appeared, late in 1916, the German High Command already realised that the Royal Flying Corps, the Royal Naval Air Service and the ground defences had proved the airship by no means the decisive weapon it had at first seemed. It therefore decided to reduce the number of Zeppelin raids in the future; at the same time some consideration was given to the possibility of bombing London with multi-engined aeroplanes. These raids by formations of long-range bombers were later to be surprisingly effective, and 1917 was destined to be a very successful year for many different operational units of the now highly efficient German Imperial Air Force.

CHAPTER II

YEAR OF ATTRITION: 1917

MANFRED FREIHERR VON RICHTHOFEN shot down his sixteenth victory, one of the new Sopwith Pup scouts, on 4th January, 1917, and less than two weeks later was awarded the blue Maltese Cross edged with gold of the *Ordre Pour le Mérite*. Almost at once, as congratulations poured in from all over Germany, he became a popular hero of the people; but 1917 was to be a year of many heroes, and Richthofen to be but one star in a glittering galaxy of splendid men.

As Richthofen left the distinguished company of Jasta Boelcke later in January to take over his first command, Jagdstaffel 11, at Douai, the Royal Flying Corps was still struggling desperately to recover from the heavy casualties it had suffered during the Battle of the Somme. Some thirty-five British squadrons, having 550 aeroplanes, were now in the field, despite the losses sustained in the autumn of 1916, but the Albatros and Halberstadt fighters of the Jagdstaffeln remained vastly superior in every way to the aircraft that opposed them. This delay in the production of first-class Allied machines, together with the strong westerly wind over the front, which so often meant a long slow struggle home for the R.F.C. pilots after a battle, were the two important factors that gave the advantage to such skilled and determined airmen as Richthofen and Werner Voss, and the Jagdstaffeln seldom failed to leave behind a trail of casualties.

The air fighting that was now a daily occurrence rose to an appalling pitch of intensity over the shell-torn battlefields of Arras in April, 1917, the month that was later to be remembered bitterly by the Royal Flying Corps as "Bloody April" and high-lighted by the loss of no less than 140 British machines, mostly obsolescent two-seaters of the F.E.2b and B.E.2c type. Manfred von Richthofen had the most halcyon days of his career that month; on the 28th April he shot down five British aircraft between dawn and dusk, and established without a doubt that

Jasta 11 was now a definite menace to the Royal Flying Corps. Also, Richthofen was the man responsible for shaking British confidence in a new fighter that had just been introduced, the Bristol F2B two-seater.

The Bristol F2B fighter, powered by a 275 h.p. Rolls-Royce Falcon engine, was a sturdy and excellent biplane, in many ways superior to the Albatros single-seater, and heavily armed with a synchronised forward-firing Vickers machine-gun and twin Lewis guns in the rear cockpit for the use of the observer. Nevertheless, it was an aircraft that required skilful handling and considerable experience by the pilot before it could be used to the best advantage in a dogfight, and initial unfamiliarity with the new machine gave it an unfortunate baptism of fire.

Six Bristol fighters of No. 48 Squadron, Royal Flying Corps, led by Captain W. Leefe Robinson, V.C., who had destroyed the first Zeppelin to fall on English soil less than a year ago, crossed the lines that ill-fated April afternoon in 1917. Almost at once they encountered five Albatros fighters, which hurtled down to meet them with deadly efficiency. Manfred von Richthofen, in the leading Albatros, opened a continuous fire on the nearest Bristol, which immediately spun down out of control. Meanwhile the dog-fight raged around him, and when the battle ended three more Bristols had been destroyed and the two who remained were staggering slowly home. Leefe Robinson managed to land his bullet-riddled machine behind the German lines and remained in captivity until the end of the war. The confident début of the Bristol fighter had turned in the space of a few moments into a tragic disaster, and Richthofen had no hesitation in reporting afterwards that the new British aircraft was a complete failure.

In the event, the Bristol fighter proved to be one of the most successful aeroplanes to appear during the Great War, and it later did much to regain the air supremacy for the Allies. With trained pilots and observers working together in close co-opera-tion, and using fighter tactics evolved in the light of experience, it became able to tackle the best German single-seaters, whose pilots for some time unwittingly continued to treat it with con-tempt, and quickly paid the price for their recklessness. Over 1,700 Bristol fighters were in action by the end of the war, and the type demonstrated its usefulness to the extreme by remaining in service with the Royal Air Force until 1930.

However, by the first week of May, when Richthofen returned to Germany on leave, the Bristol fighters had not arrived at the front in sufficient quantities to make any difference to the air situation, although towards the end of April the very fast new British single-seater scout, the S.E.5, had also been reported in action. By this time Germany had thirty-seven Jagdstaffeln dispersed about the front, but with the entry of the United States into the Great War, it was obvious that when the un-limited resources of America's material and manpower reached the Western Front a much stronger and larger German Air Force would be needed. At the same time, the tried and trusted Albatros would soon have to be replaced by a faster type of machine.

Aware that a reversal of the present situation might well already be developing, General von Hoeppner, the Commander of the Air Service, or Kommandierender General Der Luft-streitkrafte, held a conference with his senior staff officers which decided upon a general development and expansion programme for the whole German Air Force. This was formally adopted by the Supreme Command on 26th June, 1917, and on the same day Jastas 4, 6, 10 and 11 were grouped together as a single fighting unit, or Jagdgeschwader.

It was only to be expected that Manfred von Richthofen would be appointed commander of the four grouped Jagdstaf-feln. Based at Courtrai, the duties of Jagdgeschwader 1 were simple, and yet of vital importance; to maintain air supremacy in any sectors of the front as might be directed from time to time by the strategy of the High Command. To ensure complete mobility at all times, a liberal establishment of motor transport was provided.

Richthofen quickly set to work to turn his already élite units into a single powerful and decisive formation that would earn the respect of the Royal Flying Corps over the whole Western Front. He had flown a distinctive scarlet-painted Albatros since his early days with Jasta Boelcke, and all the machines of his first command, Jasta 11, had adopted the same brilliant colour, with the exception of the nose, wings, or tailplanes, which had a contrasting individual design for each pilot. Now the idea was introduced to the new Richthofen Geschwader, and the great variety of bizarre colour schemes which ensued, together with the way in which the Geschwader began to move about the front in accordance with the circumstances at the time, soon established for it the lasting nickname of Richthofen's Circus. Yet at the same time Richthofen's underlying purpose was achieved; red became a memorable colour to his opponents during the summer of 1917, and they were seldom in any doubt that the gaily painted Albatros scouts they so often encountered held the proudest and most efficient pilots in the German Air Force.

Then, just as the new Geschwader was organised on an operational basis, Richthofen himself was shot down. In a fight with six F.E.2d two-seaters and four Sopwith Pup single-seaters on the morning of 6th July, a bullet grazed his head; blinded by blood and scarcely conscious, he barely managed to land behind his own lines. He made a quick and seemingly perfect recovery, but while he was in hospital the Geschwader had a run of bad luck, and slowly the pendulum of air supremacy began to swing gently over to the Allied side. Also, the tempo of the fighting itself was steadily rising; on 26th July, the day that Richthofen resumed command of Jagdeschwader 1, ninety-four to a hundred machines battled over Polygon Wood, and a bitter engagement was fought using an even larger number the following day.

The Royal Flying Corps continued to take the offensive during the late summer of 1917. The S.E.5 single-seater scout had now established itself as an outstanding fighter, especially in the capable hands of such aces as Mannock, Bishop, and McCudden, and now a successor to the Sopwith Pup, the Sopwith F.1 Camel, was in action over the Western Front. This little machine, probably the best single-seater fighter to appear during the Great War, later gained the distinction of shooting down more enemy aircraft than any other Allied aircraft, and easily outclassed not only the Albatros D.V, but also the new Pfalz D.111, which had been hurriedly rushed to the front as a replacement. To the German airmen who faced these remarkable British fighters, this was a bitter time, and the profitable days of the previous April began to seem nothing more than a pleasant glimpse of what might have been.

Then, on 28th August, the first production batch of an entirely new German fighter arrived on the Western Front. The Fokker Dr I Triplane has sometimes been compared with the Sopwith Camel as the supreme single-seater scout of the First World War because of its brief but highly effective career; however, it sacrificed speed for manoeuvrability and rate of climb, and the Allies never had an opportunity to realise how slow it actually was, owing to its extreme dexterity. Nevertheless, the Fokker Triplane will always be associated with Germany's two leading aces in 1917—Manfred von Richthofen and Werner Voss.

Werner Voss, the son of a Krefeld dye-factory owner, began his military career as an officer in the 2nd Westphalian Hussars, transferring to the flying service in the August of 1915. After seeing some action as an observer, he became a fighter-pilot under the skilful guidance of Oswald Boelcke in 1916, and a year later was a *Pour le Mérite* holder, with twenty victories. As the commander of Jasta 10, he was an obvious competitor with Richthofen for the highest score of enemy aircraft destroyed by a pilot of the Richthofen Geschwader, but Voss was the opposite of the Red Knight in every other way. Richthofen was a strategist, a born leader like Boelcke, who had his own methods of attack and weighed the chances in a dog-fight with calculating precision; Voss always remained a brilliant individualist, a lonely warrior like his English contemporary, Captain Albert Ball, who met his end on the evening of 7th May, 1917, somewhere in a roaring dogfight over Annoeullin. For such a man, the little Fokker Triplane was an ideal machine, and during the few weeks of his life that still remained Voss reached the highest pinnacle of fame while flying the latest Fokker fighter, by shooting down twenty-two British aircraft in twenty-one days.

On 23rd September, with forty-eight victories behind him, Werner Voss crossed the lines in his silvery-blue triplane for the last time. As he dived to attack a lone S.E.5a, six more S.E.5a planes of No. 56 Squadron hurtled down to intercept him, flown by some of Britain's finest fighter pilots, including Major J. T. McCudden, V.C., Lieutenant Cecil Lewis, and the nineteen-year-old Etonian, Lieutenant A. P. Rhys Davids, M.C. The ensuing dogfight has often been considered the most epic air battle of the Great War

The S.E.5s twisted and turned around the skilfully handled Fokker Triplane, their guns firing in short spasmodic bursts, while Voss spun, dived and climbed to evade the pencil lines of tracer that sought to destroy him. For more than ten minutes he managed to elude the stammering enemy guns, avoiding them by a performance of brilliant flying that has seldom been equalled. Then came the inevitable end. Rhys Davids, who had already expended two drums of ammunition without any effect, caught the triplane briefly in his sights and fired again, using both his synchronised Vickers and the Lewis mounted on the upper wing at the same time. Immediately, the silvery-blue triplane turned and glided gently down to earth; Werner Voss, the Flying Hussar, was dead.

A nation mourned for Voss, but perhaps an enemy airman who had seen him fall provided the only epitaph he himself would have wished. Of him, James McCudden wrote afterwards, "As long as I live I shall never forget my admiration of that German pilot, who, single-handed, fought seven of us for ten minutes, and also put some bullets through all our machines. His flying was wonderful, his courage magnificent, and, in my opinion, he was the bravest German airman whom it has been my privilege to fight."

With the brief life of Werner Voss ended, Manfred von Richthofen became Germany's most renowned and leading air ace. Temporarily equipped with the Fokker Triplane, the Geschwader nevertheless continued to be hard-pressed, in common with the whole German Air Force; by 30th September the famous 56 Squadron of the Royal Flying Corps had brought down two hundred black-crossed machines destroyed or out of control.

With the opening of the Battle of Cambrai on 20th November, most of the German Jagdstaffeln were constantly in action, and the winter of 1917 proved to be a bleak period, with a number of casualties. Experienced pilots also began to fall through accidental causes, as the Fokker Triplane now revealed an important defect; in a long dive the canvas tended to tear away from the upper wing, often resulting in the collapse of the entire structure. Consequently the type was withdrawn from service after only a brief appearance on the Western Front, although Richthofen was a convinced exponent of the machine and continued to use an improved and strengthened model presented to him by Anthony Fokker.

It will be recalled that the German Naval Air Service had been sadly neglected as a fighting force for the first two years of the Great War. In 1916 the pilots who had to face the English squadrons over the Channel and the North Sea fought a losing battle against faster, more manoeuvrable and better-armed machines, simply because Germany had failed to produce a fighting seaplane that could match the neat little scout biplanes possessed in such large numbers by the enemy.

The Hansa Brandenburg W 12, a two-seater seaplane designed by Ernst Heinkel, head of the Hansa-Brandenburg Flugzeugwerke, appeared in 1917, and it was this machine that finally broke the English superiority. A biplane of conventional appearance, the W 12 had a high speed and was armed with twin synchronised forward-firing machine-guns and a free machine-gun for the observer's use; looking back over the years, it was not a revolutionary machine, but with it the German naval pilots operating from Zeebrugge and Ostend won command of the air along the Flanders coast, and never again lost it.

The much more remarkable Hansa Brandenburg W 29 monoplane was actually nothing more than a modified W 12 with the upper wing removed and an altered centre section, but it was an even better aircraft than its predecessor in action, having a rate of climb to 3,000 ft. in just under six minutes and a speed of 112 m.p.h. Often, formations of these little fighters would leave the coast and rest on the water many miles out at sea—thus saving petrol—and quietly wait for the big English flying-boats to pass nearby on patrol. Then they would take off and attack the huge boats, with such success that Friedrich Christiansen, the commander of the Zeebrugge air station, soon established himself as an ace while using the W 29.

Aged thirty-seven at the height of his fame, and therefore considered to be an elderly pilot by many of the youngsters who flew out with him from Zeebrugge, Christiansen nevertheless shot down two Curtiss flying-boats in one day, and soon afterwards destroyed three more Curtiss boats in one engagement, which resulted in a written "Bravo" by the Kaiser himself on the margin of the announcement. Christiansen was awarded the coveted *Ordre Pour le Mérite* in December, 1917, and by the end of the war he had twenty-one victories, including aeroplanes, flying-boats, balloons and an airship. During the Second World War he was responsible for the military government of the occupied Netherlands, and although later tried by the Allies for atrocities committed by SS troops in his area and sentenced to a term of imprisonment, was eventually pardoned.

During 1917 and 1918 the Albatros D.III scout was also modified for use as a seaplane, and Rumpler floatplanes were also in service. Ernst Heinkel designed a long sequence of reconnaissance and torpedo floatplanes that were used most successfully in action, but the W 12 biplanes and W 29 monoplanes, often mixed together in large formations, were the machines that led Friedrich Christiansen to glory and at the same time gained complete air superiority over the Channel for the once almost non-existent German Naval Air Service.

During the two years that the Hansa Brandenburg seaplanes fought for the sky, the Zeppelin passed into history as an air weapon. On 16th March, 1917, five airships of the Marine Luftschiffabteilung attempted to bomb London, but were scattered by a heavy gale, and one, the L.39, was destroyed by anti-aircraft fire while drifting helplessly over France. Other raids on the nights of 23rd-24th May and 16th-17th June were equally unsuccessful, although only one Zeppelin, the L.48, was shot down, falling at Theberton in Suffolk. Then, on the night of 19th-20th October, eleven naval airships set forth to attack England; this, the last Zeppelin raid of 1917, was to prove beyond all doubt that the German dreams of a London consumed by flames would not easily be realised.

Slowly gaining height as they passed over the English coast in order to reduce the risk of attack by the watchful air defences, the eleven Zeppelins suddenly found themselves fighting a tremendous gale and had to struggle homeward in a nightmare journey that left a trail of disaster. The L.44, after dropping a few bombs near Elstow, drifted across France and was shot down by anti-aircraft fire; the L.45 dropped some bombs on London, but, swept and tossed by the wind, eventually crashed near Sisteron in southern France; the L.50 passed over the front-line trenches in France, then finally disappeared for ever somewhere far out over the Mediterranean; and the L.49, which also drifted across France, was captured intact after landing near Neufchateau. Thus of the eleven majestic airships that had left Germany on 19th October, four were lost, mastered more by the weather than the British defences, for although seventy-three intercepting pilots were in the air that night, not one of them managed to reach the height at which the Zeppelins flew.

The airship campaign petered out at last during 1918. Only four raids took place that year, and it was during the last of these that Fregatten-Kapitan Peter Strasser, the energetic organiser of the Marine Luftschiffabteilung, met his death. The Zeppelin he commanded, the L.70, was shot down by Major E. Cadbury and Captain R. Leckie, falling, a mass of flames, some forty miles off Yarmouth. With the passing of Peter Strasser, the Zeppelin offensive that had failed to subdue England ended; in fifty-one raids the airships had dropped 196 tons of bombs and killed or wounded over 1,900 people, but seventy-seven of the huge dirigibles had been lost, and the faith of the German public in them had never been justified.

Some attempts to bomb England with aeroplanes had been made during 1914, and again in 1915, but it was November, 1916, before a heavier-than-air machine succeeded in bombing London. On this occasion, Deck-Offizier Paul Brandt and Leutnant Walther Ilges, in an L.V.G. C.II two-seater reconnaissance biplane, appeared at noon on 28th November over Victoria Station and dropped six small bombs before turning away for home. Shortly after crossing the French coast, engine trouble forced the L.V.G. to alight near Boulogne, and both Brandt and his observer were captured.

Early in 1917 the German High Command decided to undertake a determined aeroplane bombing offensive against England. Seven Bombengeschwader came into service, each comprising three Staffeln of Grossflugzeug ("G" Type) twin-engined heavy biplane bombers, with the exception of the special England Geshwader 3, commanded by Hauptmann Brandenburg, which had six Staffeln. Various types of multi-engined aeroplanes were in use with the German Air Force by this time, but the most outstanding heavy bomber sent against England was the Gotha G.V., which replaced the highly successful G.IV. These two types of aircraft made the name Gotha a household word in Britain during the summer of 1917.

Powered by two 260 h.p. Mercedes engines, the Gotha G.V. was a very large aeroplane for the period, having a wing span of over 77 ft. and carrying a bomb load of 900 lb. inside the fuselage and on external racks. A crew of three was usually carried, and the Gotha had a very heavy armament, being equipped with free Parabellum machine-guns in front and rear cockpits and one fixed Parabellum gun firing rearwards from under the fuselage to protect the tail. A maximum speed of 87 m.p.h. at sea level and an endurance of four hours made the Gotha an ideal machine for use against England, and its ability to operate easily in daylight indicated that it would be a precision air weapon far superior to the slower and more expensive Zeppelin.

On 25th May, 1917, German heavy bombers crossed the English coast for the first time. Twenty-one Gothas, encountering dense cloud before reaching London, turned aside and dropped their bombs in Kent, mostly at Shorncliffe and Folkestone, causing heavy civilian casualties. Thirty-seven Royal Flying Corps and Royal Naval Air Service fighters took off to intercept the Gothas, but the high-flying bombers were out of range, and returned to their base at Ghent with the loss of only one machine.

Encouraged by the obvious inadequacy of the scanty British air defences, Hauptmann Brandenburg led twenty-two Gothas over the Channel in a second raid on 5th June. Bombs were dropped at Shoeburyness and Sheerness, and although on this occasion sixty-five defending fighters went up to engage the bombers, only one was destroyed, and that by anti-aircraft fire. Nevertheless, Brandenburg was unsatisfied; his aircraft had not yet managed to reach London. Then, at 11.35 a.m. on 13th June, aeroplanes of the England Geschwader swung majestically over the English capital in an immaculate diamond formation, and Brandenburg's dream was realised. The fourteen Gothas he was leading that day dropped 118 bombs, killed 162 persons, and injured 426. "The visibility was exceptionally good," reported Brandenburg afterwards, "with perfect clearness, the Thames bridges, the railway stations, the City, even the Bank of England, could be recognised. . . . Our aircraft circled around and dropped their bombs with no hurry or trouble. . . All the aeroplanes landed safely on their aerodromes." Flying too high to be reached by fighters or anti-aircraft fire, the bombers had simply ignored the defences, and of the ninety-two British pilots who took off to intercept them, only one, a Bristol Fighter, managed to get within range and actually attack the formation. Return fire from the Gothas killed the observer.

This well-organised and determined raid aroused great public indignation in Britain, and the Air Ministry was reluctantly compelled to withdraw the élite No. 56 Squadron, flying S.E.5s, and No. 66 Squadron, flying Sopwith Pups, from the Western Front, at a time when the Passchendaele offensive was under way and every Allied aircraft was vitally needed. Within the space of a few weeks, twenty-two Gothas were over London again, dropping bombs over the East End and causing 250 casualties. As the two recalled fighter squadrons had been sent back to Flanders only a few hours before the raid, the defences again failed to resist the bombers, although one Gotha was shot down and four others crashed on landing.

As Brandenburg's impeccable formation of biplanes throbbed homeward across the Channel, the British Cabinet held an emergency meeting to discuss the situation. As a result of this conference, No. 46 Squadron, Royal Flying Corps, was urgently recalled from France, and all the elements of defence, both ground and air, were combined under one command. In the event, these precautions, which again weakened British air power on the Western Front, proved to be unnecessary; about the same time Hauptmann Brandenburg broke his leg in a landing accident, and during his absence in hospital the England Geschwader was commanded by a leader of quite a different pattern, Hauptmann Kleine.

A brave but reckless man who lacked Brandenburg's patience and careful appraisal of a situation, Kleine led his Gothas over England regardless of the weather and at various heights within reach of the defences, mostly in spasmodic raids over Essex and Kent, until, after an attack on Ramsgate on 22nd August, when three bombers were destroyed, the German High Command decided that the increasing casualties the Geschwader was suffering during the daylight raids were no longer acceptable. Moonlight bombing was therefore contemplated for the future, although it was becoming obvious that as the British defence system gradually became stronger, the Gothas would sooner or later be mastered.

Twenty-one moonlight raids were carried out against England between 2nd September, 1917, and the end of the war, using Gothas and the even larger Zeppelin-Giant bombers. Some of these attacks were highly successful, but the network of anti-aircraft guns that surrounded London by 1918, together with aprons of steel wire suspended from captive balloons, frequently kept the bombers so high that accurate bombing of the selected targets became almost impossible. At the same time, the British night fighter-pilots began to receive better aircraft, mostly Sopwith Camels fitted with powerful 110 h.p. Clerget engines; these were very fast, with an exceptional rate of climb, and operated easily from small airfields.

The last bombing attack against England for twenty-one years took place on the night of 19th-20th May, 1918, when forty-three Gothas and Giants set out to bomb London. Less than half that number managed to reach the capital, and of those, six were destroyed and two damaged by the eighty-four fighters which rose to intercept them and the anti-aircraft defences, that night firing thirty thousand shells. Courage alone could not withstand such losses, and the England Geschwader never attempted to raid England again.

During the offensive the German bombing aircraft had dropped 73 tons of bombs in fifty-two raids, killed 857 people and injured 2,058 more, not an outstanding achievement in the objective military sense. Nevertheless, the raids by Gothas and Giants had caused great disruption to industry, out of all proportion to the number of machines used or the weight of bombs dropped, and hundreds of aircraft, men and guns had been kept in England when they were badly needed on the Western Front.

The importance of another and far more vital aspect of the German air offensive against Britain was not fully realised even in 1918. This, the gradual evolution of the long-range heavy bomber as a powerful strategic weapon, brought about to a great extent by the desire of the German people to see London under aerial bombardment, would many years later result in the complete destruction of such great cities as Cologne, Dresden and Berlin.

CHAPTER III

THE BROKEN WINGS: 1918

THREE men who would play an important part in future German military aviation were flying over the Western Front during the early months of 1918. Two of these young fighter pilots were inseparable friends, and would remain so for many years, until death finally parted them; the third man was an outrageously flamboyant individualist, whose life after the war was destined to be a strange mixture of excitement and gaiety, fading away into a tragic and violent end in 1941. All three became holders of the *Ordre Pour le Mérite*, and their fame was equalled by only one other living air ace, the illustrious Manfred von Richthofen.

When Hermann Goering unexpectedly contracted arthritis at the age of twenty-one in 1914, there was little doubt that his new career as an infantry officer was already ended. Then, while he lay crippled with pain in hospital at Freiburg, Bruno Loerzer, his closest friend in the regiment, who had just trans- ferred to an air training school in the same town, opened out a completely new world for him—the kingdom of the sky. By the time he had recovered enough to hobble slowly around the ward he was determined to become an airman, but it needed patience and all his acknowledged iron resolution to overcome the reluctant authorities and eventually reach the front as Loerzer's observer. The two friends worked well together in action, and made many reconnaissance flights, mostly over the heavily fortified area around Verdun.

In the autumn of 1915 Goering was trained as a pilot, and after flying the big cumbersome A.E.G. twin-engined bombers for a while, soon managed to rejoin Loerzer, who by 1916 was commanding a fighter unit, Jasta 26. It was obvious that a man with Goering's abilities as a pilot and remarkable qualities of leadership would rapidly earn promotion, and within a year he had his own command, Jasta 27. Yet Loerzer continued to remain with him; both units shared the same field and the two

23

friends frequently led their combined formations into battle together, their individual scores steadily mounting in the hundreds of engagements that preceded the great German offensive in March, 1918.

At about the same time that Hermann Goering was lying helpless with arthritis at Freiburg, a young army despatch rider named Ernst Udet was learning to be a pilot at Darmstadt. He turned out to be a willing pupil, but recklessness and over-confidence brought a number of minor crashes. Nevertheless, after a successful year flying two-seaters and then Fokker mono-planes, he went to Jasta 15, and by April, 1917, had five victories. In June of the same year he fought the most dangerous and eventful battle of his whole career, when he encountered the brilliant French ace, Georges Guynemer, in the air. For over eight minutes the two biplanes zoomed and spun and twisted around each other, then Udet's guns jammed and Guynemer courteously turned away and left him. The experience affected Udet intensely for some time, and he had scarcely recovered his nerve when he was posted to command Jasta 37 in Flanders.

During the first two months of 1918 the headquarters of the German High Command prepared for the gigantic offensive that was intended to reverse the fortunes of war and overthrow the Allies by breaking through across the Marne. Artillery, transport and ammunition flowed to the front in an endless stream, while at the same time the Air Service was steadily expanded, mainly by reinforcements from the Russian battle areas. Many new fighter units were formed, until no less than seventy-seven Jagdstaffeln were in existence, and a number of these were then grouped together as Jagdgruppen for the purpose of the offensive.

The German Air Service Order of Battle prior to the mightiest onslaught of the Great War revealed the tremendous amount of work that had been done in implementing the expansion programme initially decided upon in 1917. Germany now had forty-eight Fliegerabteilungen reconnaissance and photography units serving in France, with a further six Fliegerabteilungen on the Turkish front; thirty Schutzstaffeln ground support units; seven Bombengeschwader heavy bombing groups; and the seventy-seven Jagdstaffeln fighter units already mentioned. On 20th March, the eve of the offensive,

Jagdgeschwader 1, under Manfred von Richthofen, was reinforced by Jagdgruppe 2 (comprised of Jasta 5 and Jasta 46) and
the southern sector of the Western Front became the responsibility of Jagdgruppe 9 (Jastas 3, 37, 54 and 56) and Jagdgruppe
10 (Jasta 16 and 34) under the command of Oberleutnant
Kohze.

At 4.45 a.m. on 21st March the artillery bombardment that
opened the battle rained down death and destruction again and
again along the British Fifth Army trenches, and four hours later
the German infantry were struggling forward through the smoke
and mist that shrouded the desolation of No Man's Land. Some
fifty-six divisions had been assembled for the attack, and by
sheer weight of numbers the initial onslaught was a success;
slowly but surely the Fifth Army retreated towards the Somme.
Despite appalling weather the Royal Flying Corps was in the air
from dawn to dusk, harassing the German troops in the forward
areas and bombing and machine-gunning transport and
infantry behind the lines, although poor visibility restricted
fighting in the air for the first three days of the offensive.

On 24th March Richthofen, in his scarlet triplane, led twenty-
five aircraft into a raging dogfight with ten S.E.5as of the
famous 56 Squadron, Royal Flying Corps, and shot down his
sixty-seventh victory, which disintegrated over Combles. Thus
began the period of his last successes; within a week he destroyed
another seven Allied machines, including three that fell to his
guns in one day. At once he was headline news again throughout all Germany, but the ardent young Manfred of the Jasta
Boelcke days had gone for ever and in his place was a man aged
beyond his years, weary of the war and the unceasing bitter
struggle for existence that now consumed his life.

During that first week of the March offensive, Richthofen
found time to tour the Jagdstaffeln in the 2nd Army area, and in
due course arrived at an airfield near Le Cateau, where he talked
for a while with Ernst Udet. The commander of Jasta 37,
already with twenty victories to his credit, had proved himself
to be a capable if somewhat reckless leader, and Richthofen,
always an excellent judge of men, asked him to join the
Geschwader. As in so many other similar instances, Udet turned
out to be well worthy of the master's selection; on his first flight
with the Richthofen Circus he shot down a Sopwith Camel.

By the end of March, 1918, the tremendous spring offensive on which Germany's hopes depended was slowly grinding itself to a standstill along the whole front. The 17th Army was halted at first, while the 18th Army fought desperately forward almost to Amiens, then paused, unable any longer to withstand the appalling casualties they were enduring every day. The air fighting continued to be waged with a fierce intensity matched only by the struggle on the ground, and the German Air Force made history in dozens of brief but savage battles, but as the weeks passed German strength in the air grew slowly weaker; only the morale of the hard-pressed Jagdstaffeln remained unwavering as ever.

The Royal Flying Corps and the Royal Naval Air Service were amalgamated on 1st April to form the Royal Air Force, which concentrated most of its strength against the German fighter formations that were now made up of as many as thirty to forty aircraft at a time. Richthofen led his brightly painted triplanes into the full heat and fury of the aerial war again and again—by 7th April he had seventy-eight confirmed victories—but the Geschwader as a whole had passed its zenith back in the late summer of 1917, and an inexorable fate was carrying the Red Knight himself remorselessly forward to the inevitable end. In the last two years he had seen many aircraft fall in flames, and now the ghastly memories returned again and again to haunt him. "The last ten I shot down burned," he said thoughtfully one day, when interviewed by a newspaper correspondent. "The one I got today burned, too. I saw it quite well. At the beginning, it was only quite a small flame under the pilot's seat, but when the machine dived, the tail stood up in the air and I could see that the seat had been burned through...." This obsession with fire, which he shared with Britain's leading air ace, Mannock, was significant for both men; it indicated clearly that mentally, if not physically, they were almost exhausted.

21st April, 1918, began much the same as any other day. Richthofen strolled out to his red Fokker Triplane in the early morning, deep in conversation with Joachim Wolff, a young pilot who was to accompany him on a hunting trip to the Black Forest in two days' time. Mechanics spun propellers, the roar of Oberursal engines disturbed the crisp spring air, then Richthofen raised a gloved hand and the six machines sped across the field to rise swiftly into the cloudy sky.

Flying westward along the Somme valley, Richthofen soon sighted two R.E.8 two-seater observation craft of No. 3 Squadron, A.F.C., and four triplanes dropped neatly away out of the formation as they dived to the attack. Simultaneously, two flights of Sopwith Camel fighters from 209 Squadron, R.A.F., led by Captain A. R. Brown, D.S.C, were attracted to the scene by the white puffs of British anti-aircraft fire around the triplanes and immediately plunged to the assistance of the besieged two-seaters In the ensuing battle, aircraft twisted and spun and dived in a bedlam of chattering guns and roaring engines; two triplanes soon weaved crazily through the dog-fight out of control, and a Camel staggered away with a wounded pilot. Amid the confusion of noise and flame Richthofen patiently circled, seeking an unwary opponent.

Then, quickly, the Red Knight selected a Camel flown by Lieutenant W. R. May, a new pilot with no battle experience, and swung skilfully on to the Sopwith's tail. May saw the pencil lines of tracer flashing past his cockpit, and glanced over his shoulder; he looked into the ugly flame-stabbing muzzles of twin Spandaus and glimpsed the outline of a goggled, black-helmeted head. Instinctively, he took violent evasive action, turning and diving until he ran out of sky and was skimming along the Somme Valley just above the ground, the merciless guns behind him hammering away in his ears. Then at last he was right down between the banks of the river, and could turn no more; it had to be the end.

Meanwhile, Captain Brown had seen the scarlet triplane attack May and plunged headlong towards Richthofen, opening fire as soon as he was within range. The three aircraft passed low over the front-line trenches, the triplane under heavy fire from Australian machine-guns and rifles on the ground. Brown held the enemy machine squarely in his sights for a moment and his tracers stitched a pattern of death along the fuselage; Richthofen turned slightly in his seat, then abruptly fell forward. The triplane faltered, but he managed to touch down, bumping heavily along the ground to a standstill. When the pilot was lifted from the cockpit, he was found to be dead, killed by a single bullet through the heart.

In the late afternoon of 22nd April Manfred von Richthofen was buried with full military honours at Bertangles. Six R.A.F. officers carried the plain wooden coffin shoulder high from the hangar where it had remained during the night, to the hearse, a Crossley tender, and then the cortege moved slowly away, preceded by a firing party of Australian airmen and followed by more than a hundred Allied mourners. At the graveside, the simple but strangely impressive words of the Church of England burial service were repeated by an English chaplain, in a silence broken only by the endless muted thunder of the guns only a few miles away. With the three sharp volleys of rifle fire that rang out over the grave, the ceremony was ended, save for that most moving of all bugle calls, the Last Post; quietly and respectfully the troops filed away, leaving Richthofen at peace among his enemies.

Thus ended the brief but brilliant life of the Red Knight of Germany. Except for the three weeks in July, 1917, when he was recoving from his head wound, he had been almost continuously in action on the Western Front from September, 1916, until the day of his death; during that period he destroyed eighty enemy aircraft, thus claiming more victims than any other pilot during the Great War, a remarkable record that was never equalled from 1914-1918.

That night, Leutnant Karl Bodenschatz, adjutant of the Richthofen Jagdgeschwader, sadly opened his commander's last will, which had remained in a sealed envelope for some weeks, locked in the unit strongbox. The single sheet of paper bore only one sentence, hurriedly written in pencil: "Should I fail to return, Leutnant Reinhard (Jasta 6) shall take over the leadership of the Geschwader." Even in death, Richthofen's word remained law in the German Air Force, and Reinhard, who was a good, steady pilot, but lacking in imagination, became his successor. At the same time the loss of Richthofen began to have a profound effect on the Geschwader and a dark cloud of despair settled over the little airfield at Cappy, spreading to almost every other unit along the front. Heavy casualties were suffered during the next few weeks, although Ernst Udet seemed to be unaffected by the general depression and soon established himself as Germany's most successful surviving fighter-pilot.

Then, on 18th June, Reinhard left for Adlershof, on the out-

skirts of Berlin, to test a new type of biplane fighter intended
to replace the now long-obsolete Albatros. At the demonstration,
the commander of Jasta 27, Oberleutnant Hermann Goering,
took the prototype machine into the air, and found that it res-
ponded perfectly; after a short flight he landed, and Reinhard
took his place. To the watching staff officers and technicians it
seemed to be an ordinary routine flight, nothing more than a
final check on an approved fighter, but at 3,000 ft. an interplane strut broke, the whole upper wing of the biplane immediately collapsed and the machine plunged to earth out of control.
Reinhard was instantly killed.

For five days every man in the Richthofen Geschwader
wondered who would be nominated as the new commander; it
was taken for granted that the appointment would be given only
to a serving member of the unit, probably Manfred's brother,
Lothar von Richthofen, or Ernst Udet. Then, on 8th July, the
long-awaited message arrived from the High Command, and the
adjutant, Bodenschatz, read it aloud to the pilots crowded
around him: "Order No. 178.654. 8.7.18. Oberleutnant
Hermann Goering has been appointed commander of the
Geschwader No. 1 Manfred Freiherr von Richthofen."

Why Goering, a man from outside the Geschwader? Difficult
though it may be to fathom the true reasons for his selection, it
probably came about because he was at that time the senior
regular Oberleutnant, and at the same time was a capable
fighter-pilot, with twenty-one victories. Also, he had recently
been awarded the *Ordre Pour le Mérite*; above all, he was a
splendid organiser and a born leader.

Within a week the new commander arrived at Beugneux airfield to join his new unit, and immediately called all flying personnel of the Geschwader to an address. A rather plump, short
man, with steady blue eyes, Goering quickly explained to the
assembled pilots his views on air fighting, and ended by saying
how proud he was to have the great honour of leading
Germany's finest airmen. Then Oberleutnant Bodenschatz formally handed him the famous geschwaderstock—a gnarled walk-
ing-stick that had been carried by Richthofen and later Reinhard, and which had become a symbol throughout the whole
German Air Force. With that brief ceremony, the inauguration
ended, and the pilots walked silently away, instinctively sensing

that the good old days had ended with Richthofen, and the methods of this new highly efficient and strict commander would seldom be to their liking.

By July, 1918, the Richthofen Geschwader, in common with many other fighter units, had almost completely re-equipped with the latest German single-seater scout biplane, the Fokker D.VII. The short-lived success of the Fokker Dr I Triplane, which failed entirely to regain the air supremacy from the S.E.5a and the Sopwith Camel types used by the Allies, aroused the German High Command to order all aircraft manufacturers to produce entirely new fighter prototypes; these were all tested together by front-line pilots at a special open competition held at Johannisthal, Berlin, in January, 1918. By far and away the most superior design was the Fokker D.VII, which was therefore put into quantity production at once, not only at Anthony Fokker's own factory at Schwerin but also in the Albatros and A.E.G. works at Berlin.

The Fokker D.VII has been immortalised as the machine that represented the ultimate achievement in German fighter aircraft types used operationally in the First World War. A sturdy, conventional biplane, the D.VII featured the usual Fokker cantilever wooden wings and a simple fuselage built up of steel tubing covered with fabric, while the interplane "N" struts and the unusual pyramidical centre-section strutting were also built up of streamlined steel tubing. The standard engine fitted was a 160 h.p. Mercedes, later superseded by a 185 h.p. B.M.W; the armament consisted of the normal twin synchronised Spandau machine-guns situated in the cowling to fire forward through the propeller The maximum performance figures of the D.VII—110 m.p.h. at 10,000 ft.—were good, but not remarkable for the period; however, it had a much more important asset, the ability to retain perfect control at heights where the Allied aircraft it opposed were slow and difficult to handle.

Like the Fokker Triplane and the Albatros fighters that had preceded it, the D.VII was flown by most of Germany's leading pilots, and by the end of the war practically every Jagdstaffel on the Western Front had been equipped with this machine, the excellent flying qualities of which were to earn it special recognition in the Armistice Agreement, which specifically named the

D.VII to be handed over to the Allies. Yet it arrived in action just too late to sway the tide of battle that had now turned completely against Germany; hampered by the British blockade at sea, the supply of raw materials had slowly dwindled away, and by August, 1918, aircraft production was seriously affected.

Meanwhile the Richthofen Jagdgeschwader continued to move to and fro about the front, always in the thick of the battle and suffering increasing casualties. Because of these losses, which gradually reduced the fighting strength of the Geschwader to that of a Jasta, operational patrols were conducted in conjunction with a Jagdgruppe under Ritter von Greim, and Jagdgeschwader 3, which had been built up some months earlier under the command of Bruno Loerzer from Jasta Boelcke, 26, 27, and 36. Other units had been combined to form Jagdgeschwader 2, commanded at this time by von Boenigk, and in this confusion of expansion and reorganisation, which strove to combat the tremendous Allied superiority in numbers, the German squadrons fought on with a dogged determination, but they could not be expected to last much longer. The sands of time were rapidly running out, and the end of the Great War almost in sight.

On 1st September, 1918, Hermann Goering reported to the High Command on the situation in the field. "... the enemy biplanes are strongly armed and operate very well in close formation," he wrote, "even when attacked by several German single-seaters. They are equipped with armoured or fire-proof fuel tanks ... On the fronts of the 7th and 2nd Army, enemy balloons have been attacked on several occasions without catching fire ..." The young commander's words revealed his despair; even his undoubted ability as a leader could not exact any greater efforts from his faithful officers and men.

During the last week of September the Allied assault on the last and greatest German network of defences, the famous Hindenburg line, was launched, and by 1st October most of that intricate system had been taken, with the capture of over 4,000 guns, 25,000 machine-guns, and more than 250,000 prisoners. The exhausted and sadly depleted German Air Force concentrated against the overwhelming numbers of British day bombers now in action, hurling into the battle as many as fifty fighters at a time, and on 30th October sixty-seven German machines were shot down for a loss of forty-one Allied aircraft. All three Jagdgeschwader roamed here and there over the disintegrating front line, their D.VIIs now supplemented by a few of the new revolutionary Fokker D.VIII fighters. These slim little parasol monoplanes, Anthony Fokker's last contribution to the German military aviation industry, were very fast and highly manoeuvrable, but unfortunately never became available in sufficient numbers to alter the desperate situation.

On 5th November the Richthofen Geschwader fought its last battle in the air during the Great War, engaging a formation of Spad fighters and shooting three down without loss. Then the weather closed in and rendered flying impossible. The pilots stood idly on the airfield in the pouring rain, waiting for the heavy fog to lift, unaware that many miles away in Germany the High Seas Fleet at Kiel had mutinied, there was street fighting in Berlin, and in a number of army units troops had refused to obey their officers. And also at this turning-point in history, while the Kaiser's empire crumbled into ruins, a young unknown corporal of the 16th Bavarian Reserve Infantry Regiment, who had been temporarily blinded in a gas attack near Ypres, lay in a military hospital at Pasewalk, in Pomerania, slowly recovering from the injury. His name was Adolf Hitler.

Three days later it was obvious that the end was now very near for Germany. Hermann Goering summoned all personnel of the Richthofen Geschwader to assemble before him, and informed them bitterly that orders had been received to demobilise. Confused and contradictory messages continued to pour in until the Armistice at last became effective, on the eleventh hour of the eleventh day of the eleventh month, 1918; at once an order arrived directing the pilots to hand over their aircraft immediately to an American receiving unit. Instead, Goering decided to lead his squadron to Darmstadt, and on the 12th November the Geschwader took off to return to the Fatherland.

At Darmstadt a revolutionary soldier-council was in control of the aerodrome, and the troops there commenced to impound the Geschwader aircraft, but an enraged Goering approached the soldiers and gave them his ultimatum—either the confiscated machines would be released or he would attack at once with every other aircraft he possessed. In his anger and desperation he undoubtedly meant every word. His authority quickly proved to be effective; without any further argument the fighters were at once returned to him.

The last order received by Goering instructed him to lead the Geschwader to Aschaffenburg, for the purpose of surrendering all his aircraft to a French commission. As a final act of defiance, all the pilots deliberately landed heavily at the airfield there, and many of the machines were almost completely wrecked by the impact with which they struck the ground. That evening, Goering made a farewell speech to the demobilised men, reviewing the achievements of the Geschwader since its inception in June, 1917, and recalling the great leader who had died in action while flying with it, Manfred von Richthofen. A total of 644 victories in the air had been gained since Oberleutnant Dostler had shot down an observation balloon on 5th July, 1917, until the last three victories on 5th November, 1918. During that time fifty-six officers and six other ranks had been killed; fifty-two officers and seven other ranks had been wounded. Thus ended Germany's most outstanding fighter wing, the élite Jagdgeschwader No. 1 Manfred Freiherr von Richthofen, the men who fought and flew in it no longer wanted, the machines they had used now in the hands of their enemies.

On 11th November, 1918, when the thunder of the guns at last faded into silence, a German pilot walked quietly to the blackboard where orders for the day were normally chalked, and wrote sadly, *"Im Kreig geboren, im Kreig gestorben"*. In those few words he summed up the whole bitter, splendid history of the Imperial German Air Force. Born in the war—died in the war; and in those dark days it seemed that such untarnished glory would never be seen again.

And, in a way, it proved to be so. The knights of the air on both sides who fought in the First World War were a class of men apart from all others, and when they departed quietly into the mists of time an era had ended. Their mettle had been wrought in the seething crucible of the Somme, and it is to their everlasting credit that it never failed to shine brighter than the most tempered steel, not only when they ruled the embattled heavens, but also in the face of their greatest enemy—defeat.

CHAPTER IV

PHOENIX RISING: 1918-1926

HERMANN GOERING returned to Germany that bitter winter of 1918 to find his country torn asunder by unrest and revolution. In Munich, the Wittelsbach King of Bavaria had abdicated, and the radical Kurt Eisner, President of the rebellious Workers', Peasants' and Soldiers' Councils, was in power, while in Berlin the streets echoed to the rattle of gunfire. Meanwhile, the President of the new Weimar Republic, Friedrich Ebert, and his moderate government struggled desperately to restore order out of the chaos that reigned everywhere. Disillusioned, and contemptuous of a Fatherland in defeat, Goering accepted without hesitation a job as aircraft salesman in Scandinavia with the Fokker organisation and departed soon afterwards for Denmark, not to see Germany again until the summer of 1921.

In January, 1919, the Allied powers met at Versailles to penalise their late enemy for plunging an unsuspecting world into four years of war, and at the same time claim the rewards they felt victory had earned for them. The carcass of Imperial Germany was carved firmly and with unswerving determination: Malmedy was yielded to Belgium; Alsace-Lorraine handed to France; Posen, West Prussia, Upper Silesia and Pomerania were ceded to Poland. Memel and Danzig were placed under mandate to the new League of Nations, while North Schleswig reverted to Denmark. As a final blow, all Germany's colonies were distributed among the victorious nations.

The list of conditions seemed to be endless. Forty thousand million marks were to be paid at once as financial war reparation, and yet another forty thousand million marks were claimed before 1926. Conscription was abolished, all military academies and bases closed and the German General Staff disbanded. A peacetime army (or Reichwehr) of 100,000 men was conceded, but tanks, aircraft and artillery were no longer allowed; indeed, the whole armament industry and all fortifications had to be destroyed. Allied control commissions would be threaded about the whole country, to ensure that the many conditions were completely fulfilled.

In despair, Ebert stated that the terms imposed on Germany were unacceptable to his government, but the fiery and unrelenting Clemenceau of France replied on 16th June by insisting upon the final acceptance—and within five days. There followed a long silence, while the war clouds hung threateningly again over Europe and the Allied troops on the Rhine prepared to march once more; then the Weimar Government reluctantly agreed to sign the Peace Treaty. On 28th June, 1919, in the Hall of Mirrors at Versailles, the war that was supposed to end all wars officially and ceremoniously came to an end.

Nevertheless, even with so many involved conditions, the Treaty of Versailles failed to cripple Germany as a military nation. The terms necessitated the complete dissolution and destruction of the entire German Air Force, and in accordance with those terms Germany was left with only 140 aircraft and 169 aircraft engines for commercial use. A seemingly important clause, which prohibited the construction or importation of aircraft or engines, actually served little purpose; it applied for a period of only six months, and the German aeroplane manufacturers needed only patience to await events and the courage to build their industries up again from the emptiness that remained.

The political scene remained in confusion. Kurt Eisner, the man who had led the powerful Bavarian revolution in November, 1918, was shot dead in a Munich street on 21st February, 1919, and his Soldiers' Councils were replaced by a Social Democratic government; this in turn was quickly overthrown by a Soviet republic. Armed communists patrolled the deserted streets, houses were ransacked and police headquarters seized in a wave of terror that ran unchecked, until regular troops together with restless ex-officers who had banded themselves into volunteer organisations known as Freikorps, regained control and restored a democratic government.

Germany in these troubled times seethed with small political parties, many of them lacking any programme or definite purpose, and the new Reichwehr, seeking a party over which they could gain control and use to further their own ends, became interested in one of these; consequently, thirty-year-old Adolf Hitler, who was employed as a political instruction officer with the Army's VII (Munich) District Command, was instructed in September, 1919, to investigate the possibilities of this small group, which was known as the German Workers' Party.

A Munich locksmith, Anton Drexler, had founded the German Workers' Party the previous year, in a vague endeavour to create a party composed of working-class members, with a somewhat obscure nationalist programme, and its activities had never really progressed beyond heated but indecisive discussions in Munich beer halls. Oddly enough, this very uncertainty and obscurity attracted Hitler, and with the approval of his superiors he decided without hesitation to join the party. The group at that time had just over forty members, yet when Hitler spoke for the first time in the Hofbrauhaus Keller in the October a hundred and eleven people were present, and by the end of the year two hundred members were attending meetings regularly to hear him. By April, 1920, he had taken over the propaganda section of the party and was devoting all his time to building up the membership, mainly by the use of frequent advertising and large display posters.

While the unknown agitator in the shabby trench-coat worked tirelessly to gain something of a reputation for an equally unknown political party, and Hermann Goering enjoyed a gay and luxurious life in Sweden, many of the airmen who had flown into battle so frequently only two years before were finding it difficult to forget the open vastness of the sky they had known so well. Gliding clubs were formed throughout the land and members patiently constructed their own craft; meanwhile, Bruno Loerzer, leader of a Jagdgeschwader in 1918, had founded the Luftsportverband, a national flying club that came into being less than a year after the Treaty of Versailles had been signed. The aircraft manufacturers and designers who had survived the landslide of defeat, among them Claudius Dornier, Junkers, and Ernst Heinkel, were already considering the possibilities of the export market for aeroplanes, and Dr. Dornier's latest flying-boat was already under construction—in Switzerland. As time passed, it became obvious that the Great War had turned Germany into an air-minded nation, and despite the Treaty restrictions many outstanding glider flight performances were

achieved during the immediate post-war years by individuals
who led the way for the tremendous organisation that in later
years turned Germany into the leading air power of the world.

In the summer of 1921 Goering returned to Munich and
enrolled as a student at the University, about the same time that
Adolf Hitler took over leadership of the German Workers' Party
—the N.S.D.A.P., or National-Sozialistische Deutsche Arbeiter
Partei. Since 1920 the party had made important strides; a little
office had been opened in an inn, and furnished with a few old
cupboards and bookshelves; a bankrupt newspaper, the *Volkische Beobachter,* had been bought, using Army funds placed at
Hitler's disposal by Ernst Roehm; and last but by no means
least, the later infamous strong-arm squads of storm troopers,
known as S.A., or Sturmabteilung, had been formed, to silence
hecklers at the mass meetings which were now a regular occurrence. By August, 1921, the S.A. men were marching noisily
through the streets in their tattered leather jackets, protecting
the party's assembly places and shouting down any political
opponents who dared to oppose them. Within a year, Hitler had
the reputation he sought. The German people suddenly
awakened to the fact that they had a spokesman—and many of
them liked the stirring violence of his words. On 18th September, 1922, he faced his audience in Munich's largest assembly
room, the Zircus Krone, and shouted, "We want to call to
account the November criminals of 1918. It cannot be that two
million Germans should have fallen in vain and that afterwards
one should sit down as friends at the same table with traitors.
No, we do not pardon, we demand—vengeance! The dis-
honouring of the nation must cease . . ." He stood there, vibrat-
ing with excitement, an incongruous, nondescript man with a
short moustache and flashing eyes, and when he had finished
speaking the applause broke around the platform in great waves,
like an endless sea. On such an evening two months later,
Hermann Goering listened to that harsh magnetic voice and
was at once captivated by the words and the man who uttered
them, so much so that the following day he went to see Hitler at
the small headquarters of the party.

The two men who met that morning in the dingy little office
were at once attracted to each other. Goering was overwhelmed
with admiration for such a brilliant and outspoken orator, and

Hitler immediately perceived that the highly decorated former leader of the Richthofen Jagdgeschwader would be a valuable asset to the party; with his social standing and remarkable war record he would give tone to an organisation still composed to a great extent of uneducated working-class members. Impulsively, Hitler explained the purpose of the S.A. and outlined its activities, ending by offering Goering the leadership of the unruly storm troopers, with the task of disciplining them until they became a credit to the brown uniforms they frequently wore. It was a job after Goering's heart, promising authority tinged with a little showmanship and glamour, and that same day he accepted.

Five weeks later Goering, only just enrolled as a member of the party, was made Commander of the Sturmabteilung, and taking his first steps on the long road that would lead him eventually to the lowest depths of degradation and suicide in a lonely prison cell.

In the autumn of 1920, when General von Seeckt became Commander-in-Chief of the Reichwehr, his small post-war army of one hundred thousand men was still not allowed the inclusion of an air force, and he was therefore faced with the problem of keeping Germany in touch with aviation developments throughout the world, while strictly prohibited from authorising the building of any military aircraft, including prototypes. During 1921 von Seeckt's Defence Ministry, the Reichwehrministerium, considered forming a secret flying department, and in the December of that year two envoys were sent to Soviet Russia, a country whose vast industrial potentiality was insufficiently organised at that time through lack of the technical knowledge required to institute a satisfactory production programme.

The Treaty of Rapallo, signed in 1922, finally opened the door for post-war German military aviation, for it contained a secret clause that gave the Red Air Force the advantage of any future German technical developments. In return for this vitally needed assistance, Russia agreed to put a lonely disused airfield, sparsely equipped with runways, a few hangars, uncomfortable living quarters and little else at the disposal of the Reichwehr. This was Lipetzk aerodrome, about two hundred miles south-east of Moscow.

For the next twelve months ammunition, tools, engines and other aeroplane parts were smuggled aboard Russian ships at Stettin and other Baltic ports and transported to Leningrad. Over two hundred Reichwehr officers, all specialists in aerial strategy, bombing, armament or reconnaissance, travelled to Russia in civilian clothes, using assumed names and forged passports. Many of these men who trained the Soviet Air Staff and worked in the experimental centre at Lipetzk became the highly efficient tacticians who launched the German air weapon against Europe less than twenty years later. Student, who later became an expert in airborne invasion, passed through the secret flying ground, as did Kesselring, Stumpff and Sperrle, who commanded the three main air fleets that threatened England in the summer of 1940.

While Germany's professional airmen were exiled in Russia and seeking to provide the Reichwehr with the nucleus of an air force, the aeroplane industry of the nation gradually revived. The general ban on the construction of civil aircraft had been raised by the Allies on 3rd May, 1922, although certain restrictions on size and performance still remained, and at once a number of leading manufacturers were again openly in business. Claudius Dornier's impressive flying-boat, the "Wal" twin-engined monoplane, was an immediate success, and Hugo Junkers, who during the war had designed a number of all-metal armoured ground-attack machines, was now building his F. 13 air-liners for the many air transport contractors anxious to take advantage of the renewed public interest in aviation. Ernst Heinkel had been approached by the Reichwehr to design a small biplane that could be used as a reconnaissance plane and this machine, the He 17, was followed by two training aircraft, the He 18 and the He 21, types that were well within the regulations on size and performance, and outwardly displayed as light civil aeroplanes.

Meanwhile, the Albatros concern in Berlin was once again hard at work, and the new Arado Works was also in the field. Ernst Udet, once an outstanding fighter pilot with the Richthofen Jagdgeschwader and now a touring stunt pilot, decided to join the industry and formed a company at Ramersdorf, near Munich, at about the same time that a young and unknown designer named Willy Messerschmitt opened his first small works in Augsburg. His little two-seater sporting monoplane, the M-17, was to be the predecessor of a whole series of neat little light aeroplanes that culminated in Messerschmitt's most successful design—the Bf 109 fighter.

The cause of much of this activity—the Reichwehr—supervised the technical testing of the new aircraft and the training of the pilots in Russia by opening a special secret section of the Reichwehrministerium in Berlin. Here, the German airmen of the future were carefully selected, and the strength and disposal of the world's air forces studied, by a small but highly efficient organisation that remained in existence for ten years and in that time outlined the mass production programme for various types of military aircraft and prepared more than five hundred trained crews for the day when they would be needed.

In this way, thirteen years before Adolf Hitler came to power, General von Seeckt founded the air strength of Germany that would later be considered by many as the greatest achievement of the future Commander-in-Chief of the Luftwaffe, Hermann Goering.

On a grey November day in 1925 Manfred von Richthofen, who had lain at rest since the war in Fricourt Cemetery with some eighteen thousand other German dead, was brought home to his native Germany. Throughout the land flags were flown at half mast and bells were sorrowfully tolled after the special train carrying the coffin had crossed the frontier, and for two days people filed past the dimly lit catafalque standing in the Gnadenkirche in Berlin to pay their last respects to the young airman who had been idolised by a nation. Upon the casket, ablaze with floral tributes, glittered Richthofen's decorations and a Uhlan officer's sword, together with the simple wooden cross that had marked his grave in Fricourt War Cemetery.

The state funeral on 20th November was a highly significant occasion that pointed a warning finger at the whole world, for it was the first time since the war that an impressive full military parade had been openly held in Berlin. Manfred von Richthofen's coffin was borne to a shining horse-drawn gun carriage by eight holders of the *Ordre Pour le Mérite*, including Ernst Udet, and then the long sad procession moved off through the crowded streets to the Invaliden Cemetery. Behind the hearse walked Richthofen's mother, her only surviving son, Bolko, and Field Marshal von Hindenburg, the President of the German Republic, followed by other dignitaries of the state, high-ranking officers of the Reichwehr and many ex-members of the Richthofen Geschwader. Hindenburg was the man who scattered the first handful of earth on the casket as it was lowered into the open grave.

The following year a large tombstone to Richthofen's memory was ceremoniously unveiled over his grave, and the full homage to a national hero had been paid, eight years after his death. Yet at the same time another more important purpose had been served. The almost forgotten memories of Germany's military greatness were deliberately revived, and the men who had known Richthofen were stirred into remembrance of the reckless, carefree days of 1918. The healing hands of time had softened the bitterness of war, and now only the happy times were recalled. The cold tombstone in the Invaliden Cemetery failed as a monument to wasted youth, but symbolised instead a glorious death, and the longing for another age of immortal heroes.

CHAPTER V

AWAITING EVENTS: 1926-1933

GERMAN civil aviation came into existence in 1917, when the Deutsche Luftreederei, a small air freight company, was formed, and continued to operate with some success until immediately after the Great War, when a regular service commenced between Berlin and Weimar, flying uncomfortable converted military aeroplanes. Soon afterwards, Hugo Junkers founded his own airline, using his famous all-metal F. 13 cabin monoplanes, which covered the routes between Munich, Zurich and Geneva, Munich and Berlin, Munich and Frankfurt, and Munich, Vienna and Budapest, and eventually linked most of the major cities in central Europe. With the revival of popular interest in aviation during the 'twenties, some thirty independent air transport operators entered the field, including not only such experienced and established aviation industrialists as the Rumpler and Albatros companies, but also a number of individuals with wartime flying experience who saw the opportunity to jump headlong into an unexpectedly profitable business.

Unable to compete successfully in such an overcrowded market, and faced one by one with bankruptcy, the various independent operators soon had to consider amalgamation and were incorporated into one airline, the Deutsche Aerolloyd, which then had only one rival, the prosperous Junkers organisation. Finally, the Junkers airline joined Deutsche Aerolloyd to become the Deutsche Lufthansa, which was formed in 1926 as a state monopoly airline.

Looking back over the years, it is difficult even now to realise that in a Germany still shaken by the aftermath of defeat the calculating brain and guiding hands of General von Seeckt were secretly at work behind the outwardly innocent façade of Lufthansa, manipulating his chosen men into the important positions in German civil aviation, and ensuring the future development of military projects in a civilian disguise that successfully blinded the world to the deadly underlying purpose. Erhard

Milch, an ambitious man who had been a pilot in the Great War and subsequently works manager of the Junkers company, became the first Managing Director of Lufthansa, thus taking the first step on what proved to be a swift and unswerving rise to power as a dominating military personality. Working in close liaison with the Reichwehr, Milch gradually built up a reserve of trained airmen by incorporating lectures and practical instruction into the Lufthansa training programme that could only be of value from a military point of view, and a surprising number of the men who led fighter and bomber formations into battle in 1939 had been transferred just before the outbreak of war from civil aviation.

It was only to be expected that the great depression which began in 1929 would have an effect on the aircraft industry, and in Germany the crisis overwhelmed a number of experienced and well-known manufacturers. Ernst Udet, still as gay and uninhibited as ever, had discovered that a good fighter pilot does not necessarily make an efficient business executive, and the Udet Flugzeugbau factory had gone into liquidation and been taken over by the Bayerische Flugzeugwerke, a new works sponsored by the Bavarian Government. Undismayed, Udet returned to the carefree but dangerous existence of a freelance touring stunt pilot. The famous Albatros works vanished almost without trace, and only amalgamation with the Bayerische Flugzeugwerke saved the little Messerschmitt factory; very few people in the early 'thirties could afford to buy the young designer's light sporting monoplanes, and his thoughts were already turning to mailplanes and fast, single-engined bombers.

The Junkers, Heinkel and Dornier organisations survived the disastrous years unscathed, mainly because of the tremendous advances they had made since the early days of aviation. Ernst Heinkel continued to design various conventional training machines and also some ship-borne aircraft, mainly for export to Sweden, Japan and even Russia, although he had also built two very successful catapult mail seaplanes intended to operate from the new 50,000 ton Norddeutscher Lloyd passenger liner, the *Bremen*. Meanwhile, the series of increasingly larger and better flying-boats produced by the Dornier works had finally culminated in the huge Do X, which was completed at Altenrhein on the shores of Lake Constance in 1929. Initial cooling difficulties with the twelve Siemens Jupiter engines mounted above the wide monoplane wing with a span of over 157 ft. led to the substitution of American Curtiss Conqueror motors on the Do X, and on 21st October, 1929, this vast machine took the air with 169 persons on board, including nine stowaways. A year later it visited Calshot for a few days, after which it undertook a journey of 28,000 miles, returning to Germany via Lisbon, the Canary Islands, Bahamas, Rio de Janeiro, the West Indies, Miami, New York, Newfoundland, the Azores and Spain.

The interest shown at that time by Claudius Dornier in very large aircraft was shared by Hugo Junkers, whose extensive factory was still concentrating on airliners for use with the new Deutsche Lufthansa. His big G-38 monoplane was first produced in 1928, and subsequently remained in service with the Lufthansa until the outbreak of war in 1939. A vast and undoubtedly ugly machine powered by four Junkers Jumo 750 h.p. engines, the G-38 employed a remarkably thick wing section, the inboard sections of the wing leading edges actually containing passenger cabins, while the square, unstreamlined fuselage was fitted with two separate passenger decks. Thirty-four passengers and a crew of seven were carried and the wing span was just over 144 ft., but the cruising speed of only 129 m.p.h. reflected the most pressing German aviation problem of the period, the lack of high-powered engines because of insufficient development resulting from the time lost during the idle post-war years. Nevertheless, the G-38 was a good, steady machine, and the two airliners used by Lufthansa, the *Deutschland* and the *General Feldmarschall von Hindenburg*, carried many hundreds of passengers during the 'thirties, while a militarised version of the G-38 was also built under licence in Japan as a heavy bomber for the Japanese Army.

Seemingly uninterested in the political changes that were taking place in Germany, events that within the space of a few years would alter the whole pattern of their industries, the aircraft designers of the nation continued to foster the steady growth of civil aviation by the introduction of many varied types of aeroplanes, ranging from the enormous Dornier flying-boats and Junkers airliners already mentioned to the curious tail-first, unstallable, unspinnable Focke-Wulf Ente monoplane, an experimental design by Kurt Tank which attempted to overcome aerodynamic problems later mastered in some degree by the development of the helicopter.

Despite the failure of the military airships used during the Great War, progress with lighter-than-air craft had not been neglected, largely due to the unceasing efforts of Hugo Eckener, an airship pioneer who had remained a close friend and adviser of Graf Zeppelin until the aristocratic old inventor died in March, 1917. Using two dirigibles constructed immediately after the war, and named *Lake Constance* and *North Star* respectively, Eckener established a successful air service between Friedrichshafen and Berlin in 1920, with the intention of extending these regular flights to Stockholm and later other European cities. However, soon afterwards the Allies intervened, forbidding Germany to operate airships or to build them, and at the same time confiscating the two passenger Zeppelins already in use. Within a few weeks the huge hangars at Friedrichshafen stood empty and neglected, and Eckener's dream of a regular airship service seemed to be at an end.

But Hugo Eckener found it impossible to relinquish his struggle against the ill luck that had pursued the development of lighter-than-air craft for over ten long years. Aware that the Zeppelin company simply could not afford to wait until the Allied restrictions were lifted, he searched for a solution to the problem, and at last had a brilliant, ingenious idea. The Allies were at that time demanding reparations in cash from Germany to replace the warships scuttled at Scapa Flow in 1918, and Eckener decided to offer the United States a new airship in lieu of a cash payment—not a profitable transaction for the Zeppelin works but one that would at least serve to keep his factory in business for a while. The American authorities agreed to the proposal and on 11th October, 1924, the latest Zeppelin dirigible, the LZ. 126, took off from Friedrichshafen on the first direct transatlantic flight made by an airship. Just over three days later it landed at Lakehurst naval airport, where it was afterwards ceremoniously redesignated the ZR. 111 and named *Los Angeles*. As Eckener had hoped, the resulting publicity, together with the launching of the Zeppelin-Eckener fund and a whirlwind lecture tour to arouse national enthusiasm, raised the four million marks needed to finance the building of another transatlantic airship, legally possible now that the ban on German aviation had been abolished.

Completed in the summer of 1928, the LZ. 127, named the *Graf Zeppelin*, soon became the most famous airship ever built in Germany. It was powered by five Maybach engines which developed 2,650 h.p., had a gas capacity of some 3,950,000 cubic ft. and was 775 ft. in length. Cruising speed was 60 m.p.h and twenty passengers and twelve tons of freight could be carried for up to 6,000 miles, thus being capable of crossing the Atlantic in three days with all the spaciousness of an ocean-going liner.

After a number of test flights, the *Graf Zeppelin* took off for Lakehurst on 11th October, 1928, with twenty passengers and a crew of forty. Surviving appalling weather, it arrived in the United States four days later, receiving a tremendous welcome from the thousands of people who awaited it. On his triumphant return to Germany, Eckener decided to display the latest Zeppelin airship on a series of special publicity flights designed to arouse interest in lighter-than-air craft throughout the world, and that winter the *Graf Zeppelin* carried a number of distinguished passengers on a cruise over the warm countries of the Mediterranean, reaching Palestine and circling the Dead Sea before returning to Friedrichshafen. A year later the airship journeyed round the northern hemisphere of the world in twenty-one days, landing at Tokio and Los Angeles to replenish the fuel and gas supplies, and the year 1930 saw it undertaking a number of successful ventures, including an intercontinental "triangle flight" from Friedrichshafen over Seville to Recife, and then proceeding via Rio de Janeiro to Lakehurst and from there back to Seville and Friedrichshafen. A charter flight was also made to Iceland, then the *Graf Zeppelin* flew to Russia on a goodwill mission, returning to undertake various shorter passenger flights inside western Europe. The popularity of this most beautiful of all the Zeppelin dirigibles was therefore at its height when the tragedy that became a staggering blow to the future development of lighter-than-air craft shook the world.

Great Britain had been interested in rigid airships since before the Great War, and two Government-sponsored craft, the R. 34 and R. 38, had met with some success until the latter broke in two in the air over Hull in 1921 with a loss of forty-three lives. This disaster ended airship development in England for nearly ten years, but the remarkable achievements of the *Graf Zeppelin* indicated a happier future for the craft, and by 1930 the British Government had again entered the field with two large airships, the R. 100 and the R. 101. After a successful flight to Canada by the R. 100, her sister ship rose from Cardington on 4th October, 1930, bound for Egypt and then India. Immediately after crossing the Channel the R. 101 suddenly dipped towards the ground near Beauvais, in Northern France, momentarily righted itself, then plunged into a low hill and exploded into a mass of flames. Of fifty-four passengers and crew on board, forty-seven were killed, among the dead being Lord Thomson, the Secretary of State for Air, and Air Vice-Marshal Sir W. Sefton Brancker, the Director of Civil Aviation.

With the loss of the ill-fated R. 101, the death knell of airship development in England had finally been sounded, and all construction programmes under consideration were immediately abandoned. To the great relief of Hugo Eckener, German enthusiasm in lighter-than-air craft remained largely unaffected and the many successes of the *Graf Zeppelin* enabled it to survive the catastrophe unscathed. In April, 1931, the airship flew to Egypt, and on 24th July it left Friedrichshafen on a special Arctic flight, carrying a group of international scientists on a research expedition over the glittering ice-fields that surround the North Pole. Later in the same year the *Graf Zeppelin* commenced regular passenger and mail flights to South America, flying from Friedrichshafen to Pernambuco, and competing successfully against the French Aero Postale aeroplane service which operated via West Africa.

Nevertheless, Eckener had known for some time that a transatlantic airship required much more power, a higher speed and a greater capacity than his airship possessed. It had possibilities as a passenger craft, but basically it remained an experimental dirigible, and bigger airships would soon be needed for the carrying of passengers and freight on a regular transatlantic service. While the *Graf Zeppelin* flew steadily back and forth on the South American route, with full bookings on every trip, Eckener continued to gaze ahead into the future, dreaming of a new, vast and even more beautiful airship, the predecessor of a fleet of Zeppelin dirigibles that would end the eternal airship-

versus-aeroplane controversy for ever and prove to the world
that the two methods of aerial transport could work side by side
for the common good and the benefit of mankind.

Triumph and tragedy awaited Hugo Eckener in the tumultuous decade that preceded the Second World War, but in that
summer of 1931 his faith in lighter-than-air craft had never
been more secure. It was not the work that had occupied so
much of his life that troubled his thoughts in those days; only
one man haunted his mind, the insignificant, tempestuous new
politician who was rising so swiftly to power, and whose name
was on the lips of every man and woman in Germany. "The
man who preaches force to Germany preaches Germany's destruction," Eckener had once said in a speech to university
students in Prague, and now Adolf Hitler had appeared to lend
emphasis to his words, like a cloud lingering on the horizon to
warn Europe of the coming storm.

CHAPTER VI

AIR FORCE IN EMBRYO: 1933-1935

ON 5th March, 1933, the day of the last democratic elections to be held in Germany, the National Socialists led the polling with over 17,000,000 votes. Two weeks later, at a ceremony held in the Potsdam Garrison Church, amid the crash of drums, the blaze of great swastika banners and the thunder of jackbooted feet, Adolf Hitler was formally accepted as the Chancellor of Germany. At last he could strike back at those who had treated him with contempt and dismissed him as an Austrian vagabond, a street-corner orator with wild ideas. The miracle had taken place and Hitler had become all things to all men, able to ignore or eliminate as he chose all who sought to oppose him.

With Hitler's rise to power, Hermann Goering became the second most important man in the Third Reich. He already held a variety of posts, and was in control of most of the economy of the new government. Also, one of his more recent appointments, that of Minister of Aviation, was a job he welcomed, despite the problems it threatened to bring him. Hitler had entrusted him with the secret task of creating a completely new German Air Force, and thus forging the most decisive air striking weapon the world had ever seen, not as a steady development over a number of years, but in the shortest possible time. To the former commander of the illustrious Richthofen Geschwader this was an inspiring challenge that could not be denied; and he never paused to reflect that an outstanding fighter-pilot does not necessarily make a brilliant air strategist. Had he done so, many wasted young lives might have been spared in the years that followed, and perhaps a little of the glory he gained over the Western Front in 1918 would have survived the ignominious years with Hitler that eventually destroyed him.

Many years after Goering had been entrusted with the formation of a new German Air Force, he liked to point out that in 1933 there had not been a single modern fighter or bomber available to equip the new squadrons, and yet he and his

subordinates had managed by 1939 to build up the strongest air
force in the world. Such statements were, of course, far from the
truth. Goering owed much of his success to his predecessors, in
particular General von Seeckt of the Reichswehr, who had
worked for years for just the day when the re-armament of
Germany would commence on a large scale. During the five
years that preceded 1933, almost every German aircraft designer
had paid special attention to the development of military aeroplanes, and although the new German Air Force—to be known
as the Luftwaffe—could not be equipped immediately after
Hitler came to power with the latest fighters and bombers, a
great variety of types were already in existence and ready for
service.

In 1928, the many training machines and catapult seaplanes
designed by Ernst Heinkel with the Reichwehr in mind had led
to the building of the Heinkel He 37, a neat little racing and
experimental biplane. From this was evolved the He 38, which
became the most widely used single-seater fighter in the still
secret Luftwaffe. A sturdy and reliable biplane, armed with two
machine-guns, the He 38 was powered by a 750 h.p. B.M.W.
VI engine which gave it a top speed of 186 m.ph and therefore made it faster than the Bristol Bulldog, the standard British
fighter in service at that time. Other Heinkel types ready in
1933 to equip the new squadrons were the He 49 single-seater
fighter, which also had a 750 h.p. B.M.W. engine, and was
capable of a top speed of 202 m.ph, and the two-seater reconnaissance biplane He 45, which had a top speed of 170 mp.h.
These aircraft were followed soon afterwards by the He 46, a
high-wing monoplane designed for army co-operation duties,
and the He 59, a large twin-engined multi-purpose seaplane that
remained in service until the end of the Second World War.

At about this time the Dornier concern had decided to turn
its attention to multi-motored landplanes designed as such and
not improvised from flying-boats as had occasionally been
attempted in the past. In 1931, a large high-wing monoplane
with a fixed spatted undercarriage, designated the Do Y, was
produced in Switzerland. From this machine was developed an
experimental bomber, the Do F, which masqueraded as a mail
transport aircraft, and the Do F in turn led to the twin-engined
Do 23, which formed the standard medium bomber equipment

of the Luftwaffe in 1933. To all intents and purposes an improved version of the Do Y, the rather ungainly Do 23 was in much the same class as the Fairey Hendon, and featured similar defensive positions in the nose and aft of the wide wings. Although it could not be considered a highly successful bomber for the period, the Do 23 was ordered into quantity production pending the arrival of vastly superior types under consideration.

Hugo Junkers provided the unofficial Luftwaffe with its first heavy bomber, the big three-engined Ju 52/3m, which had been designed in 1932 as an airliner for the Lufthansa, with the proviso that it could easily be converted for military use. This slow and cumbersome aeroplane appeared in the first bomber squadrons of the Luftwaffe with a gun ring fitted in the roof to replace the emergency exit, makeshift bomb bays inside the angular fuselage and a retractable "dustbin" turret below, just behind the wide spatted undercarriage. Comparatively useless as a bomber, it nevertheless eventually became a successful freighter and paratroop carrier, and was to remain in service as the principal German transport aeroplane until the end of the Second World War.

Of the many other types which the industrious German aircraft designers were developing in 1933, the Arado Ar 64 and 65 were also chosen for the Luftwaffe, while the prototype Ar 67 biplane was under consideration as a possible single-seater fighter. Apart from the Heinkel seaplanes, Germany still lacked naval reconnaissance craft, and the Dornier Wal, a flying-boat that was a predecessor of the basically similar but far more successful Do 18, was therefore contemplated as temporarily suitable for the purpose.

For the improvement and administration of this varied collection of good, bad and indifferent aircraft that were the nucleus of the new German Air Force a secret Technical Department, known as "C-Amt", was formed, made up chiefly of engineers and officers who had been transferred from the Reichwehr and old comrades of Hermann Goering who had remained faithful to him since 1918. Erhard Milch, who had proved himself such an energetic chairman of Lufthansa, became the new Deputy Air Minister. Lieutenant General Wever, formerly a Reichwehr officer, was selected by Goering as Chief of the General Staff, while General Stumpff, another Reichwehr soldier, became Chief of Personnel. Karl Bodenschatz, once adjutant of the Richthofen Geschwader, was appointed Goering's personal assistant at the Air Ministry. One by one, the almost forgotten fighter pilots and officers of the old Imperial Army came out of retirement to supply the new Luftwaffe with the administrative and technical staff it required, all anxious to grasp at the opportunity of a new life and rapid promotion that Goering was now prepared to offer those who had served him in the past.

Thus, by the end of 1933 Goering commanded a collection of men who varied in ability almost as much as the aircraft they hoped to build up into a powerful air force. Many of these new staff officers in the higher echelons of the Luftwaffe were men who either did not fly at all or had not flown since 1918, and refused to abandon the views on aerial warfare they had formed so many years ago on the Western Front. The few exceptions—Kesselring, the new Chief of Administration, and General Wever were two of these—who realised that in a future war the strategic bomber fleet would be the backbone of an air force, struggled patiently to overcome the welter of stubborn, hidebound ideas that surrounded them. General Wever, in particular, was an ardent champion of the heavy bomber, and soon after he took office he realised that such aircraft as the Junkers Ju 52/3m were far from being the ideal striking weapons the Luftwaffe needed. His energy and persistence eventually led to the development of a four-engined long-range bomber, the Dornier Do 19, and in still later years to the production of other four-engined aircraft, such as the big Junkers Ju 89 and the Focke-Wulf Fw 200 Kurier. This endeavour to build up a strategic bomber fleet, based on the theory of the Italian General Douhet, who considered that continuous air attack on enemy cities and industrial installations would weaken morale and might well bring a future war to a swift conclusion, was unfortunately never to meet with more than initial success. In the summer of 1936 General Wever lost his life in a tragic air crash, and without his guiding hand the development of heavy bombers was gradually abandoned. Therefore, in much the same way that the German High Command in the early days of the Great War had envisaged the aeroplane only in a secondary, almost unnecessary role, the men who founded the Luftwaffe in 1933 continued to advocate the employment of aircraft in direct support of the ground forces, a short-sighted policy that later became of vital importance when Germany decided to launch a major bombing offensive against England.

The secret training of German aircrew at Lipetzk experimental centre and other auxiliary airfields in the Caucasus had now been going on for a number of years, and Hermann Goering decided that with the forming of a Luftwaffe the Russian project had served its useful purpose and could be brought to an end. However, he appreciated that the personnel of the new Luftwaffe still needed considerable practical experience in modern military aviation, and here the close friendship of Adolf Hitler with Benito Mussolini, the dictator of Italy, began to play a vital part in the German plan for a powerful air force. Provided that international complications could be avoided, the Duce was prepared to allow selected Luftwaffe aircrew to train with the Regia Aeronautica, at that time one of the most efficient and modern air forces in Europe. In July, 1933, the first batch of German pilots travelled secretly across the border into Italy, and, posing as South Tyrolean soldiers, were taken to selected airfields of the Italian Air Force. The German airmen, many of whom were already in the service of Lufthansa, were then issued with Italian Air Force uniforms and accepted as students on an air battle training course. One of these enthusiastic young men, an expert glider pilot at the age of nineteen and now anxious to become an efficient fighter-pilot, was destined within ten years to be hailed as a second Manfred von Richthofen, become General of the Fighters in the Luftwaffe, and receive Germany's highest decorations for valour in the air. His name was Adolf Galland.

In their disguise as officers of the Italian Air Force the aircrew of the Luftwaffe practised every aspect of modern aerial warfare in the warm summer months that followed, developing the new theory of lightning war (or *Blitzkrieg*) by concentrating on low-level support of an invading army. Day after day the German pilots skimmed over the heads of the Italian soldiers who crouched in the trenches below them, firing at the toy balloons waved unwillingly in the general direction of the fighters as they hurtled past. Then, in the autumn of 1933, the course came to an end, and the now highly trained fighter pilots returned to Germany and the unexciting, monotonous routine of the airline pilot—but not for long. Within six months all the graduates of the training course in Italy had been placed on the Air Force active list, and a year later most of them, including Galland, were commissioned officers on the strength of the Luftwaffe.

During 1934, while Germany staggered under the impact of the Roehm blood purge, Hermann Goering and his lieutenants worked energetically to improve upon the basic equipment that General von Seeckt's foresight had contrived to provide for them. State architects were requested to submit plans for a magnificent Air Ministry building in Berlin, and Goering, always with his old comrades in mind, decided to found a Haus de Flieger, or Airmen's Club, that they could use as a meeting place. Aerodromes and factories began to appear all over Germany as the aircraft industry expanded at a remarkable speed. Ernst Heinkel, whose various types of aeroplane equipped most of the new Luftwaffe, chose, with the assistance of General Kesselring, a much larger and more suitable site at Marienehe for his growing organisation, while the famous Henschel locomotive concern at Kassel now had a new aircraft factory outside Berlin, and soon produced their first prototype, a single-seater advanced trainer. In Bavaria, the young Technical Director of the B.F.W. works, Willy Messerschmitt, emerged into the limelight with his latest design, the little four-seater Bf 108 cabin monoplane, an aircraft that led the way for the outstanding Bf 109 fighter, which played such a vital part in the Second World War. The Bf 108 competed in the 1934 "Challenge De Tourisme Internationale" and soon became so popular as a light sporting aeroplane that it was accepted by the Luftwaffe as a communications aircraft and remained in service for many years.

Looking back at the variety of thinly disguised military aeroplanes Germany blatantly displayed to the world in the early 'thirties, it seems difficult to believe that so many "high-speed mailplanes" and "sporting monoplanes" were accepted as such by an innocent and trusting aeronautical community who should have known better. Perhaps it was only reasonable to accept the Junkers Ju 52 as an airliner, for any military possibilities were carefully concealed, but Ernst Heinkel stretched incredulity to the limit with his slim and beautiful He 70, blithely introduced as a mail carrier for four passengers but in reality an experimental military two-seater, and the direct predecessor of the He 111 bomber. Considered purely as a civil aircraft, the He 70 was remarkable for a very high speed, inadequate baggage space and cramped, uncomfortable passenger accommodation, yet despite the widespread publicity it received suspicions in England and France were apparently lulled by the fact that it did actually enter service with Lufthansa on the Berlin, Hamburg, Cologne and Frankfurt routes, if only for a short time. In the summer of 1933 a leading Lufthansa pilot, Flugkapitan Untucht, won eight international speed records with the He 70, later designated the Blitz, which had a maximum speed of 234 m.p.h. at a time when the world speed record for land planes—with a special American racing aircraft—was just over 259 m.p.h Oddly enough, the perfectly streamlined fuselage and elliptical wings of the He 70 made such a favourable impression in England that Rolls-Royce bought one of the machines to use as a test bed for the famous Merlin engine which later equipped the Spitfire and Hurricane fighters of the Royal Air Force.

During this first "undercover" phase of the Luftwaffe, which lasted until March, 1935, Hermann Goering settled into his new post and made use of his most capable officers, Milch and Wever, to gain experience in modern military aviation, although in 1934 he also took the opportunity to become a General of the Reichwehr. Endowed with a genuine love of animals, he had already assumed the title of Reichsjagermeister, or Master Hunter, taking a great interest in the breeding and preservation of wild game. Particularly attracted by a magnificent stretch of forest and heathland beyond Berlin known as the Schorfheide, he arranged for the building of an enormous stone and marble palace for his own use, which he named Karinhall. Situated between two lakes, it included a majestic mausoleum where the body of his late wife, brought from Sweden, was laid to rest. Endowed with the same restless energy and lust for power that was so much a part of Adolf Hitler, Goering was a man who also craved great wealth, and now that he was the second most important personage in the Third Reich all the luxury he had ever wanted began to surround him at Karinhall and his other imposing mansion in the centre of Berlin.

At the end of this busy year, on the eve of his greatest glory,

Goering was already the most popular man in Germany, not a political genius like Hitler to be idolised by the people, but a beaming, rosy-cheeked jester who laughed when he was called "the fat man" or "good old Hermann", and slapped his huge thighs with mirth as he listened to the many jokes about his bulk and hundreds of bemedalled uniforms. Yet behind the jolly exterior lurked always that other Goering who had organised the mass executions on the "night of the long knives" and took more than a casual interest in the new policy for the complete sub-jugation of the Jews, an odd mixture of ruthless efficiency and good-humoured devilment that had served Hitler well in the past but would be slowly consumed by luxury and wealth until it could no longer stand the test of time.

In March, 1935, the Luftwaffe officially emerged into the open as an independent arm of the Reichwehr, which General von Blomberg was in the process of steadily reorganising on such a vast scale that later, as the Wehrmacht, it became the most modern and mechanised army in the world. Goering at once assumed the rank of General der Flieger, or General of the Airmen, and declared to an astonished Europe that Germany demanded immediate equality in the air, while his technical advisers prepared to turn the new German Air Force into a powerful striking weapon in the shortest possible time. Hitler had always remained insistent on this point, and now Goering and Milch were in the position openly to hammer it home.

Of the several new types of aircraft which the leading German designers had been carefully developing since 1933, two —the Heinkel He 51 and Arado Ar 68 fighters—were chosen as standard equipment until 1937, when it was visualised that the industry would be ready to put into mass production the ex-tremely fast and efficient machines that were already available as prototypes.

The Heinkel He 51 and Arado Ar 68 single-seater fighter biplanes were aerodynamically far superior to the variety of fighters that had formed the temporary equipment of the Luft-waffe since 1933, proving to be almost 20 m.p.h. faster than the standard types used during the clandestine period that had now come to an end. Powered by a greatly improved version of the 750 h.p. B.M.W VI in-line engine, both machines were well streamlined and remarkably similar in general appearance, and the He 51 in particular had a performance not unlike that of the then standard single-seater fighter of the Royal Air Force, the famous Hawker Fury. The Arado Ar 68 was a successor to the sturdy Ar 65 already in service with the Luftwaffe, and had been developed by way of the Ar 67, a prototype fighter experimentally equipped with a Rolls-Royce Kestrel 12-cylinder liquid-cooled engine.

When the existence of the Luftwaffe was formally announced, the bomber squadrons had progressed in equipment hardly at all since 1933 and continued to retain the ponderous three-engined Junkers Ju 52/3m and the far from satisfactory twin-engined Dornier Do 23. However, the strangely uncomfortable "high-speed mailplanes" so beloved of the German designers during the previous two years had served their purpose, and other more modern types were either on the drawing-board or had just reached the prototype stage. Two of these, the excellent Heinkel He 111 and the less successful Junkers Ju 86, were to emerge as medium bombers within a year. Meanwhile, Goering and his lieutenants had to be content with the obsolescent material at hand, while the designers, ignoring the general impatience, worked steadily on with the confidence that they were looking ahead into a brilliant future.

A special order signed by Hitler on 14th March, 1935, authorised the formation of the Jagdgeschwader Manfred von Richthofen 2, which was organised into two Gruppen, each of approximately forty aircraft. The first Gruppe was established with Arado Ar 65s (later replaced by Ar 68s) at Doberitz-Elsgrund near Berlin, and soon afterwards Gruppe II came into existence with Heinkel He 51s at Juterborg-Damm. The commanders and many of the senior officers were airmen who had served during the First World War, and all the Geschwader aircraft sported bright red cowlings in order that the colourful traditions instituted so many years ago by Manfred von Richthofen might be revived. Many of the new fighters at first bore deceptively innocent German civil registration letters, but soon after they entered service the familiar black Latin crosses adopted in 1918, together with the swastika of the Third Reich, appeared as the formal national markings of the Luftwaffe.

On 10th April, 1935, thousands of cheering people lined the streets in Berlin as the long wedding procession of Hermann

Goering and his actress bride, Emmy Sonnemann, moved away from the Reich Chancellory in the direction of the Town Hall where the civil ceremony was to be held. Goering, resplendent in the uniform of a General der Flieger, and heedless of the light rain that was falling from a grey sky, waved to the excited crowds, beaming with pleasure as the cries of "*Hoch Hermann!*" and "*Heil Hitler!*" mingled with the thunder of aero engines and the fighters of the new Richthofen Geschwader swept in perfect formation overhead. Ten days after the wedding, on the occasion of Hitler's birthday, the fighter force of the Luftwaffe was expanded with a further squadron of Heinkel He 51 biplanes which was named the Horst Wessel Geschwader and presented to the Fuehrer as a birthday present to mark the double event. The fact that the disreputable S.A. leader Horst Wessel, killed in a Nazi street brawl, should be considered a hero fit to be honoured alongside Manfred von Richthofen apparently had little significance for those who remembered Germany's most outstanding airman, but it was a striking example of the power that lay behind Joseph Goebbels' propaganda machine and the declining standards that were following in the wake of National Socialism under Adolf Hitler.

One of the men who had served in the original Richthofen Geschwader was at this time working in the Technical Department of the Luftwaffe, to the surprise of his many friends, who found it impossible to imagine him fettered to a desk, his life bounded by the dull monotony of office routine. But Ernst Udet, the gay, reckless fighter-pilot of the Great War, the flying acrobat of the 'twenties, the film stunt man of the early 'thirties, had never really changed since 1918. The rise of the Nazi Party meant absolutely nothing to him, and Goering, despite his wealth and power, remained only "the fat man" to Udet, who for years had treated him with a mixture of contempt and amused indifference. Frivolous, light-hearted and yet always an ardent nationalist, Udet disliked working for anyone except himself, and danger was the spice of his life. He had no ability as an executive—his brief career as an aircraft industrialist had ended in complete disaster—and he enjoyed his irresponsible life as a stunt pilot far more than the money it brought him. The love of adventure and passion for flying that was so much a part of him attracted thousands of admirers and hundreds of reliable friends, but he also had a sensitive, artistic temperament that made him at home with famous actresses such as Leni Riefenstal, and he had a reputation as an enthusiastic sportsman.

Why, then, should Udet be interested in the Technical Department of the Luftwaffe? The answer lay to a great extent with Hermann Goering, who knew perfectly well that he needed as many experienced airmen as possible in the new German Air Force, and though he had little in common with Udet, the flying skill and popularity of "Udlinger", as he was often called, could not be denied. When Goering asked him to join the Luftwaffe, saying that Germany needed practical men with imagination, Udet hesitated, then finally agreed—but only in his own characteristic way. He wanted no official status, had no desire to wear uniform again, and firmly refused to enter the dangerous whirlpool of Nazi politics. He simply wanted to fly and do exactly as he liked, yet to his great surprise Goering was still anxious to accept him, and slyly suggested an immediate trip to America to study the development of military aviation there. Delighted at such an opportunity to travel outside Europe again, Udet said no more, and so the decision that would eventually prove to be a fatal one was made.

While touring the United States, Udet discovered a new air weapon that was to have a serious effect on the whole policy of the Luftwaffe, with disastrous consequences that did not become fully apparent for many years. The dive-bomber, an aircraft which could fall almost vertically from a great height on to a selected target, drop a heavy bomb and then zoom away, was at that time under consideration in America, where such machines were popularly known as "Hell Divers", and the Curtiss factory was building a number of prototypes. The idea was, of course, not completely unknown in Germany, for the Swedish plant of the Junkers company had produced an aircraft in 1928 designated the K. 47, which was publicised as a two-seater interceptor fighter but proved to be an experimental dive-bomber and the direct predecessor of the infamous Ju 87. Ernst Heinkel had also provided at least one type of aircraft which could be used as a dive-bomber, and this machine, the He 66, did, in fact, go into temporary service with the Luftwaffe. Nevertheless, when Udet returned from America the dive-bomber suddenly became no longer an interesting novelty but a subject of the utmost importance, for Goering's interest had been aroused and the German aircraft industry was eager to fulfil his demands.

However, it was no easy matter to convince such professional airmen as Milch and Kesselring, and Udet therefore persuaded Goering to buy two of the new Curtiss dive-bombers for demonstration purposes. After they had been delivered he spent many hours flying the new machines, until at last he was completely familiar with their amazing ability to plunge headlong towards the earth, engines screaming with power, only to pull easily out of the power dive at a movement of his skilled hands and rise swiftly away. But at Tempelhof, Udet lost control of the Curtiss he was flying when an elevator abruptly jammed, and he barely escaped by parachute before it crashed. He refused to be discouraged and decided to demonstrate the remaining Curtiss at Rechlin before an audience of high-ranking Luftwaffe staff officers. The ensuing magnificent flying display failed to impress those who saw it, not because they could honestly find any obvious faults in the performance of the machines, but because most of them considered Udet to be nothing more than a likeable jester, an aerial comedian who enjoyed being in the limelight. With a strength of character totally at variance with his usual careless acceptance of events, Udet bitterly resisted any criticism of the dive-bomber as a modern air weapon, but as a civilian, a mere outsider fortunate enough to have the ear of Hermann Goering, he found it impossible to oppose the views of the general staff. Unwittingly, of course, he had played directly into Goering's hands, for now, unless he was prepared to let the dive-bomber idea fizzle away, he had to join the Luftwaffe, take a high military rank and acknowledge the existence of the Nazi Party. Reluctantly, Udet decided to accept the responsibilities of high office and became an Oberst in the Technical Department, realising at last that Goering's patience and diplomatic skill had, as usual, been rewarded.

Now that Udet was able to use his new influence in the Luftwaffe a specification was soon drawn up for aeroplanes to be used as dive-bombers and fighters. The first machine to be built to fulfil this specification was the Henschel Hs 123, a sturdy single-seater biplane with a large 800 h.p. B.M.W. 132 air-cooled radial engine and a fixed, spatted undercarriage. The prototype Hs 123 was first flown, and by Udet, in May, 1933, and later this machine was demonstrated at the Nazi Party rally at Nuremberg that year. Not entirely successful as a dive-bomber, and with a maximum speed of only 214 m.p.h. at 4,000 ft. that made it a hopeless proposition as a fighter, the Hs 123 turned out to be more of a ground attack (close support) aircraft than anything else, and it was therefore eventually placed in production as equipment for the Luftwaffe's first Schlachtgeschwader, or close support wing. Strangely enough, the subsequent history of the Hs 123 more than justified Udet's unswerving faith in the type, for it served with the Legion Condor during the Spanish Civil War, and although obsolescent by 1939 flew in support of the German invasions of Poland and France, was used in some numbers on the Russian Front and actually remained fully operational until 1943.

Despite the fact that he gained little official support from the German Air Ministry (the Reichsluftfahrtministerium) and continued to be opposed by most of the leading Luftwaffe staff officers, Udet remained an ardent exponent of the dive-bomber, and by the end of 1933 the Junkers, Heinkel and Arado factories were building prototypes for his consideration. Meanwhile, General Wever was demanding the heavy strategic bombers that Germany would need so badly in the near future, Goering was inclined to feel that fast twin-engined medium bombers should compose the main striking force of the Luftwaffe, and a few lonely voices in the wilderness were suggesting that a strong fighter arm should not be overlooked. Uncertainty and indecision reigned supreme, but the professional airmen shrugged their shoulders and reflected that all the main difficulties were merely the birth pangs of the new Luftwaffe, and time and the technicians would overcome them.

In Berlin Adolf Hitler, preparing for the war in which air power would play such an important part, was one of the few people who knew that in 1935 there was very little time, and within four years there would be no time at all. Unfortunately, the passing years only brought more revolutionary ideas and greater problems, while the wavering, unsettled policy of the men who had founded the Luftwaffe meandered on and on, until eventually it contributed in no small measure to the downfall of what might have been the most powerful air striking weapon in the world.

CHAPTER VII

INTO THE ARENA: SPAIN, 1936

THROUGHOUT the autumn and winter of 1935, while Mussolini was waging his highly mechanised war against helpless Abyssinian tribesmen and Britain and France were preoccupied with futile attempts to frustrate the blustering Fascist dictator, Adolf Hitler quietly bided his time. Then the Franco-Soviet Pact, which had been signed the previous year after Germany had rejected the Treaty of Versailles, and still awaited ratification, finally came before the French Chamber of Deputies in February, 1936. It was approved by 353 votes to 164, and immediately Hitler had his excuse for a startling and decisive move. On the pretext that the Franco-Soviet treaty was incompatible with the terms of the Locarno Pact, he issued orders for the reoccupation of the demilitarised zone of the Rhineland.

On the morning of 7th March, 1936, a comparatively small body of German troops, stated afterwards by General Jodl to comprise only one division, moved into the Rhineland, three battalions crossing the Rhine to Aachen, Trier and Saarbrucken. The Luftwaffe, still little more than a collection of old and new aeroplanes, was totally unprepared for even such a small-scale military operation as the reoccupation of the Rhineland, and many years afterwards Adolf Galland recalled in his memoirs that the only school for fighter-pilots then in existence had to be dissolved because the aircraft were needed to display the strength that still existed only on paper. Out of the three Jagdgeschwader raised with some difficulty to an operational status, only about ten aircraft could have fought in action, the remainder being virtually unarmed. To give an impression of greater numbers, the same machines were displayed over and over again to the public at different aerodromes, but the air screws and cowlings were repainted in new colours between appearances, usually the previous night. The scarcity of pilots, which might well have aroused the suspicions of foreign air attachés, was overcome by using mechanics dressed in flying clothing, who posed for press photographs beside the machines they had never flown. The whole mobilisation was an elaborate masquerade—a few airworthy fighters shielding behind a cardboard façade—but the fact remains that it worked, and was accepted as proof of Germany's new power.

During the forty-eight hours that followed the march into the Rhineland, which Hitler later admitted were the most nerve-racking in his life, the German generals trembled in their polished boots and awaited disaster. However, the news had been handed to the French, British and Italian ambassadors with remarkable new proposals for peace, for the Fuehrer had judged public opinion within the Western Powers with amazing accuracy, and soon afterwards it became obvious that his outrageous bluff had succeeded. Anthony Eden saw no reason to suppose that Germany threatened hostilities, a sign that France would meet with little support from Great Britain, and both nations wavered and hesitated. The Locarno Powers conferred, Germany's action was condemned as an assertion of strength, but there was little talk of mobilisation, and in the end nothing was done. In less than two days, without a shot being fired, Hitler had won a staggering victory, increased the popularity of the Nazi Party and at the same time taught his generals a decisive lesson in diplomacy and military affairs.

Determined to convince those in Germany who might still have an uneasy feeling that he had used his position as Supreme Commander of the Armed Forces of the Third Reich to gamble recklessly with the nation, Hitler abruptly dissolved the Reichstag soon after the reoccupation of the Rhineland. The election that followed was a direct invitation to the German people to pass judgement on his policy, and the results quickly subdued the few officers on his staff who still vaguely criticised him. 45,001,489 (99 per cent) of the German electorate actually voted, and 44,461,278 (98.8 per cent) of the votes cast were for Hitler, establishing beyond a doubt complete national approval of his action. Freed at last of the shackles of Versailles, backed by the German people and with the Rhineland as tangible evidence that Europe was uncertain of his power, the Fuehrer retired quietly again into the background to complete his preparations for the moves that would lead inexorably to war.

When the smouldering powder keg of south-west Europe

finally exploded into life in July, 1936, and civil war broke out in Spain, a number of far more powerful and certainly much wealthier nations grasped at the unexpected opportunity to try out their latest military aircraft and other equipment under operational conditions, in the belief that invaluable battle experience with modern weapons would thus be gained. Had the Spanish people been left to fight out their quarrel among themselves much unnecessary bloodshed and distress would probably have been saved, for at first the air side of the civil war was fairly evenly matched, with part of the small Spanish Air Force flying with the Government forces and part with the Revolutionary forces, but unfortunately both sides soon began to receive aid from foreign countries. The Communist Government armies were sent quantities of I-15 and I-16 fighters and some SB-2 bombers from Russia, as well as a continuous flow of new aircraft from France. However, following the example of Mussolini, Adolf Hitler decided to give active assistance to General Francisco Franco Bahamonde, the principal leader of the insurgents, and thousands of men and hundreds of tons of supplies were sent to Spain in the course of the next three years, including the Luftwaffe "Volunteer" Corps identified officially by its unit number of "88" and popularly known as the Legion Kondor.

Luftwaffe personnel selected for service in Spain initially reported to a secret drafting office in Berlin, where civilian clothes, documents and Spanish currency were provided before the enthusiastic airmen were sent on the next stage of their journey to Doberitz, a central assembly point for the batches of "volunteers". Dressed in their civilian clothes, and posing as innocent *Kraft durch Freude* (Strength through Joy) tourists, the various experts and technicians of all kinds then moved to Hamburg for embarkation on liners supposedly bound for Genoa, but actually destined for Spain. Personal mail, which could have presented a tricky security problem, was handled with typical German efficiency, for friends and relatives who wished to correspond with a pilot were asked to write him "c/o Max Winkler, Berlin, S.W.68", a postal address that existed only as a secret clearing house for the onward transmission of letters. On arrival in Spain, the protégés of "Max Winkler" donned olive-brown Spanish uniforms and were appointed to a rank one grade higher than their normal status in Germany, with correspondingly increased pay that was welcomed by all concerned, although in the event they more than earned it.

In the summer of 1936 the first personnel for the Legion Kondor left Hamburg on the S.S. *Usaramo*, which also carried six Heinkel He 51 biplanes and spares for Junkers Ju 52/3m bombers. Meanwhile, the Hisma air transport organisation, comprising a number of the big three-engined Junkers machines, had already flown across the Mediterranean to their Spanish bases and were soon engaged in transporting General Franco's Moorish troops from North Africa, the main base of the revolutionaries, across the Straits to the Spanish mainland. By September, 1936, estimates gave the total number of troops flown from Morocco to Spain as 14,000, in a remarkable airlift that assisted Franco to consolidate his position during the first two months of the civil war, with the result that San Sebastian and then Badajoz soon fell to the insurgents and the march on Madrid began.

During the autumn of 1936 large shipments of aircraft for the Government forces continued to pour into Spain from France and Russia, and Franco subsequently appealed to Hitler and Mussolini for further assistance. In due course the main strength of the Legion Kondor was despatched by sea to Cadiz, where a brief ceremonial parade to welcome the new arrivals was held before the Luftwaffe aircraft commenced a series of bombing raids on Mediterranean ports in Government hands. These early attempts to practise precision bombing on towns and centres of communication actually met with only moderate success, for the cumbersome Ju 52/3m aircraft encountered icing difficulties that winter when crossing the Sierra Nevada and had to be transferred to bases in Spanish Morocco, but the first steps had nevertheless been taken on the road that would eventually lead to Warsaw, Rotterdam and Belgrade. Initially commanded by General Hugo Sperrle, the Legion later came under the leadership of General Volkmann, who was responsible for forming these first bomber units in Spain.

The fighter force of the Legion Kondor, designated Jagdgruppe J/88, comprised in the beginning three Staffeln, or squadrons, each possessing twelve aircraft when at full strength, and all equipped with Heinkel He 51 biplanes until 1937, when the first and second squadrons received the new Messerschmitt Bf 109B monoplane fighters then entering service with the Luftwaffe. The original bomber force of the Legion, established as Kampfgruppe K/88, was made up of four Staffeln of three-engined Junkers Ju 52/3m bomber-transport aircraft, which proved to be so slow and vulnerable that they were suitable only for daylight operations, and then only with a strong escort of fighters. The obvious inferiority of the Ju 52 machines later led to the introduction of a few Junkers Ju 86D bombers, but these were already obsolescent, sadly lacking in speed and defensive armament, and had to be withdrawn after only a brief period in service. More successful were the very fast Heinkel He 70 mono-planes that equipped the only reconnaissance squadron of the Legion and the Heinkel He 59s and He 60s used by the solitary German seaplane squadron in Spain, although they did not have to play such a vital part in the struggle for supremacy that soon became a characteristic of the first great battles fought in the air since 1918.

While the Legion Kondor was enduring an unexpectedly savage baptism of fire in Spain, the extremely modern aircraft intended to form the backbone of the Luftwaffe were beginning to leave the assembly lines for flight testing and evaluation prior to entering squadron service. The most important of these new types proved to be the Heinkel He 111K and Dornier Do 17 twin-engined medium bombers and the Messerschmitt Bf 109 single-seater fighter, although the angular Junkers Ju 87 dive-bomber, which also appeared in 1936, soon acquired the highest reputation, due mainly to the influence and determination of Ernst Udet. During the same year three prototypes had also been built of the Dornier Do 19, a four-engined heavy bomber of the type advocated by General Wever, but in the event the development of this interesting aircraft was abandoned, owing to a tragic accident involving an entirely different machine, the Heinkel He 70.

The Heinkel He 70 Blitz, at that time the fastest German aeroplane in service, was chosen by General Wever for his personal use in 1935, although he could not be considered a very experienced pilot, having been taught to fly only the previous year. Unfortunately, Wever was unaware that a small lever situated in the cockpit of the He 70 locked the control column while the aircraft was on the ground, and when he took off on 3rd June, 1936, after a conference at Dresden this catch had not been released. The He 70 became airborne, but with the ailerons immovable failed to gain any height and crashed at high speed, with the result that Wever was instantly killed. With the loss of this remarkable man, later acknowledged to be one of the best brains the Luftwaffe ever possessed, died all hopes that Germany would ever have a powerful strategic bomber force, although his persistence and foresight led to the issue a year after his death of a new Reichsluftfahrtministerium specification for a four-engined long-range heavy bomber—intended primarily for shipping duties.

The development of the Heinkel He 111K was undertaken by the leading Heinkel designers Walther and Siegfried Gunther, who successfully managed to fulfil a Deutsche Lufthansa specification for a high-speed airliner, and at the same time include in their design all the basic requirements of a medium bomber for the Luftwaffe. An orthodox cantilever low-wing monoplane of metal stressed-skin construction, the prototype He 111 was demonstrated in public at Tempelhof, Berlin, in January, 1936, and a year later aircraft of this type—the first mass-produced German bomber—were already being delivered to the Luftwaffe. These early versions of the He 111K were fitted with twin Daimler-Benz DB 600 engines rated at 1,000 h.p. and did not feature the fully glazed nose that later became a trade mark of the type, which soon proved so adaptable that it could be produced not only as a bomber but also as a mine layer and torpedo aircraft. Meanwhile the civil prototypes had failed to interest Deutsche Lufthansa, but served a useful purpose when they were transferred to a highly secret Luftwaffe unit commanded by Oberst von Rohwehl at Staaken and undertook special long-range reconnaissance flights over Britain, France and the Soviet Union. A civil version of the He 111 was also used as a personal transport by Erhard Milch.

Heinkel He 111B-1s were chosen to re-equip the bomber force of the Legion Kondor in 1937, replacing the Junkers Ju 52/3m machines then in service and thus providing Kampfgruppe 88 with the opportunity of launching daylight raids with unescorted bombers fast enough to evade even the latest Republican fighters sent from France and Russia.

Unlike the He 111K, the attractive Dornier Do 17, popularly known as the "Flying Pencil", was initially designed as a commercial airliner, but the prototypes were rejected by Deutsche Lufthansa and the project was therefore abandoned. However, the star pilot of Lufthansa, Flugkapitän Untucht, considered that the Do 17 might well make an excellent high-speed bomber, and aroused the interest of Goering and the Reichsluftfahrt-ministerium to such an extent that a new series of prototypes was ordered to examine the possibilities of the Do 17 in the bombing role. A slim and graceful shoulder-wing monoplane powered by two 600 h.p. B.M.W. VI upright Vee motors, the Do 17 made a spectacular appearance at the International Military Aircraft Competition at Zurich in 1937, having such a high speed that it proved to be 25 m.p.h. faster than the standard biplane fighters then in service with the Royal Air Force.

In the summer of 1937 the first Do 17 squadrons began to appear in the Luftwaffe, and a year later a number of the latest E-1 bombers were sent to Spain for testing under operational conditions. The success of these aircraft in the bombing and reconnaissance role led to the formation in the Legion Kondor of a special unit composed of a further fifteen Do 17s, of the F-1 type.

The strangely psychological effect created by the sight and noise of the ugly, vulture-like Junkers Ju 87 dive-bomber succeeded in weaving around it a reputation actually far in excess of its worth as a weapon of war. Commonly called the Stuka, from the term *sturzkampfflugzeug*, applied to all dive-bombers regardless of type, the Ju 87 was slow, unwieldy, and easily one of the most vulnerable of warplanes, yet by a curious quirk of fate it came to be selected as the standard dive-bomber for the Luftwaffe. A year after Ernst Udet had been appointed to the Technical Branch a special competition was held at Rechlin to select the most suitable type of aircraft for the dive-bombing role out of the four prototypes entered, the Arado Ar 81 biplane and the Blohm and Voss Ha 137, Junkers Ju 87 and Heinkel He 118 monoplanes. The final choice rested between the Junkers and Heinkel machines, and Udet therefore decided to flight test both these prototypes himself before making decision, but his lack of experience with the automatic airscrew pitch-change of the He 118 resulted in disaster when the aircraft shed its propeller and crashed. Udet baled out, stunned but comparatively uninjured, and soon afterwards the Junkers concern was awarded a contract for the mass production of the Ju 87.

In the spring of 1937 the first Junkers Ju 87A dive-bombers began to reach the squadrons, the Sturzkampfgeschwader Immelmann being the first unit to receive the new equipment, and later that year the Henschel Hs 123 biplanes then serving in Spain with the Kondor Legion were supplemented by an experimental trio of Junkers Ju 87As. These machines initially went into action at Teruel and proved to be so successful— always operating under a protective umbrella of Nationalist fighters—that in 1938 they were joined by large quantities of the latest Ju 87Bs, which had a better performance, increased armament and a heavier bomb load. They also featured a typical invention of Ernst Udet, the high-pitched sirens commonly known as "the trumpets of Jericho", which produced the almost unbearable noise that gave the Ju 87 its dreaded reputation during the first phase of the Second World War.

The design of the Messerschmitt Bf 109 fighter evolved slowly but surely from the various little Messerschmitt sporting aeroplanes that appeared in the 'twenties, and more directly from the Bf 108 communications monoplane. The first prototype of the Bf 109, which successfully competed against the Arado Ar 80, the Focke-Wulf Fw 159 and the Heinkel He 112, was powered by a Rolls-Royce Kestrel V engine, for the German aero engine industry had failed to keep pace with the breathtaking progress of military aviation; however, subsequent prototypes were fitted with Junkers Jumo 210A engines and the type was sufficiently developed by 1936 to be demonstrated in public at the Olympic Games held in Berlin. Meanwhile, the Reichsluftfahrtministerium had already accepted the Bf 109 for service as a standard single-seater fighter with the Luftwaffe, although it is extremely doubtful if any of the experts concerned realised at the time that they were officially approving an aircraft destined to be one of the most formidable fighters in the world, equalled only by the legendary Supermarine Spitfire and to gain the distinction of being manufactured in larger quantities than any other warplane used during the Second World War.

The first production model of the Bf 109, the B-1 version

armed with three machine-guns, was issued to the resurrected Richthofen Jagdgeschwader (JG.2) shortly before a special team under the command of Major Seidemann gave a practical demonstration of the new fighter's capabilities at the Zurich international flying meeting in July, 1937. The remarkable performance of the Bf 109 in Switzerland completely vindicated Messerschmitt's faith in his design, and soon afterwards a number of Bf 109B-2 fighters arrived in Spain to re-equip the first and second Staffeln of Jagdgruppe J/88 in the Legion Kondor. The Heinkel He 51 biplanes initially in service with all three squadrons of J/88 had proved to be inferior in speed and armament to the latest Soviet I-15 and I-16 fighters that opposed them, but the unexpected appearance of the new Bf 109s immediately altered the situation. Vastly superior in every way to all other fighters flying over Spain, they were eminently suitable for escort duties with the fast Heinkel He 111 bombers that had recently replaced the Junkers Ju 52/3ms of Kampfgruppe K/88 and were also employed from time to time on low-level ground staffing duties behind the enemy lines. However, the third Staffel of Jagdgruppe J/88 retained its Heinkel He 51 fighters, and these aircraft, armed with fragmentation bombs, were relegated almost entirely to the ground attack role. In the summer of 1937, under the command of Adolf Galland, who was already establishing himself as a born leader and a skilful tactician, they wrought havoc among the Republican forces, although they were extremely vulnerable to ground fire and were suffering heavy losses by the end of the year.

This new Luftwaffe policy of testing the latest German military aircraft, including types not yet ordered for mass production, under operational conditions in Spain led to the development of various techniques which at the time were considered by Goering and his staff to be of inestimable value in the future conduct of modern air war. For example, in their encounters with the Republican I-15 and I-16 fighters, the German Bf 109 pilots soon realised that the close wingtip-to-wingtip formations used by almost every air force in the world, including the R.A.F., were impracticable for combat, as the high speeds of modern fighters, made it necessary to pay more attention to avoiding collision than watching for enemy aircraft. These tight "V" formations were therefore abandoned in favour of the loose pair, or *Rotte*, making up a finger-four, or *Schwarm*, three of these finger-fours forming a Staffel of twelve aircraft.

Another new technique was developed after using the Heinkel He 111 bombers of Kampfgruppe K/88, which were found to be so fast that they were able to evade most of the interceptor fighters in Republican service. A policy of unescorted daylight raids was therefore adopted and proved successful enough in Spain but resulted in complete disaster when used during the German onslaught against Britain in 1940. Oddly enough, however, Adolf Galland and his obsolescent He 51 fighters were responsible for pursuing the technique of saturation, or "carpet" bombing, which in the spring of 1937 had already turned the eyes of the world on an almost unknown Spanish town and given a terrifying glimpse into the awful future that lay ahead for Rotterdam, Dresden and Hiroshima.

Monday was the traditional market day in the little Basque town of Guernica, and on 26th April, 1937, the Monday that Guernica died, the jostling streets and the wide plaza were thronged with thousands of peasants from the surrounding countryside, shepherding their sheep and donkeys to the market, their ungainly oxcarts laden with the richest farm produce in Spain. High above the red roofs of the town, bright dots in the early morning sky, circled two aircraft, too high for the peasants who crowded the plaza to see that they belonged to the dreaded Legion Kondor of Hugo von Sperrle. Lazily, contemptuously, the German reconnaissance machines turned slowly over unprotected Guernica, then, satisfied at last, set course for their base, leaving behind them 10,000 people innocently unaware that they were about to participate in a typical German experiment—to assess the value of mass bombing from the air.

At 4.30 p.m. the church bells rang out in Guernica an urgent warning that a heavy formation of enemy bombers was on the way. Ten minutes later, while the streets were still crowded with frightened, uncertain people, the He 51 fighters of the Legion Kondor, suddenly hurtled across the roofs of the town at less than 600 ft., their machine-guns stammering violent death at the screaming men, women and children who fought desperately to get under cover. The plaza became a shambles of bullet-riddled bodies, laden carts overturned as the fear-crazed oxen that drew them stampeded wildly through the streets, people

scattered for the open fields outside the town and were ruthlessly mown down from the air. Then, abruptly as they had
arrived, roaring away in perfect formation, the fighters were
gone.

The second phase of what von Sperrle calmly envisaged as
an "act of force" brought the thundering, majestic might of the
German bomber squadrons. With terrible precision, the He 111s
swung over Guernica, then, as if released by a single giant hand,
the huge bombs rained down. Smoke and flame erupted in the
reeling town, buildings crumbled into ruin and cellars buried
their dead, but the bombardment continued until the earth
trembled beneath the concussion of the bombs, while the
victims, human and animal, cowered and waited for the deluge
to end.

The medium bombers passed overhead for the last time, and
immediately Guernica was compelled to endure the agony of the
third and final phase of her destruction. Thousands of incendiary
bombs, clustered in containers that broke apart in the air,
tumbled down on the shattered town, turning the broken streets
into raging infernos, consuming at least one hospital and burning hundreds of people alive. Communications were cut and all
transport in the town completely destroyed, bombed houses
became cauldrons of fire, but for hour after endless hour the
bombardment went on, until nothing moved in the desolation
of Guernica. Hugo von Sperrle's "act of force" was being conducted with a thoroughness and precision hitherto unequalled
in any war.

Three hours later, at 7.45 p.m., it was all over, and the dazed
survivors were left in peace to search in the smoking ruins for
their relatives, and, having found them, bury their dead. That
night, the staff officers of the Legion Kondor, the men who wore
the badge of a diving condor eagle with a bomb clutched in its
claws, were able to congratulate themselves on yet another
interesting theory proved in action, yet another satisfactory
report to be sent back to Germany and carefully filed away in the
vaults of the Reichsluftfahrtministerium in Berlin. The reaction
of the more civilised world that existed outside the borders of
the Third Reich, so intense that it staggered even Franco and
his supporters, not surprisingly showed little appreciation of
either the efficiency or the necessity of the bombardment.

Appalled at the devastation they found in Guernica, the foreign
correspondents in Spain immediately condemned the wholesale
slaughter of 1,600 men, women and children as a terrible crime.
"In the form of its execution and the scale of the destruction it
wrought," ran one detailed statement, "no less than the selection
of the objective, the raid on Guernica is unparalled in military
history. . . ."

Undisturbed by the thunderbolts of criticism hurled at
Germany from every side, the Goebbels propaganda machine
had no difficulty in washing the blood from the wings of the
Legion Kondor. "Everyone regrets the fate of Guernica," commented a spokesman in Berlin, "but as no German aeroplane
took part in the bombing Germany is not concerned in the affair."
To ensure that public opinion in England was silenced once and
for all, von Ribbentrop, the German ambassador to Great
Britain, officially protested to Anthony Eden against "the in-
correct . . . allegations made in parts of the British Press and in
the House of Commons with reference to the alleged destruction
of the Spanish town of Guernica." The uncertainty of German
guilt, deliberately fostered in a world not yet accustomed to
Hitler and his methods, to some extent still remains; Adolf
Galland, who was not in Spain at the time, has written that the
bombing of Guernica was an error, caused by primitive bomb
sights and inexperienced crews, but he admits that the members of the Legion Kondor had a certain reluctance to discuss
the matter.

Hugo von Sperrle was a monocled, bull-necked soldier of the
old school, with no political axe to grind and little regard for the
value of public opinion. In 1939, when Franco was dictator of
Spain and Hitler was plunging a delirious Germany towards the
precipice of war, Sperrle stated openly that aircraft of the Legion
Kondor were responsible for the bombing of Guernica. Unfortunately, by 1939 the dusty, bloody slaughter of the Spanish
civil war had faded into history, and it no longer seemed very
important, or even interesting, that the former commander of
the Legion Kondor was proudly boasting that his aeroplanes
had, after all, been "concerned in the affair".

Probably Hermann Goering had the last word on the subject
of Guernica. Endowed with that astonishing, twisted German
logic that obligingly provides an explanation for the inexplic-

able, in two simple sentences he dismissed from his conscience the first town in Europe to be destroyed by bombing from the air. Questioned about the raid while on trial for his life at Nuremberg in 1946, he stated: "Guernica had been a testing ground for the Luftwaffe. It was a pity; but we could not do otherwise, as we had nowhere else to try out our machines."

It was indeed a pity. The people of Guernica—not to mention the thousands who died in Hamburg and Dresden—would undoubtedly have agreed with him.

CHAPTER VIII

THE END OF THE AIRSHIPS: 1936

AWAKENED into vigorous protest at the startling revival in German military aviation, aeronautical experts all over the world were soon pointing out that too many other leading air forces had been sadly neglected, and indeed had scarcely improved in equipment since the end of the First World War. The day of the romantic fighter biplane, with its manoeuvrability, wire-braced varnished struts and bulky cowling-mounted machine-guns, was slowly coming to an end, but it was true that tradition died hard and the Hawker Furys and Gloster Gauntlets, the Fiat CR. 32s and Grumman Hawks lingered on as if determined to survive for ever. Outside observers contemplated with alarm the replacement for the Gloster Gauntlet in the R.A.F. of the Gloster Gladiator, for it had a performance inferior even to that of the latest German bombers, although in the event it proved to be the last of the British biplane fighters. The standard R.A.F. day bomber in service since 1930, the two-seater Hawker Hart, had a maximum speed of only 184 m.p.h., while the Handley Page Heyford night bomber, ungainly and inadequately armed with three Lewis guns, struggled along with a ridiculous bomb load at a mere 142 mp.h.

The French Air Force in 1936 boasted one good single-seater fighter type, the Dewoitine D. 510 monoplane, which had been successfully tested in the dusty arena of Spain, and preceded the excellent D. 520, to gain some distinction in the early summer of 1940. The bombers of the Armée de L'Air were mostly ponderous, under-powered machines with apparently dozens of imposing glazed turrets and very few defensive guns, although new streamlined types such as the Amiot 351 and Liore et Olivier LeO 45 were on the way. Even Japan, influenced for so many years by German designs, had just discarded the biplane; the latest Nipponese fighter, already in action over China, was the sturdy Mitsubishi 96 monoplane, the direct predecessor of Jiro Horikoshi's outstanding A6M Zero-Sen, undoubtedly one of the best aeroplanes to be used during the Second World War. Italy, with an air arm supposedly at least as powerful as the Luftwaffe, continued to some extent to live in the past by continuing the development of the Fiat CR. 32 biplane which had already suffered the same disadvantages as the He 51s of the Legion Kondor when used in Spain. However, the new three-engined Savoia-Marchetti Sm. 79 bombers of the Regia Aeronautica were extremely modern in appearance, and were to form the backbone of Italian air striking power for almost a decade.

Fortunately for the people of Great Britain, the R.A.F. and the Air Ministry had watched with more than a casual interest the whirlwind rebirth of military aviation in the Third Reich, and, without any fuss, acted accordingly. The biplane-versus-monoplane controversy came to an abrupt end with a series of specifications sent out in 1934 and resulting in the appearance only two years later of some of the finest military aircraft in the world—all monoplanes. These included the Supermarine Spitfire and Hawker Hurricane single-seater fighters and the Vickers-Armstrong Wellington and Handley Page Hampden heavy bombers. Other new aircraft for the R.A.F. were the Fairy Battle and Bristol Blenheim light bombers and the Armstrong Whitworth Whitley, a rather ugly but efficient night bomber. All these machines were at least as good as the latest equivalent aircraft Germany possessed, and some were infinitely better. For instance, the formidable armament of the production Spitfires and Hurricanes—eight Browning machine-guns with a rate of fire of 1,200 rounds per minute—was so novel at the time that it aroused considerable doubts in the minds of men who still thought of aircraft armament in terms of twin Vickers guns and Aldis sights, but the destructive power of the R.A.F. eight-gun fighters proved to be a decisive factor when put to the test during the Battle of Britain.

Another aircraft, not very interesting at the time, but destined to be one of the most powerful weapons used against the Third Reich, was during this period flying in the U.S.A. The Boeing XB-17, the prototype of the famous B-17 Flying Fortress, was a large attractive monoplane bomber intended to operate from 20,000 to 25,000 ft., a height band then considered to be beyond the reach of fighters and anti-aircraft fire. Powered by four

1,000 h.p. Pratt and Whitney radial engines, the original Flying Fortress carried an insignificant bomb load and had a hopelessly inadequate defensive armament of four hand-operated .303 in. machine-guns in glazed streamlined blisters aft of the wings, with provision for a fifth machine-gun in the nose, but fortunately the basic design had tremendous possibilities. The graceful XB-17 of 1936, which seemed much too beautiful an aircraft ever to make a weapon of war, probably signified nothing to Hermann Goering and his air staff, who could never have visualised that the final B-17G as used in 1944 would have a withering fire power brought about by no less than thirteen .50 in. defensive machine-guns in chin, nose, dorsal, centre fuselage, ventral, waist and tail positions, and also be so heavily armoured that it could penetrate deep into the heart of Germany with devastating effect. The Heinkel He 111s of the Legion Kondor had proved that daylight bombing from the air could turn an undefended town into a shambles; in due course the Flying Fortresses of the U.S. Eighth Air Force would turn the dagger into a sword and exact a terrible vengeance.

But in the winter of 1936 General Wever was dead, and the long-range strategic bomber regarded as an unnecessary luxury by those in the Luftwaffe who followed him. His immediate successor, General Kesselring, and later the uninspired General Stumpf, considered that the Luftwaffe now needed a large force of twin-engined medium bombers, massed behind a spearhead of dive-bombers—the new Blitzkreig technique—and priority was therefore given to the mass production of Heinkel He 111, Dornier Do 17 (later Do 217) and Junkers Ju 87 machines. The German designers were encouraged to benefit from the great deal of information about horizontal and dive bombing that had been acquired during the first twelve months of the Spanish civil war, and in the light of this experience a specification was issued by the Reichsluftfahrtministerium for a medium bomber with a range of at least 2,000 miles and a speed of over 250 m.p.h. This specification, later to be fulfilled by the highly successful Junkers Ju 88, stated that the new bomber must be able to dive at a very steep angle; the influence of Ernst Udet and his supporters was at work again.

At least one man in the higher echelons of the Luftwaffe

bitterly resented Udet's unexpected popularity following upon the successful baptism of his dive-bomber brain-child. With the German aircraft industry rapidly expanding to place it on a war-productive basis, Erhard Milch, long established as a brilliant organiser, not without reason considered himself overdue for promotion; he was not to know that certain of his colleagues were working against him. Instead of a higher post, he soon found that Goering was gradually divesting him of the power he already had, relieving him of various routine but nevertheless important matters and placing others in command. When Ernst Udet was appointed director of the technical side and became responsible for future aircraft production, he gained a considerable opponent in the experienced Milch, who knew perfectly well that the uninhibited one-time fighter ace was totally unsuitable for such a responsible task. Despite the apparent success of the Junkers Ju 87, Milch suspected that the excitement over Stuka aircraft now raging like a whirlwind through Luftwaffe Headquarters was misplaced, and he blamed Udet for leading Goering astray in the first instance. That such a man could be promoted over his head appalled Milch; it seemed to him that Goering could not have made a more hopeless choice.

In fact, Hermann Goering never believed for a moment that Udet was the best man for the job, but he had sound personal reasons for placing him in it. For some time, the stout, jovial commander-in-chief had been suspicious of Milch, and recalling his reputation as an ambitious organiser, had decided it was time to replace him with someone less likely to covet his throne. While it is quite possible that Milch—who openly criticised Goering on more than one occasion—hoped one day to thrust his commander out of office, the higher ranks of the Luftwaffe were seething with jealousies and intrigues calculated to blacken the character of any man whose ability might lead to rapid promotion. Goering, well aware of his own inefficiency in air staff matters, turned a ready ear to all rumours and chose to believe that he could secure his position by surrounding himself with men who shared a similar weakness. In doing so, he disregarded the fact that he was sowing the seeds of a greater discontent that sooner or later would bring confusion and disaster.

Meanwhile, as the extremely modern Luftwaffe visualised by the German air staff in 1933 gradually became a reality, it emerged as a "bombing" air force, a strictly offensive weapon with the emphasis placed on speed and striking power. The Heinkel He 111 and Dornier Do 17 types in production during 1937 were very fast and had proved their bombing efficiency when used in Spain, but they lacked the range necessary for destroying industrial targets in a possible global war. The Achilles' heel of the Luftwaffe lay in the fact that it was arming only for a European war of limited duration. In direct support of advancing ground forces, the German bombers had the ability to pin-point military objectives quickly and with devastating force, but they were incapable of waging a long offensive against an enemy country and thus gradually reducing resistance and weakening civilian morale. This short-sighted policy, utterly at variance with the views of the brilliant Italian general, Giulio Douhet, who had long ago stated that a modern war could no longer be limited to order and that it was impossible to devise an effective defence against the long-range bomber, was dictated to a great extent by Adolf Hitler. The Fuehrer had no intention of waging a long and exhausting struggle against increasing odds, and his plans called for a series of lightning offensives calculated to overthrow Europe in the shortest possible time.

During those tumultuous years that preceded the Second World War, with the voice of Hermann Goering loudly proclaiming that Germany demanded equality in the air and the menacing thunder of the new Luftwaffe increasing in volume from East Prussia to the Rhine, the continuing achievements of that most successful of all lighter-than-air craft, the *Graf Zeppelin*, seemed after all to be of only minor significance. Nevertheless, the greatest European exponent of the airship, Hugo Eckener, was still hard at work in the friendly solitude of Lake Constance, looking ahead, as always, into the future and seeking to make a dream come true. No longer the adventurous, inspired young man who had seen such famous commanders as Mathy and Strasser take their Zeppelins out into the wind and rain over the North Sea, Eckener remained as determined as ever to build a transatlantic airship, a splendid passenger liner of the clouds that would be a true successor to the *Graf Zeppelin*. Lack of funds, the everlasting problem that had haunted Eckener for so many years of his life, was a hurdle crossed this time without any great difficulty, due mainly to unexpected government support in the form of Goering himself, who was quick to appreciate the publicity value to the Third Reich of a second highly successful German airship. Acting on his orders, the Reichsluftfahrtministerium contributed large sums of money for the construction of what turned out to be the last and most beautiful of the Zeppelin dirigibles, but the price that had to be paid for the government assistance was a hard one for an individualist like Eckener. Slowly but surely, the vast bureaucratic machinery of the Air Ministry overwhelmed him, until with the founding of the German Zeppelin Line by Goering in 1935, much of his original influence had been carefully whittled away.

Eckener took the changes in his administration with a studied calmness that amounted almost to contempt. As a man of peace, he had always disliked the rise of National Socialism and all it meant to Germany, but the end more than justified the means; without financial resources, it would have been another long and weary battle against hopeless odds, and he had a feeling that time was no longer on his side.

For over a year the new airship LZ. 129, later named the *Hindenburg*, took shape on the shore of Lake Constance. Eight hundred feet in length, with a gas capacity of 7,000,000 cubic ft. and powered by four Daimler-Diesel engines that developed 4,400 h.p., the new dirigible was obviously superior to the smaller *Graf Zeppelin*, proving yet again that Eckener's unswerving faith in a new design had been justified. Now, at last, the passenger flights to America could be resumed, and the work of almost a lifetime fully rewarded.

With the construction of the *Hindenburg* almost at an end, Eckener travelled to the United States and outlined to President Roosevelt his plan to carry out at least ten scheduled flights a year between Germany and America. Somewhat doubtful at first, the President was encouraged by Eckener's obvious sincerity and enthusiasm, and finally gave permission for the transatlantic service to begin, allocating Lakehurst air station as the American terminal. When all the necessary arrangements had been completed to his satisfaction, Eckener returned to Europe and on a fine March day in 1936 the *Hindenburg* took the air and passed gracefully over the waters of Lake Constance for the first time.

After all the trials had been successfully carried out, the new dirigible was soon in service with the *Graf Zeppelin* on regular passenger flights to America. The *Hindenburg* proved beyond a doubt Eckener's belief that it was technically possible to build the perfect transatlantic airship; it was spacious, comfortable, and highly popular with passengers and crew, and the fact that it boasted a cruising speed of only 86 m.p.h. did nothing to lessen that popularity. The rapid development of the aeroplane had for years been a devil at Eckener's heels, but in 1936 it seemed that the high-speed mailplanes and multi-engined airliners effortlessly circling the world had not completely replaced the airships, despite the long record of failures with lighter-than-air craft, tinged only occasionally with the brightness of success.

Yet even the splendid *Hindenburg* was doomed. On the evening of 6th May, 1937, a day of gusty, stormy weather over Lakehurst, the gleaming silver airship arrived at her American terminal as a light rain was falling, and began the normal landing procedure, flying north into the fairly strong wind and gradually losing height. The many watchers on the ground who had come to welcome the arrival saw the nose of the *Hindenburg* abruptly swing around as the wind changed direction, and, still perfectly under control, the airship turned neatly towards the landing mast. Then, at a height of 200 ft., the *Hindenburg* drifted gently with reversed engines and the land lines were thrown.

In that moment, when the land lines actually touched the ground, a tremendous explosion took place inside the *Hindenburg*, setting the whole stern of the airship ablaze. Burning fiercely, the stern dropped almost immediately, and the stricken *Hindenburg* reared up at an acute angle, allowing the flames to roar along the full length of the hull until they erupted out of the bows. In less than a minute the watchers on the ground were confronted with an appalling sight as the *Hindenburg* became incandescent and collapsed, burning from end to end with the intense, white heat of ignited hydrogen gas.

Of those on board the *Hindenburg* that tragic day, sixty-five people miraculously escaped, and thirteen passengers and twenty-two members of the crew, including the commander, lost their lives. When Eckener arrived at Lakehurst, nothing remained except a tangled heap of blackened girders to show that on the now desolate and smouldering earth he saw before him the last and greatest of the Zeppelin airships had come to such an abrupt and terrible end; yet there had to be a reason for the disaster. The investigation that followed brought evidence to indicate that the tight turn which the *Hindenburg* had made on landing probably strained the long hull, wrenching a bracing wire out of position. The wire had then lashed back, cutting open a gas cell near the stern and allowing the hydrogen to stream out and escape through the outer envelope of the hull. With the storm overhead creating a high degree of atmospheric electricity, contact with the ground by the wet land line brought a spark, which in turn ignited the escaping gas at the stern. Seconds later, the *Hindenburg* was a gigantic torch, consumed by the mixture of hydrogen and diesel oil that could so easily bring disaster.

The funeral pyre at Lakehurst was the end of everything for Hugo Eckener and his beloved Zeppelins, just as the R. 101 tragedy had finally brought airship development to a close in Great Britain. The *Graf Zeppelin* lingered on as a symbol of past glory until soon after the outbreak of war, when the Reichsluftfahrtministerium recalled the vast amount of valuable aluminium that was going to waste and gave orders for the airship to be dismantled in order to recover it, together with the LZ. 130, a sister ship to the *Hindenburg* that had been under construction at Friedrichshafen since 1936. At about the same time, the vast new Zeppelin Line hangar near Frankfurt was destroyed.

As for Eckener, broken by misfortune and then disillusioned by the war, he died on 14th August, 1954, at the age of eighty-six, a tired old man whose life's work had brought little reward except the friendship of Count Zeppelin, Heinrich Mathy and all those others who, like himself, had dedicated themselves to a cause fated always to lead them no further than the brink of success.

CHAPTER IX

AUSTRIA TO POLAND: 1938-1939

ON the afternoon of 12th March, 1938, less than twenty-four hours after his troops and aircraft had moved forward into Austria, Adolf Hitler himself crossed the frontier and motored triumphantly through a cascade of flowers and decorations to Linz. In the little town where many years ago he had attended secondary school, the Fuehrer spoke to the cheering crowds who thronged the streets to welcome him. ". . . If providence once called me forth from this town to be the leader of the Reich, it must, in so doing, have charged me with a mission," he said, "and that mission could be only to restore my dear homeland to the German Reich. I have believed in this mission, I have lived and fought for it, and I believe I have now fulfilled it. . . ." The following morning the Anschluss became a reality, and Austrian girls were garlanding the German troops with flowers, innocently unaware that there would be no more laughter when the black-clad henchmen of Reinhard Heydrich settled down to work in Vienna. Hitler's audacity had succeeded yet again—and this time there had been little risk of a major war.

The German troops and aircraft had crossed the frontier in an invasion that curiously enough revealed little of the vaunted military efficiency of the Third Reich. Indeed, General Jodl stated at the Nuremberg trials in 1946 that seventy per cent of all armoured vehicles and cars were stranded on the roads from Salzburg and Passau to Vienna, and the breakdown of so many motorised units probably contributed in some extent to the lapse of almost three days before Hitler made his triumphant entry into Vienna. The Luftwaffe organisation worked more smoothly, and considering that many of the latest aircraft were in action with the Legion Kondor, quite an impressive display of German air power was achieved at very short notice. Yet in 1938 the Luftwaffe was still not ready for anything that Hitler might demand of it, for behind the scenes the Anschluss had brought the same haste and confusion that had marked the occupation of the Rhineland. On paper, the German Air Force possessed an increasing number of operational units, but very few pilot schools and training establishments existed as yet, and consequently there remained an acute shortage of fully experienced aircrews. Hitler's tendency to risk everything on a single throw of the dice, when the German armed forces had no reserves and were scarcely ready for action at all, was a constant nightmare to the Luftwaffe and Wehrmacht generals, who were compelled to put everything "in the shop window" at times when the military organisation was stretched to the limit preparing for what in 1938 seemed to almost everyone an inevitable war.

Nevertheless, the German rearmament programme was in full swing, and not all of it was merely sounding brass and voices; General Jodl also testified at Nuremberg that twenty-seven divisions were in existence by April, 1938. The mechanical difficulties encountered during the conquest of Austria undoubtedly caused Hitler some annoyance and more than a little serious thought, but within a few weeks his agile brain was planning the next moves on the great chessboard of Europe. Czechoslovakia was, of course, the prize; and the Sudeten Germans under Konrad Henlein, aroused by the exciting success of the Anschluss, were already staging violent demonstrations against the Czech Government. Why not strike again, almost at once, while the world was still awed by his strength and audacity? To Hitler, it seemed the time was ripe, but Europe was tiring of his aggression, and he was running too hard a race.

Then Hitler received an unexpected surprise. On 13th September, 1938, twenty-four hours after he had vented his anger against President Benes of Czechoslavakia in a savage speech that thundered out abuse from the microphones in the great stadium at Nuremberg, he received an urgent message from London; the British Prime Minister, Neville Chamberlain, proposed to fly at once to Germany and try to find a peaceful solution to the Sudeten problem. Hitler was delighted at the prospect; it pleased him immensely to think that the man in charge of Great Britain's foreign policy, who had never flown in an aeroplane in his life, and was then sixty-nine years of age, had to come to a one-time street corner agitator to plead the Allied cause. When he received Chamberlain at Berchtesgaden, he attempted, as usual, to drown his audience in a sea of words. "Three hundred Sudetens have been killed," he shouted, "and . . . the thing has got to be settled at once. I am determined to settle it; I do not care whether there is a world war or not. I am determined to settle it and to settle it soon; I am prepared to risk a world war rather than allow this to drag on."

But Chamberlain was no coward, to be bullied and threatened into submission. "If the Fuehrer is determined to settle this matter by force," he interjected angrily, "without even waiting for a discussion between ourselves to take place, what did he let me come here for? I have wasted my time."

Taken aback by the objection, Hitler hurriedly began to retrace his steps, replying that : ". . . if the British Government were prepared to accept the idea of secession in principle, and to say so, there might be a chance then to have a talk." Chamberlain said that he would have to consult his Cabinet, and left the Berghof the next day with Hitler's assurance that he would not take any military action against Czechoslovakia until they had met for a second time.

A week later, Chamberlain was received by Hitler again, this time at Godesberg, on the Rhine. He brought with him a plan for the transfer of the Sudetenland to Germany; intense pressure brought against the Czech Government by Britain and France had, in effect, forced it to surrender. But Hitler had an unpleasant surprise in store for Mr. Chamberlain. Shielding himself behind a rambling monologue, he quietly turned the proposals down, without giving any clear reason for doing so; the truth was that he did not want the Sudetenland handed to him on a plate, he wanted German troops in Czechoslovakia. Later, he made that perfectly clear by delivering what amounted to an ultimatum. Now he not only claimed the Sudetenland, but demanded that it accept a military occupation by Germany— and within a week. Angry and disillusioned, Chamberlain argued bitterly with the Fuehrer for some time, but Hitler remained unmoved. The British Prime Minister returned to London and the following day, 26th September, Great Britain pledged support to France if she fulfilled her treaty obligations to Czechoslovakia as a direct result of German aggression.

During that last week in September the war clouds hung heavily over Europe. In Berlin the air of tension had given way to a strange foreboding of disaster, as if the people sensed that

Germany was ill prepared for war behind the imposing military façade. There was no reckless enthusiasm, as there had been in 1914; sadly, and in almost complete silence, the crowds watched the mechanised divisions rumbling through the streets. The general despondency made a deep impression on Hitler, and finally roused him to send a letter to Mr. Chamberlain that again stressed his demands, but hinted that hope still remained of a peaceful settlement. In a last appeal, the British Prime Minister replied at once by suggesting an international conference.

On 29th September the historic meeting between Chamberlain, Deladier, Hitler, and Mussolini was held in Munich. Beginning as a discussion, it soon deteriorated into a confusion of individual conversations and arguments that terminated in the early hours of the following morning with the Munich Agreement, a document that substantially accepted all the terms of the Godesberg memorandum. By taking Germany to the very brink of war, Hitler had persuaded Britain and France to hand over to him the vitally important Czechoslovakian defensive frontier, and thus achieved his greatest triumph in the political field. The German generals were staggered at his success. On the night of the Munich conference, General Jodl wrote in his diary: "... The genius of the Fuehrer and his determination not to shun even a world war have again won victory without the use of force..." All previous doubts were scattered to the winds; Hitler was now the Man of Destiny, who could twist the statesmen of Europe around his little finger and do with them as he wished

Mr. Chamberlain took the opportunity to ask the Fuehrer to sign a declaration that in future any questions would be dealt with only by consultation between the great Powers. Hitler signed the paper promise without the slightest hesitation—it meant nothing to him at such a time—and Chamberlain returned to London. When he stepped from his aeroplane at Croydon, holding his famous umbrella in one hand and waving the useless scrap of paper at the crowds who awaited him, the Prime Minister was elated. "It is peace with honour," he told the people of Britain, but Winston Churchill saw only the tarnished side of the coin. "Silent, mournful, abandoned, broken, Czechoslovakia recedes into the darkness," he said, during the Munich debate in the House of Commons, and it was so; on 1st October German troops were marching across the frontier into the Sudetenland.

Only six months later, in March, 1939, Hitler decided to occupy the remainder of Czechoslovakia. The chain of events, so familiar by then that they no longer aroused the world to anger, began with the usual violent outcry in the German newspapers against imaginary Czech atrocities directed at the German minority in Bohemia and Moravia, and ended when President Hacha of Czechoslovakia arrived in Berlin to plead with Hitler to spare his country. A tired old man, so troubled by ill health that he fainted during the audience and had to be revived by Hitler's doctor, Hacha was no match for the Fuehrer in his most threatening mood. Convinced that war must be averted at any price, he ". . . confidently placed the fate of the Czech people in the hands of the Fuehrer," and, with those few words, the deed was done.

On 15th March Hitler arrived in Prague, accompanied by Keitel, Ribbentrop and Himmler. The swastika flags were flying gaily from the battlements of the Hradschin Castle overlooking the city, the tramp of German jackboots resounded through the streets, and far away in Berlin the British and French Ambassadors were protesting loudly, but in vain. Surrounded by the sprawling grandeur of the Hradschin Castle, Hitler signed the documents to finally encircle with steel fingers another little nation that had never desired anything except independence. "Czechoslovakia," he wrote firmly, "has ceased to exist. . . ."

Sitting in the Hradschin Castle that bright spring afternoon, Hitler might well feel confident of his power as the modern Man of Destiny, but in reality he had gambled and won for the last time; never again would the pitcher return unbroken from the well. The Munich crisis and the final annexation of Czechoslovakia shattered a thousand illusions, and proved that peace cannot always be bought at any price, that only too often futile words are of little avail against the sword. In London, Mr. Chamberlain stated that Hitler would never be able to deceive him again; Britain had been taught a hard lesson, and was girding her loins for war.

The military operations against Czechoslovakia were marked

by the usual frenzied activity within the higher ranks of the Luftwaffe. The vast bulk of Hermann Goering had remained conspicuously absent during most of the negotiations, although he made an appearance at the conference with President Hacha to remind that ailing old man of the Luftwaffe's ability to bomb Prague into smoking rubble should Czechoslovakia try to resist the mighty forces of the Third Reich. In fact, Goering had a very real fear of war, and he did not want to be too deeply involved in any moves that might lead to it; also, less than six months before the invasion of the Sudetenland he had stated openly that Germany had no designs on Czechoslovakia. All things considered, including a slight illness, he decided it would be better to linger in the background and await events, which were moving at far too rapid a pace for his peace of mind.

Then the crisis reached a climax and came to an end, and Goering found himself able to relax again. Now, while the eyes of the world were on Germany, he could use the occupation of Czechoslovakia to display his Luftwaffe for all to see; never would there be a better opportunity to awe the Allied Powers with the might and splendour of German air power. He followed Hitler to Prague, while overhead thundered the élite squadrons of the Luftwaffe; the Messerschmitt Bf 109s of J.G.2, the Richthofen Jagdgeschwader; the Junkers Ju 87s of the first unit to receive that equipment, the Stukageschwader Immelmann; the latest Heinkel He 111 and Dornier Do 17 medium bombers. Goering's own parachute regiment, the former Standarten Feldherrenhalle, tumbled out from behind the spread wings of Junkers Ju 52s over Karlsbad; on the ground, the jovial Luftwaffe Commander-in-Chief inspected over fifteen hundred Czech aircraft, mostly obsolete biplane fighters of the Avia B-534 type, now legally the property of the insatiable Third Reich. "The Axis is stronger than ever," he commented afterwards, once more full of the old boisterous confidence.

But Hitler was on the rampage again, while the shock and tumult of his latest aggression still echoed around the world. Immediately after the occupation of Czechoslovakia he demanded the return to the Reich of Memel, a city lost to Germany by the Treaty of Versailles, and in less than a week the Lithuanian Government had accepted his ultimatum. Poland, however, was actually scheduled to be Hitler's next victim, his initial aims the Free City of Danzig—separated from Germany in 1919 that Poland might have unrestricted access to the sea—and the construction of a German extra-territorial road and railway across the Polish Corridor which divided East Prussia from the remainder of the Reich. On 26th March, the Polish Government rejected the German demands, and five days later Mr. Chamberlain announced in the House of Commons: "In the event of any action which clearly threatens Polish independence, and which the Polish Government accordingly consider it vital to resist with their national forces, H.M. Government would feel themselves bound at once to lend the Polish Government all support in their power." The French Government at once issued a similar guarantee; the shameful ghosts of Munich were being banished into the shadows.

Hitler flew into a raging temper when he heard the news. Never before had he encountered such determined opposition, but his success at Munich had raised his prestige to such giddy heights that now there could be no question of retreat. On 23rd May, he called a meeting of his senior Army, Navy and Air Force officers, and told them; "We cannot expect a repetition of the Czech affair. There will be war. Our task is to isolate Poland. The success of the isolation will be decisive. . . " In fact, the plans for Case White (the attack on Poland) had already been prepared, and by 22nd June the German general staff had drawn up a detailed time-table for the invasion

Meanwhile, Hitler had been considering the obvious danger from Russia should he become involved in a major war with the Western Powers in the near future. His tentative overtures to Moscow proved distinctly promising; Stalin had been negoti-ating for a pact with France and Britain for some time, and was tiring of the endless discussions that seemed to be getting nowhere. Now Hitler stepped forward to interest the Soviet dictator with an agreement to divide the whole of Eastern Europe between Germany and Russia—more bluntly, to share the spoils of war—and incidentally never to become involved in war against each other. Invested with plenipotentiary powers, von Ribbentrop flew to Moscow, and in the early hours of 24th August the German-Soviet Non-aggression Pact was signed. Ribbentrop returned the same day trailing clouds of glory, to be hailed in Berlin as "a second Bismarck", although he had done very little except utter the words put into his mouth by Hitler and append his signature to the agreement.

Goering who had never liked Ribbentrop, remained unimpressed by the German Foreign Minister's apparent success in Russia. Despondent at the worsening political situation, worried by Luftwaffe matters as the trinity of Milch, Udet and Loerzer hurriedly prepared for war, he sought refuge behind a shield of blustering speeches that years later he would recall with bitterness and shame. Returning to Berlin after travelling down the Rhine in his new yacht on a tour of the sadly inadequate Ruhr anti-aircraft defences, he said: "I have inspected personally all measures for the defence of the Ruhr territory. I shall look after every single battery which it may be necessary to install. The Ruhr will not be submitted to a single bomb of enemy airmen!" The vaunted Western Air Defence Zone, or Luftverteidigungs-zone, to which he referred, was a straggling line of guns not yet sufficiently co-ordinated to oppose even a minor bombing raid, but Goering was trying to convince himself even more than his audience. "If an enemy bomber reaches the Ruhr," he told the German people, "my name is not Hermann Goering; you can call me Meier!" The joke seemed amusing enough at the time, but it was never repeated after a thousand bombers had raided Cologne.

Despite his outward display of confidence, Goering's spirits were at a low ebb as the last hopes of peace faded away. At last, he decided to make a final attempt to localise the now inevitable war; Poland was doomed, but Britain and France might yet be persuaded to grasp his extended hand. He arranged a meeting with Mr. Birger Dahlerus, a Swedish industrialist who had business connections in Germany and Britain, and this in turn led to a conference between Goering and a number of important British business men. But his argument that there need not be a European war if Britain would give Hitler a free hand in Poland was not a very satisfactory one; and now the Fuehrer himself no longer cared what happened when he invaded Poland. Nevertheless, Goering struggled to keep the negotiations alive, and Dahlerus flew back and forth between Germany and Britain a number of times to report on the progress of his mission.

It was too late. On the evening of 31st August, while Goering, harassed and tired, was still in conference with Dahlerus, S.S. men acting on the orders of Reinhard Heydrich were staging a faked Polish attack on the German radio station at Gleiwitz, near the Polish frontier. The station was "seized" with typical S.S. efficiency, a short proclamation broadcast over an emergency transmitter and a few haphazard pistol shots fired, then the attackers vanished, leaving behind them the scattered bodies of a dozen condemned criminals dressed in Polish uniforms and thoughtfully given fatal injections by a doctor before being shot down. These dead men played an important part in Heydrich's amazingly simple little scheme; they provided mute, but convincing, evidence that Polish forces were acting with deliberate provocation by attacking German border installations.

The Gleiwitz frontier incident was Hitler's manufactured excuse for renewed aggression, the "suitable opportunity" he needed to go to war. In the early hours of the following morning the bombers and fighters of the Luftwaffe thundered into the air, hundreds of tanks and armoured vehicles rolled ponderously forward along the roads that led to war, and 1,500,000 troops of the Wehrmacht crossed the frontier into Poland. The roar of aircraft engines and the urgent clamour of machine-guns roused simple peasants from their peaceful slumbers to face a violent, incredible dawn; dive-bombers plunged, ugly and screaming, to strike with hammer blows at unsuspecting targets; men shouted orders, sweated behind huge artillery pieces, fought hand to hand—and sometimes died; and soon the stench and smoke of burning villages was drifting lazily over the Polish countryside.

All these things happened on 1st September, 1939, the first day of that five and a half years of struggle commonly known as the Second World War.

When the British ultimatum was delivered at the Reich Chancellery on Sunday, 3rd September, Goering and Dahlerus finally acknowledged that they could do no more. The worried Commander-in-Chief of the Luftwaffe, his aircraft already in action over Poland, listened in silence to the news that destroyed his hopes of peace for ever, perhaps in that moment recalling an earlier war and the nervous, hopeless existence of a fighter pilot on the Western Front in 1918. Then, his world had been encompassed by the tiny cockpit of a Fokker D.VII, and death had never been very far away, but he had also been his own master, with little to lose; now he had a wife and baby daughter he loved, a magnificent home, untold wealth and priceless art treasures. All the rich tapestry and splendour of his life as the second most important man in the Third Reich seemed to be in danger, and on this Sunday morning he faced a bleak, uncertain future, entangled in the golden web he had so willingly allowed Adolf Hitler to weave around him.

"If we lose this war, then God help us," said Goering at last, uttering the despairing words of a man who lacked the courage of his convictions, had never been dedicated to any greater cause than Hermann Goering, and now was afraid to accept responsibilities that would soon be the price of a decade of pleasure. His attitude of mind, not so uncommon in the twilight world of Nazi Germany, where personal power was more often achieved by threats and broken promises than skill and bitter experience, drove some men to madness and others to suicide. Goering chose instead to ignore the reality of war and pretend that nothing would ever happen to disturb the tranquil security of Karinhall.

CHAPTER X

BLITZKRIEG! POLAND, 1939

WHEN the Luftwaffe went to war in September, 1939, it was generally considered to be an extremely modern and powerful air force, technically and numerically superior to every other major air arm in the world, including those of the United States and Japan. In fact, the experience of the Legion Kondor in Spain had brought to light various deficiencies in the latest German aircraft when used under operational conditions, and in any case Spain was a far from realistic testing ground. One of the few men qualified to select the wheat from the chaff in the Legion Kondor's battle experience was Wolfram von Richthofen, a cousin of the famous Manfred, and himself once a member of the Richthofen Geschwader. As Chief of Staff to Hugo von Sperrle, and afterwards in command of the Legion Kondor from 1938 until its disbandment, von Richthofen had tested Hitler's Blitzkrieg technique in the field, and was responsible for developing an efficient system of R/T liaison between ground troops and supporting aircraft that later proved to be of inestimable value in Poland and France. The Heinkel He 51s of Adolf Galland, soon replaced in Spain by Messerschmitt Bf 109s, and, during 1938, backed by Junkers Ju 87As, were thus able to pinpoint targets of opportunity with remarkable success under von Richthofen's active supervision—but always operating under a strong protective fighter umbrella. During 1938 and 1939, von Richthofen's Stukas brought dive-bombing to a fine art by wreaking fearful havoc in the port areas of Valencia and Barcelona, and the Legion Kondor commander's reports were studied with enthusiasm by Udet and his supporters, who failed to realise that no experience had been gained of dive-bombing against heavy fighter and anti-aircraft opposition.

In large numbers for operational use against Poland the Luftwaffe therefore possessed the highly praised Junkers Ju 87 dive-bomber, the Heinkel He 111 and Dornier Do 17 medium bombers and the Messerschmitt Bf 109 single-seater fighter. All these types had seen active service in Spain, and their deficiencies had to some extent been overcome, although certain problems, particularly in armament, still had to be ironed out. However, two entirely new machines, the Junkers Ju 88 dive-bomber and the Messerschmitt Me 110 two-seater escort fighter, were in squadron service by 1939, and great faith was placed in the capabilities of both these aircraft. The Ju 88—Erhard Milch's "wonder bomber"—did, in fact, eventually become the true backbone of the Luftwaffe, being produced in greater numbers than all other German bombers combined, and successfully performing literally hundreds of tasks for which it was never originally intended.

A very fast, slim, twin-engined aircraft, the Ju 88 was conceived in 1935 in response to a Reichluftfahrtministerium requirement for a high-speed medium bomber, and then fitted with dive brakes to satisfy Ernst Udet's desire to incorporate a twin-engined dive bomber in the Luftwaffe. Surprisingly, it also proved suitable in a variety of other roles, including those of heavy fighter, close support and reconnaissance, and was destined to operate in various forms during the entire period of the war in Europe. Ubiquitous to the end, the Ju-88 has been acknowledged one of the few truly outstanding aircraft to enter service with the Luftwaffe.

The Messerschmitt Bf (later Me) 110 was to have an entirely different history. During the expansion of the Luftwaffe, Willy Messerschmitt had emerged as one of Germany's most successful aircraft designers, becoming so established by 1938 that the shareholders of the Bayerische Flugzeugwerke decided it was time to rename the company Messerschmitt A.G., with Messerschmitt to hold the joint post of General Director and Chairman of the Management Committee. The remarkable successes achieved by the Bf 108 and Bf 109 types had inspired the brilliant young designer to attempt a repetition in the twin-engined field, and thus in due course the prototype Me 110 appeared on the aviation scene.

Designed in order to meet the need for a heavy two-seater fighter capable of escorting bomber formations deep into enemy territory, the attractive twin-engined Me 110 was seriously under-powered and lacking in armament from the beginning, and soon proved so useless as an escort fighter that during the Battle of Britain Me 110s had no chance in action unless they were themselves escorted by Bf 109s. However, Goering, who recalled the achievements of two-seater fighters in 1918, was captivated by the idea of the Me 110, and in 1939 he formed special Zestorerstaffeln, or destroyer units, indicating that these would now be the strategic fighter élite of the Luftwaffe. The Me 110 was soon found to be unsatisfactory in many respects, but basically it was simply not a good airframe, and various attempts to adapt it for specialised roles met with little success. Goering's faith in the type came to a very abrupt end when the Me 110 formations were cut to pieces by the Hurricanes and Spitfires of the Royal Air Force in 1940, and he soon lost interest in his Zerstorerstaffeln, yet somehow, with typical German persistence, the Me 110 managed to remain in production until 1945.

A glance at the effective strength of the Luftwaffe in September, 1939—some 4,300 aircraft—shows that German air power still depended entirely on the nucleus of a few aircraft types that had either been in production with very few modifications since 1936 or were only just off the drawing-board and therefore still suffering acute teething troubles. While imposing in numbers, the Luftwaffe was technically by no means the formidable force it appeared to be, not only to the outside world, but also to Goering and his air staff, who believed that German air superiority was so firmly established in 1939 that it would be maintained for many years.

Let the figures speak for themselves. The official report of the Quartermaster-General of the Luftwaffe at the outbreak of war gives the following distribution of aircraft :

Thirty Bomber Wings—1,180 medium bombers.
   18 equipped with Heinkel He 111F and He 111P aircraft;
   11 equipped with Dornier Do 17M aircraft;
   1 equipped with Junkers Ju 86G aircraft.
Thirteen Day Fighter Wings—771 single-seater fighters.
   12 equipped with Messerschmitt Bf 109E aircraft;
   1 equipped with Arado Ar 68 aircraft.
Nine Dive-Bomber Wings—336 dive-bombers.
   9 equipped with Junkers Ju 87A and Ju 87B aircraft.

Ten Attack Wings—408 escort fighters or "destroyers".

    10 equipped with Messerschmitt Me 110C and a few Bf 109D aircraft.

One Army Support Wing—40 dive-bombers.

    1 equipped with Henschel Hs 123B aircraft.

Two Transport Wings—552 transport aircraft.

    2 equipped with Junkers Ju 52 aircraft.

Twenty-three Reconnaissance Squadrons—379 reconnaissance aircraft.

    23 equipped with Dornier Do 17 aircraft.

Thirty Army Reconnaissance Squadrons—342 scouting aircraft.

    25 equipped with Henschel Hs 126B aircraft;

    5 equipped with Heinkel He 45 and He 46 aircraft.

Eighteen Naval Squadrons—240 aircraft.

    14 equipped with Dornier Do 18, Heinkel He 115, Blohm und Voss Bv 138 and Arado Ar 196 aircraft.

    2 equipped with Arado Ar 196 aircraft only;

    2 equipped with Heinkel He 59 and He 60 aircraft.

Sundry Units—55 aircraft.

Of the above machines, only the Junkers Ju 87, Dornier Do 17 and Messerschmitt Bf 109 types had to some extent fulfilled the hopes of Hermann Goering and his staff. The Junkers Ju 86 was obsolete by September, 1939, and the Henschel Hs 123, Arado Ar 68 and Heinkel He 45 and 46 biplanes dated back to the earliest days of the Luftwaffe.

The actual framework of the German Air Force remained not unlike that of the old Imperial German Air Force Service in 1918, the basic operational unit being a squadron, or Staffel, comprising ten to a dozen aircraft. Three Staffeln made up a wing, or Gruppe, and three or occasionally more Gruppen completed a Geschwader, roughly 100 aircraft, and usually of the same type. Above these field formations were the groups of machines intended for different functions, but working together in close co-operation, mixed forces of 250 to 500 bombers, fighters, reconnaissance machines, etc. These were classified as Fliegerkorps, and for administrative purposes were controlled by Luftgaue, or Air Districts.

The highest Luftwaffe headquarters in the field were the Air Fleets (Luftflotten), each commanded by a General. In 1939, four Luftflotten were in existence, all directly subordinate to the O.K.L. (Oberkommando Der Luftwaffe) or, in other words, to Goering, Milch and, later, Jeschonnek. These four Luftflotten controlled eight Fliegerkorps, though not necessarily in the exact proportion of two Korps to each Air Fleet, and the strength in aircraft varied considerably according to the situation.

For economic reasons and in order to withhold as many reserves as possible, Germany's main air assault against Poland had of necessity to be carried out by about twenty operational Kampfgeschwader of Heinkel He 111 and Dornier Do 17 medium bombers, some five Stukageschwader of Junkers Ju 87s and ten or twelve Jagdgeschwader of Messerschmitt Bf 109 (or Zerstorergeschwader of the Me 110 fighters). General Alexander Loehr, more keenly aware than Goering of the imperfections of these aircraft, wrote later: "At the outbreak of war we felt tense, torn between confidence in victory, and the torturing question whether we would employ the right methods at the outset, and how much we should have to pay in losses to learn our lesson." Loehr's doubts were, of course, to prove unjustified, but if the Luftwaffe had not been troubled with so many small, but important, weaknesses he would never have felt any qualms in the first place.

From the beginning, Erhard Milch and Ernst Udet had been convinced that light and medium bombers should provide the nucleus of the German Air Force, and these two men were largely responsible for the concentration on a few basic types produced in large numbers. After Generals Kesselring and Stumpf had in turn served as Chief of Staff, a successor was appointed by Goering in the person of Hans Jeschonnek, often known as "the youngster" because he was then not forty years of age. Like Udet, the new Chief of Staff believed that the dive-bomber was the most suitable weapon for the Luftwaffe, and soon after he took office the German aircraft industrialists received instructions that all new types under consideration must be able to dive. This curious idea, which delighted Goering and Udet, had little effect on the capabilities of the Junkers Ju 88, but proved highly impracticable when applied to the Dornier Do 217 and later delayed production of Germany's one and only heavy bomber type, the ill-fated Heinkel He 177.

Yet Jeschonnek was a brilliant and enthusiastic young officer, unlike so many of Udet's supporters, and he had definite reasons for favouring the dive-bomber and its tactical abilities. He was convinced that Germany lacked the resources to produce large numbers of heavy four-engined bombers, and felt that a twin-engined medium machine with dive-bombing capabilities such as the Ju 88 could, in a vertical dive, hit the target with the same effect as a squadron of heavy bombers "carpeting" the area in horizontal flight. Jeschonnek shrewdly realised that dive-bombers would be of use only in a strictly localised war, but he saw no reason to suppose that they would ever be needed outside their limited range of approximately 300 miles. His only weakness was his devotion to Hitler, who had already proved that Great Britain was unwilling to go to war over Austria or Czechoslovakia, and therefore unlikely to worry unduly about the fate of Poland. Why build multi-engined strategic bombers, reasoned Jeschonnek, when they would obviously never be needed?

As Chief of Staff of the Luftwaffe, Jeschonnek's policy was simple in outline, and he never swerved away from it, even when faced with disaster. Whatever Hitler demanded of the Luftwaffe, Jeschonnek was determined it should be carried out; the bomber requirements, fantastic in numbers though they might be, must somehow be fulfilled. In 1939, dive-bombers were inexpensive and put into quantity production with very little trouble, thus satisfying not only Hitler, but also Goering, who was able to bask in the reflected glory of Jeschonnek's achievement.

Nevertheless, even before the outbreak of war, the dive-bombers so dear to Ernst Udet and his supporters had shown themselves to be far from invincible in service. In August, 1939, two Staffeln of Junkers Ju 87s took part in manoeuvres over Neuhammer-am-Queis, using live bombs for the first time, the main event being a formation dive for the benefit of some of the most important staff officers in the Luftwaffe, including Wolfram von Richthofen, Hugo von Sperrle and Bruno Loerzer. Through their binoculars, the group of observers watched the squat, ugly machines climb slowly up into the early morning sky, bank gently over the target area and then begin the long, ear-piercing plunge to earth, the wail of their sirens rising and

falling as they hurtled through the clouds. It was a perfect formation dive, with every aircraft exactly in position; it was also
the last dive all but one of the Stukas ever made.

The court of enquiry established two days later heard the full
story, although no finding was reached, and the whole affair
quickly and conveniently came to an end in the dusty archives
of the Luftwaffe. Thin ground mist, drifting over the target area
that tragic morning, had thickened until it became a grey fog
extending to over three thousand feet. The Stuka pilots, warned
of heavy cloud at six thousand feet but expecting only a light
mist directly over the target, hopelessly misjudged their dives
and thundered at full speed into the ground, only one aircraft
managing to pull out in time. As it tore through the branches of
a dozen trees and struggled aloft to safety, explosion after explosion shook the forest, and smoke and flames erupted into the
sky to mark the funeral pyre of thirteen dive-bombers and
twenty-six men.

Ernst Udet was aghast when he heard the news from Neu-
hammer, but a fortnight later Germany was at war and he had
no time to ponder on any other weaknesses that might soon come
to light in the aircraft he had introduced to the Luftwaffe. As it
happened, the nine Gruppen equipped with the Junkers Ju 87,
some 330 aircraft of that type, more than lived up to their in-
flated and undeserved reputation when used in Poland, for the
very good reason that once again they encountered no effective
air opposition. Wolfram von Richthofen, then in command of
Fliegerkorps VIII, operated his aircraft in perfectly co-ordinated
liaison with the advancing Wehrmacht, employing much the
same tactics that he had used with such success in Spain. Always
a man who liked to hurl everything he commanded into action
regardless of losses, von Richthofen now had at his disposal
three Geschwader of Junkers Ju 87s and a Gruppe of
Henschel Hs 123s, with Messerschmitt Bf 109 fighters for protection, and he seldom spared them. With clockwork precision,
Polish factories, lines of communication and aerodromes were
systematically dive-bombed into smoking rubble, while beyond
the Stukas' limited range Dornier Do 17s and Heinkel He 111s
were on hand to harass the retreating armies. Within two days,
the Polish campaign had become an excellent example of the
new German strategy, Hitler's famous Blitzkrieg technique no

longer merely a theoretical possibility, but carried to its ultimate conclusion.

However, despite the strength of the German onslaught, and contrary to popular belief, the Polish Air Force was not destroyed on the ground within three days. To oppose the Luftwaffe it possessed some 800 aircraft, of which roughly 430 could be considered as first-line operational machines, and these fought valiantly against impossible odds, shooting down 126 German aircraft during the eighteen days of the campaign. The backbone of the Polish fighter force, the sturdy but outdated little PZL P-11 and the obsolete P-7A, were responsible for interception of most of the German bombers attacked, and never failed to enter into battle, regardless of the fact that they stood no chance whatsoever against the Bf 109 fighters of the Luftwaffe, while almost all the two hundred P-23 Karas bombers of the Polish Air Force were destroyed in vain attempts to halt the advancing German armoured columns. From the first day it was an unequal struggle, but Poland was determined to go down fighting, and for the Luftwaffe it proved to be a hard and exhausting campaign.

Cracow fell on 6th September, and a fortnight later Warsaw was encircled. Hitler, worried that the campaign might deteriorate into a long siege of the Polish capital, requested a supreme effort by the Luftwaffe, and Goering in turn ordered Kesselring to use all the forces at his command to bomb the city into submission. The resulting large-scale attack, conducted on a far greater scale than the raid on Guernica in 1937, was supposedly directed at the Okecie airfield and the main Warsaw railway stations, but civilian casualties were very heavy in such a densely populated area. Kesselring was charged at Nuremberg in 1946 with various war crimes, including the deliberate and unnecessary bombing of Warsaw, and stated then and afterwards that only the military targets were destroyed and artillery fire was responsible for most of the damage in the city centre; his aircraft had never at any time been used to terrorise helpless women and children. Nevertheless, the raid was a splendid opportunity for the German propaganda machine to remind the Allies that the Luftwaffe was the most powerful air arm in Europe, and with victory assured it did not matter very much to Dr. Goebbels how many civilians had been killed. Consequently, the German documentary films of the Warsaw bombardment shocked not only the Allies, but the whole world, depicting as they did the fearful devastation that could be wrought by the same "carpet" bombing considered to be of so little importance by Goering, Udet and Jeschonnek.

On 27th September, 1939, Warsaw finally surrendered, and the campaign in Poland was at an end. To Goering and his air staff, it seemed that the Luftwaffe had lived up to its formidable reputation, encountering few mechanical difficulties and suffering negligible losses, but it was acknowledged that perfect flying conditions—"Goering weather"—and the scattered, if intense, opposition had made the outcome an inconclusive victory. The new Junkers Ju 88s were still largely untried in action, the Messerschmitt Me 110 twin-engined fighters had been used only in a limited supporting role, and the Heinkel He 111 and Dornier Do 17 bombers had yet to show their worth when battling through to attack a heavily defended target. The important question still remained to be answered; how would the Luftwaffe stand up to the supreme test when pitted against the air forces of Great Britain and France?

Even after enjoying such overwhelming success in Poland, many of the German generals felt that neither the Wehrmacht or the Luftwaffe were ready to undertake an immediate offensive in the west. On the other hand, Hitler was eager to attack at once, and on 9th October, 1939, he issued one of his famous Fuehrer Directives for the Conduct of the War, ordering preparations for: "... an attacking operation on the northern wing of the western front, through the areas of Luxembourg, Belgium and Holland. This attack must be carried out with as much strength and at as early a date as possible..." The generals, particularly Halder and von Brauchitsch, pointed out that such an autumn offensive, probably reaching its height in the depths of winter, was fraught with dangers, but Hitler remained adamant; and the arguments raged on without respite for over a month.

Finally, von Brauchitsch threw in what he hoped would be his trump card. He stated that after being driven so hard in Poland the Wehrmacht would not be ready to undertake any large-scale offensive before 26th November, seeking to gain, if nothing else, more time for discussion with the other senior commanders. Hitler retaliated by angrily issuing a revised military directive for the western offensive, now code named *Fall Gelb*, or Case Yellow, and deliberately settling the date for the initial thrust as 12th November—and not a day later. Temporarily defeated by the Fuehrer's insistence, Brauchitsch sought the combined support of the other leading German generals, including the commander of Army Group A on the western front, Generaloberst Gerd von Runstedt.

General von Runstedt was an outstanding officer and a brilliant tactician, but he had a reputation for carefully avoiding what he considered to be political problems outside his sphere. His cautiously worded arguments in support of Brauchitsch were vague and of little assistance, with the result that once again Hitler refused to be persuaded. The question of unfavourable weather he dismissed at once with the brisk comment that the spring weather might be no better; the need for more training he considered to be of no importance. In a raging temper before the interview came to an end, he thundered at last, "The Army does not want to fight!" and would hear no more.

Fortunately for the uneasy professional soldiers, the Fuehrer's plans had to be postponed on 7th November owing to even worse weather than anyone had anticipated. During the winter of 1939, Hitler spoke frequently and at length about his proposed offensive in the west, but he no longer seemed inclined to specify any definite date, and not until the January of 1940 did he make up his mind and order the attack to commence; on the 17th of that month, at dawn. The literally heaven-sent excuse—unfavourable weather—that had been used by the generals to delay the offensive for over three months was no longer of any avail, and reluctantly they settled down to direct the troop movements that would be the opening stages of the campaign.

Then, a week before the fateful day, everything had abruptly to be postponed again. On the morning of 10th January a Messerschmitt Bf 108 Taifun courier aircraft took off from Loddenheide airfield, near Munster, carrying two Luftwaffe staff officers, Majors Reinberger and Hoenmanns, on a special mission to Cologne. The day was fine, but fairly cloudy, and Hoenmanns, the pilot, who had little experience of blind flying in this type of machine, soon realised he was off course in the clouds. Confused by the unexpected turn of events, Hoenmanns apparently set his course to south-south-west, and then lost height in an attempt to locate the Rhine. In his excitement, he accidentally cut off the petrol supply of the Bf 108, which immediately stalled and abruptly dived to the ground, tearing away the wings as it hurtled between two trees. Shaken but unhurt, Hoenmanns and his companion climbed out of the wrecked aircraft, Reinberger holding his bulging leather brief-case in both hands.

Unfortunately, the river which Hoenmanns had spotted just before the machine crashed was not the Rhine, but the Meuse; they had landed on Belgium soil, not far from Maastrict, and frontier guards were already hurrying to the scene. Particularly unfortunate for Reinberger was the fact that his brief-case contained the general outline of the forthcoming German offensive in the west, and detailed information regarding the airborne landings, with a timetable of the campaign. He made two reckless attempts to destroy the secret documents after being arrested by the Belgium soldiers, but sufficient papers were salvaged to reveal most of the plans, and within a few hours the Allies had been informed. Soon afterwards, the Belgiums began to strengthen their scanty defences in the Maas area and the Ardennes.

For the Oberkommando der Wehrmacht, the loss of the plans amounted to a catastrophe. Hitler, in a towering rage, could do nothing about Reinberger and Hoenmanns, who were now prisoners of war, but he sacked their immediate superiors, General Felmay, the commander of Luftflotte 2, and his chief of staff, Kammhuber, on the spot and treated all his generals to a lecture on security and the care of secret documents. Then, after some thought and indecision, he decided to revise the plans for the offensive completely: "in order to ensure secrecy and surprise." Thus, in due course, he presented the generals with *Fall Gelb* in its final form, the plan that would turn the full might of the German armed forces simultaneously against Belgium, Holland and France on 10th May, 1940.

CHAPTER XI

THE BATTERING RAM: FRANCE, 1940

IN Great Britain they were calling it the Phoney War or the Bore War; and many people thought it would all be over by Christmas. The men of Lord Gort's British Expeditionary Force, supposedly "equipped in the finest possible manner that could not be excelled," in the words of the then Secretary of State for War, Leslie Hore-Belisha, had settled down in France to await the arrival of the German military machine. Meanwhile, there was simply nothing to do. The weeks slid by, troops dug their useless slit trenches and sang the old songs of their fathers' war. They were light-hearted, supremely confident and secure behind the apparently invincible walls of the Maginot Line; fatally unaware that the old days of trench warfare had gone for ever and they would never "hang out the washing on the Siegfried Line".

The war in the air began in much the same casual, hopeful manner. On 4th September Blenheim and Wellington bombers of the Royal Air Force attacked the German naval bases at Wilhelmshaven and Brunsbuettel, inflicting negligible damage on the pocket battleship *Admiral Scheer* and the cruiser *Emden* for the loss of seven aircraft. During the next six months, the R.A.F. accordingly restricted its activities to leaflet dropping and long-range reconnaissance flights; while the Luftwaffe seemed no more inclined to undertake risky offensive operations against the Allies. On 16th October a dozen Heinkel He 111s of Kampfgeschwader 26 bombed British warships in the Firth of Forth and were immediately intercepted by Spitfires of 602 Squadron, which shot two of the Heinkels down—the first enemy aircraft to be destroyed over Britain since 1918. The following day, another small raid was undertaken, this time against Scapa Flow, and the obsolete training battleship *Iron Duke* was damaged and later had to be beached in shallow water.

And so the winter passed away, with occasional German reconnaissance raids over Britain and France, the odd Dornier

Do 17 or Heinkel He 111 destroyed, and a few inconclusive battles between Messerschmitt Bf 109s and the Hurricanes of the B.E.F. which proved only that the German fighter was, on the whole, faster in the dive and slightly more responsive in action. Goering was anxious to launch heavier mass attacks against British ports and shipping, particularly the naval units based at Scapa Flow, but Hitler at that time had no desire to wage war directly against England and chose to keep the Luftwaffe in reserve for the forthcoming land offensive in the west.

Also, during the winter of 1939 the Fuehrer was taking an increasing interest in yet another new project—the simultaneous invasion of Norway and Denmark. The Commander-in-Chief of the German Navy, Admiral Raeder, had pointed out the advantages of securing naval bases in Norway on a number of occasions, but not until after the British destroyer *Cossack* had intercepted the German prison ship *Altmark* in Norwegian waters and rescued her prisoners did Hitler tend to agree and decide to appoint a commander for the operation. Thus was born *Fall Weseruebung*, or Weser Exercise, which took place on 9th April, 1940, only four days after Neville Chamberlain commented that the Germans had failed to take advantage of their initial superiority, and in the same speech uttered the sadly complacent words: "Hitler has missed the bus." His statement reflected the British attitude of mind at the time; not until Winston Churchill became Prime Minister would the pipe-dreams of a quiet war be shattered for ever.

The invasion of Norway was almost entirely a naval amphibious operation, and initially the Luftwaffe was used mainly for landing assault units in the Oslo area and pin-pointing targets of opportunity. The Sola airfield near Stavanger was attacked by Messerschmitt Me 110s in the early hours of 9th April, parachute troops were landed soon afterwards, and within a few hours the ubiquitous Junkers Ju 52s were flying in infantry reinforcements. The only Norwegian fighter wing, based at Fornebu, near Oslo, and equipped with nine obsolescent Gloster Gladiator biplanes, managed to shoot down two or three Heinkel He 111s before huge formations of twin-engined bombers attacked the airfield. Four of the Gladiators were destroyed on the ground while refuelling and the remainder were shot down in rapid succession. Meanwhile, Junkers Ju

52s began to land at Fornebu, despite the still intense anti-aircraft fire, and soon German infantry had dispersed and surrounded the airfield. In Denmark, the Luftwaffe met no opposition at all and the Aalborg airfield was in use within forty-eight hours of its capture.

To the Allies, the unexpected German attack on Norway and Denmark fell like a thunderbolt out of an untroubled sky. The Chamberlain government wasted valuable time in the vain hope that Sweden would come to the aid of her neighbours, and the Wehrmacht had therefore secured most of the key positions in both countries before it was decided to hurriedly despatch an expeditionary force to Namos and Aandalsnes in an attempt to capture and hold Trondheim. A week later, in response to urgent requests for air support, a single R.A.F. squadron of Gloster Gladiators was flown in from the aircraft carrier *Glorious* to operate from the frozen surface of Lake Lesjeskog, thirty-two miles to the south-east of Aandalsnes. Immediately, German bombers arrived on the scene, and within two days the Luftwaffe had efficiently blasted the lake into great pieces of ice and destroyed or disabled all but one of the Gladiators. On 20th April, the Luftwaffe began a series of concentrated attacks on Namsos, and without air support the assault on Trondheim ended in dismal failure. Under continuous air bombardment, the remnants of the British expedition retreated to the coast and were evacuated, bringing the hopeless campaign in central Norway to a close. An Allied assault on Narvik, in northern Norway, met with greater success, particularly after the little airfield at nearby Bardufoss had been made operational as a base for Gladiators and Hurricanes; but the launching of the German offensive in France and the Low Countries radically altered the strategic situation. Before the end of May, Norway was becoming a relatively unimportant theatre of war, and Narvik had no sooner been captured by the Allied forces than it had to be abandoned.

So ended *Fall Weseruebung*, a truly remarkable example of well-organised planning in combined operations and the tactical use of air power. The vastly superior British naval forces, while able to inflict serious damage on the German Fleet, had been powerless to resist the land-based aircraft of the Luftwaffe, which not only poured reinforcements into the vital landing points and destroyed the defences, but also compelled the Allies to evacuate Namsos and Aandalsnes. Much of the credit for the excellent Luftwaffe organisation during the attack on Norway must go to Erhard Milch, who arrived in Oslo on 16th April to command the new air fleet headquarters, Luftflotte 5, established to control all Luftwaffe operations in Norway. Three weeks later Milch returned to Germany in order to finalise preparations for the western offensive, his successor in Norway being General Stumpf, who remained in command of Luftflotte 5 until 1944. This was, in fact, the only occasion on which Milch left his desk to undertake a command in the field; he was an administrative genius whose abilities were wasted outside the main headquarters, and neither Udet nor Jeschonnek were capable of grasping in quite the same way the vast potentialities of air power.

Once Norway and Denmark were in German hands, Hitler was "beside himself with joy", according to General Jodl, but before the campaign came to an end he was fully occupied with other, now far more important matters. During the night of 9th May the Fuehrer's special train was rumbling across Germany towards the Belgium frontier, and dawn the following morning found Hitler and his staff in his new forward headquarters some twenty miles south-west of Bonn. Behind the bleak concrete walls of the bunker they bent over the maps that covered a front of nearly 400 miles, from the Ems estuary on the North Sea coast to the Swiss border at Basle, aware that seventy-five German divisions were at that very moment surging across the frontiers of Holland, Belgium and Luxembourg. Within the hour, the reports that Hitler nervously awaited were pouring in; the great western offensive—*Fall Gelb*—had begun, and, for better or worse, nothing could stop it now from thundering on to victory or defeat.

In the grey light of early morning on 10th May, 1940, the people of Rotterdam and The Hague were awakened by the heavy drone of aero engines as the bombers of Albert Kesselring's Luftflotte 2 passed overhead. German fighters skimmed the roofs and spires of The Hague to rake the streets with machine-gun fire, and, even as the armoured columns of Army Group B under von Bock were moving ponderously forward into Holland, a fleet of 475 three-engined Junkers Ju 52s was embarking the parachute troops and airborne units calculated to break all Dutch resistance within a matter of hours. The initial concentrated bombing of airfields, military barracks and other important objectives lasted for an hour, and was immediately followed by the first waves of transport aircraft. The defenders of the three main airfields at The Hague, dazed by the deluge of bombs, had no time to recover before they found themselves under fire from parachute troops, while a second airborne assault, under General Kurt Student, dropped out of the skies to capture and hold the vital Moerdijk Bridge near Rotterdam. By the afternoon of this first day of the campaign, some twelve hundred airborne troops had been landed on Waal-haven airfield, and reinforcements, including light artillery, were pouring in from successive waves of Junkers Ju 52 troop carriers.

It was the now familiar Blitzkrieg technique all over again, but not always a victory without losses. Large numbers of airborne troops attempting to capture the airfields of Ypenburg and Valkenburg encountered strong resistance, being driven back with heavy casualties; the lumbering Ju 52s continued to land in the face of point-blank anti-aircraft fire and the runways soon became a shambles of wrecked and burning aircraft. Meanwhile, the few Dutch fighters that had managed to get into the air wrought fearful havoc among the crowded and almost un-armed transports before hordes of Bf 109s hurtled down like avenging eagles to even out the score. As in Poland, it soon became an unequal struggle, but Student's Fallschirmjaeger and airborne infantry suffered such heavy losses that not until a year later were they fully up to strength again.

On 10th May the Netherlands Army Air Service had available, and also mobilised for action, some 132 serviceable air-craft, including forty obsolescent Fokker C.V. and C..X and Koolhoven F.K.51 reconnaissance machines. The most modern Dutch fighters available were the twin-boomed Fokker G1A "bomber destroyer" and the little single-seater Fokker D.XX1; both were excellent aircraft, but only twenty-three G.1As were in service at the time of the German attack and the D.XX1 was handicapped by a maximum speed of only 286 m.p.h. and an inadequate armament. The few Dutch fighters that survived

the initial bombardment were always hard pressed and outnumbered, but they fought valiantly to the end against the far
superior Bf 109s, until the Army Air Service fighter regiments
no longer possessed a single airworthy machine and most of the
pilots and other aircrew had been killed or wounded.

The bomber regiments of the Netherlands Army Air Service
possessed only two modern types on 10th May, 1940, the Fokker
T.V. medium bomber, of which only eight were available, and
the Douglas DB-8A-3N two-seater attack bomber, eighteen of
which had recently been acquired from the U.S.A. All the T.V.
bombers were lost during the first four days of the campaign in
vain attempts to halt the advancing columns of the Wehrmacht,
and the majority of the Douglas DB-8A-3N aircraft were destroyed on the ground at Ypenburg in the first German onslaught;
the remainder were engaged by the cannon-armed Bf 109Es
and Me 110Cs of the Luftwaffe and shot out of the skies in a
matter of hours.

By 13th May the war in Holland was almost over. However,
the Dutch forces were still holding Rotterdam, and von Bock
had been ordered to "liquidate Holland speedily" before moving
his divisions into France in support of von Runstedt; this in
turn led to a decision by Goering to launch the dive-bombers of
Fliegerkorps IV, temporarily attached to Kesselring's Luftflotte
2, against the strongpoints surrounding the Rotterdam bridgehead. That evening, Queen Wilhelmina and the government
left The Hague aboard two British destroyers bound for London,
and the following morning a German staff officer entered
Rotterdam under a white flag with a typewritten demand that
the city be surrendered.

The wires continued to hum at Luftwaffe headquarters.
Goering changed his mind about the Stukas, hesitated, and
finally instructed Kesselring to launch a saturation raid, with
the result that in the early afternoon Kampfgeschwader 54,
equipped with Heinkel He 111 medium bombers, was ordered
into the air. The target was the heart of Rotterdam; the purpose,
to hasten the Dutch capitulation; the outcome, one of the most
controversial incidents of the Second World War.

Shortly after noon, a Dutch officer named Captain Bakker
arrived at the Corps headquarters of General Rudolf Schmidt
to negotiate the surrender of Rotterdam, and an hour later he

returned to the city bearing the detailed German terms. General Schmidt, acutely aware of the impending aerial bombardment, immediately ordered the firing of red flares in an attempt to warn off the approaching bombers; he was, perhaps, five minutes too late. As the flares struggled vainly to pierce the smoke of battle that drifted over Rotterdam, the He 111s of Kampfgeschwader 54 appeared overhead, and simultaneously the bombs came raining down.

At Nuremberg, both Goering and Kesselring denied any knowledge of the surrender negotiations, but in retrospect there seems little doubt that the bombing of Rotterdam was yet another deliberate "act of force" inspired by Goering; it was intended to hasten the Dutch capitulation, and in this it succeeded. The heart of the city was totally destroyed, some eight hundred civilians were killed, several thousand wounded and 78,000 rendered homeless, while intense fires aggravated by burning oil from a bombed margarine factory raged for many hours and overwhelmed the fire services. That evening the Dutch commander-in-chief, General Winkelmann, issued a proclamation of military capitulation, and soon afterwards German airborne troops and armoured units were entering Rotterdam. The campaign in Holland—the amazing five-day war—was at an end.

By that date, 14th May, the fate of Belgium had also been sealed. The main frontier defences of that country were apparently formidable, consisting of extremely powerful fixed fortifications, including one of the most modern fortresses in the world at Eben Emael, north of Liège. At dawn on 10th May troop-carrying gliders towed by Junkers Ju 52s appeared over Aix-la-Chapelle, the gliders were efficiently uncoupled, and within minutes a silent army was descending rapidly on the unsuspecting Belgium defences. The early morning stillness was abruptly shaken by the crash of gunfire as the gliders landed to disgorge men near the three bridges carrying the main highways from Maastricht into Belgium—and also directly on the top of Fort Eben Emael. Assault troops with powerful explosive charges blew great holes in the fort's armoured turrets, and flame-throwers directed into loopholes and other openings quickly silenced the defenders; within ten minutes the great fortress had been blinded and virtually put out of action. Nevertheless, the garrison put up a desperate resistance, despite more explosive charges dropped down shafts into the depths of the casemates, causing tremendous detonations in the confined space. Twenty-four hours later, German infantry and von Richthofen's dive-bombers arrived to support the airborne assault groups, and after severe hand-to-hand fighting had taken place in the underground chambers Fort Eben Emael surrendered. Over a thousand prisoners were taken, against German losses of six killed and nineteen wounded.

Meanwhile, two of the three vital bridges over the Albert Canal behind Maastricht had been captured by the glider-borne troops before the defenders could light the fuses to blow them. The attack on the third bridge had, by contrast, proved a total failure; heavy defensive fire wiped the German assault group out and the bridge was blown up. By noon on 11th May, at about the same time Fort Eben Emael surrendered, General Erich Hoepner's XVIth Armoured Corps was thundering across the two intact bridges, with waves of Stukas ranging ahead to blast all before them out of existence.

After seven Belgian aircraft out of a force of nine had been shot down in a vain attempt to destroy the bridges, the Advanced Air Striking Force of the Royal Air Force undertook the almost impossible task. On the morning of 12th May five Fairey Battle two-seater bombers, protected by an escort of six Hawker Hurricanes, dive-bombed the now heavily defended bridges through a veritable wall of anti-aircraft fire. The Hurricanes were immediately engaged by dozens of Bf 109s, and fought valiantly until all but one of the British fighters had been destroyed, while four of the Battles were shot down over the targets and the fifth was so crippled that it crashed on the return flight. On the credit side, one Battle, manned by Flying Officer D. E. Garland and Sergeant T. Gray, both to be posthumously awarded the Victoria Cross, had temporarily knocked out the Veldwezelt bridge before plunging headlong to earth out of control. The German advance was slightly checked, but soon reinforcements and supplies were again pouring through the Maastricht gap, driving the Belgium forces back to the Dyle defensive line.

Meanwhile, much had been happening in France. At first light on 10th May the German forces had opened their assault with simultaneous air attacks on the *Armée de L'Air's* main bases at Dijon, Lyon, Metz, Nancy and Romilly; below the bomber formations, von Kleist's armoured columns were driving almost unopposed through the Ardennes. By 12th May, the 7th Panzer Division, commanded by Generalmajor Erwin Rommel, had reached the Meuse, preceded by the inevitable Stukas, and was poised for the breakthrough that would take von Runstedt's Army Group A to the Channel coast within a fortnight.

Never before had there been such perfect co-operation between ground and air forces. The Luftwaffe had available some 3,500 aircraft to cover this tremendous assault, the units being divided between Albert Kesselring's Luftflotte 2 and Hugo von Sperrle's Luftflotte 3, these being sub-divided into five Fliegerkorps of about 750 aircraft each; Richthofen's Fliegerkorps VII, Keller's Fliegerkorps IV, Grauert's Fliegerkorps I, von Greim's Fliegerkorps V, and Bruno Loerzer's Fliegerkorps II. Against this formidable force the French Armée de L'Air could muster some twenty-four single-seater fighter Groupes and six Escadrilles of twin-engined Potez 631 fighters, a total of some 800 machines. These were supported by two squadrons of Gloster Gladiators and four squadrons (increased to ten squadrons on 10th May) of Hawker Hurricanes of the R.A.F. component of the British Expeditionary Force. The French and British bomber arms could almost at once be discounted, as vain attempts to stem the grey flood of German armour had decimated them in the first two days; the Advanced Air Striking Force of the R.A.F. numbered 135 serviceable Battles and Blenheims on 10th May and only seventy-two at midnight on 12th May, while by 14th May forty of these had also been lost.

The standard first-line fighters of the Armée de L'Air were the Morane-Saulnier MS.406, the American built Curtiss Hawk 75A and the new Dewoitine D.520. For various reasons these three types proved to be generally outclassed by the Messerschmitt Bf 109 Es they opposed, and hitherto unknown German fighter pilots rocketed to fame and glory during the brief campaign in France. Wilhelm Balthasar of the Richthofen Jagdgeschwader amazingly shot down an enemy aircraft every day for twenty-one days; between 10th May and 21st June he gained twenty-two victories, including nine in one day. Adolf Galland, whose Geschwader was attached to Wolfram von Richthofen's Fliegerkorps VIII in support of the advance at Maastricht, shot down three Hurricanes in one day on 12th May and ended the campaign with seventeen victories. Other aces in embryo at that time were von Bulow, then commander of the Richthofen Jagdgeschwader; Helmuth Wick, who once said, "I want to fight and die fighting"; and the man acknowledged by Galland to be "an excellent officer and splendid pilot" —the unequalled Werner Molders.

One of Germany's leading fighter pilots at the height of the Second World War, and already in this spring of 1940 a contemporary of Adolf Galland, young Werner Molders had entered the Luftwaffe in 1935 with little opportunity to demonstrate his enthusiasm and skill until he was posted to Spain in April, 1938, to take over command of the third Staffel of Jagdgruppe J/88 from Galland, whose tour of duty was completed. In the few months that remained before the Legion Kondor was disbanded, Molders gained fourteen victories, thus becoming the most outstanding German fighter pilot in Spain; he was also an exponent of the "finger-four" fighting formation adopted by the Luftwaffe and later used by the Royal Air Force in the Battle of Britain. During the campaign in France, Molders was in command of Gruppe III of Jagdgeschwader 53, and destroyed a further twenty-five enemy aircraft before the conquest was achieved, although he had a narrow escape from death on 5th June when a French fighter surprised him over the Forest of Chantilly and he had to bale out of his burning Bf 109. A calm and disciplined leader: this was Werner Molders, popular with his men not only for his undoubted skill and courage in action, but also because, like Galland, he seldom failed to voice his opinion of Goering, and frequently dared to criticise the whole administrative structure of the Luftwaffe.

The vapour trails wove strange patterns high over the flat green fields of France, and beneath the twisting wings the fighter and bomber units of the Armée de L'Air were falling back in complete confusion. The speed and efficiency of the German advance was almost unbelievable; innumerable French fighters had to be abandoned simply because their pilots, on returning to base, found that German tanks were approaching the airfield and the ground crews had been evacuated. Despite grievous losses during what proved to be the worst six weeks in the history of French military aviation, the Armée de L'Air fought tenaciously to stem the German onslaught, destroying or badly damaging some two thousand enemy aircraft before the campaign came to an end. The Luftwaffe casualties made little difference to the outcome on the ground; by 24th May Guderian's tanks had captured Boulogne, and were within twenty miles of Dunkirk.

In London, Neville Chamberlain had resigned and Winston Churchill had been commissioned by his king to form a coalition government. On 16th May, he confronted the French Premier Reynaud and General Gamelin in Paris. "Where is the strategic reserve?" he asked Gamelin, and, in his own words, "was dumbfounded" when the Commander-in-Chief of the Allied armies merely shrugged his shoulders and answered, "*aucune*—there is none." Three days later, General Maxime Weygand replaced Gamelin, but his plan for the British and French forces to meet by cutting through the wedge of German armour thrusting at the Channel ports failed because its implementation was no longer possible. The Belgian Army surrendered on 28th May, leaving only the "Dunkirk pocket" in possession of the Allies, a corridor less than fifty miles long and fifteen miles wide containing the nine divisions of the B.E.F. and ten divisions of the French First Army. General von Runstedt's Army Group from the south and Bock's from the north should on that day have been rapidly converging to destroy them; but in fact Hitler had surprisingly lost his nerve and intervened.

On 24th May the Fuehrer paid an unexpected visit to von Runstedt's secluded Charlesville headquarters and staggered his generals by personally ordering Guderian's armour to be halted and for the time being attempt no further advance. His decision was prompted to some extent by von Runstedt, who felt that the armoured columns had outrun themselves and were about to break down under the strain, and Goering had also already telephoned Hitler to point out that the Luftwaffe could, unaided, turn Dunkirk into another Warsaw and Rotterdam. The more humanitarian Brauchitsch and Halder, on the other hand, raised violent objections, and the argument raged at command level for three days, while the Wehrmacht waited for the storm to subside and six transport ships packed with British troops departed without any difficulty from Dunkirk.

At last, Hitler again ordered his armour to advance—but only to within thirteen miles of Dunkirk. It was up to Goering now to finish the job; but his enthusiasm and buoyant confidence met with little response from Albert Kesselring, whose battleworn Luftflotte 2 had to undertake the spadework. The dawn-to-dusk air war in France had already reduced many of his units by fifty per cent, and the speed of the advance had left the Luftwaffe lines of supply and communication stretched to the limit, while the Stuka squadrons so vitally necessary in an operation of this kind were, men and machines, either weakened or exhausted. Nevertheless, Goering was insistent. "I will leave no stone on another in Dunkirk," he stated, and added boastfully, "I will not only take Dunkirk, but Calais too, if necessary!" With Hitler in full agreement, Kesselring's arguments fell on deaf ears, and reluctantly he ordered Luftflotte 2 into action.

Meanwhile, the evacuation of the British Expeditionary Force from Dunkirk—code named Operation Dynamo—had begun. An armada of some 850 vessels of all shapes and sizes, many of them manned by civilian volunteers, converged on the port, which was by now under a continuous deluge of heavy artillery fire. On the first day of the evacuation, 27th May, these little ships from England took off over 7,000 troops, and the next day 17,800 men were evacuated, despite the increasing numbers of German bombers overhead, which were gradually turning the whole dock area and harbour of Dunkirk into a sea of flames. The town itself was in ruins, the streets littered with debris or blocked with the rubble of fallen houses, dead men and horses everywhere, but somehow the weary British troops struggled through the chaos to the beaches beyond, and soon long, unbroken lines of men stretched out into the sea. Unchecked by the most appalling conditions, the evacuation went on; 47,300 on 29th May; 53,800 on 30th May; and, amazingly, over 68,000 on the last day of the month.

Kesselring had entrusted three Fliegerkorps with the destruction of the Allied forces in the Dunkirk area. These were Fliegerkorps I, commanded by General Grauert; Fliegerkorps IV, commanded by General Keller; and Fliegerkorps VIII, commanded by General von Richthofen. Junkers Ju 87s and Ju 88s, escorted by Messerschmitt Bf 109s, were the aircraft largely used, and all three units, with Jeschonnek's approval, were ruthlessly committed in a task that hampered the evacuation but never stopped it, and served mainly to highlight the Luftwaffe's limitations as a decisive weapon of war. The bombed and burning oil tanks of the Dunkirk refineries, belching greasy smoke to a height of 15,000 ft., frequently obscured the targets; the sea was dotted with hundreds of tiny ships and boats that were nevertheless not easy to sink from the air; and the sandy beaches blanketed even the heaviest bomb explosions and saved many lives. Goering had promised his Fuehrer the impossible—but over 250 German aircraft were to be lost over Dunkirk in proving it.

These last days of the B.E.F. in France brought the Royal Air Force Fighter Command up in strength to cover the Dunkirk area, and many of the German attacks were broken up with heavy losses, although the Spitfires and Hurricanes were always outnumbered. The first day of June brought a fiery climax to the air battles, when the British fighters were literally fought to a standstill and the Luftwaffe succeeded in sinking ten ships, including three destroyers. Some thirty aircraft were shot down on either side.

This was Kesselring's most powerful attempt to prevent the evacuation, but despite all his efforts it ended in failure; by midnight on 1st June over 64,00 men had been taken from the shell-torn beaches. The following day, five Fighter Command Squadrons wrought such appalling havoc in the attacking Luftwaffe formations that only scattered bombs were dropped and the evacuation continued without interruption. Beaten and discouraged, the Luftwaffe never tried seriously to interfere with Operation Dynamo again.

Dunkirk held out until 4th June, when the German tanks and infantry finally moved in to capture the town and harbour. By that day 338,226 British and French soldiers had been evacuated to fight another day, weary men who no longer by any stretch of the imagination resembled soldiers, but had nevertheless miraculously escaped what Churchill feared would be "the greatest military disaster of our long history". The long, agonising nine days was at an end, but even the Germans would find it hard to believe that the British Army had been defeated; the little ships snatching men out of the smoke and flame of Dunkirk brought not only deliverance but a legend that was destined to remain for ever.

Dunkirk was undoubtedly a bitter blow to Hermann Goering, but it came as no surprise to the more cautious Kesselring, who had foreseen the failure of the Luftwaffe if used as a decisive strategic weapon against shipping and harbour installations. Operating under difficult conditions, and already seriously weakened by the intensive fighting, it had been confronted for the first time over Dunkirk by a determined and skilful enemy air force—and found wanting. The Supermarine Spitfire had proved itself to be a match for the Messerschmitt Bf 109; the Boulton and Paul Defiant, a new British two-seater turret fighter, had shown itself to be an excellent destroyer of bombers; and, given certain advantages of height, the sturdy Hawker Hurricane had outflown everything the Luftwaffe put into the air. Since 10th May the Royal Air Force had lost a thousand aircraft, but twice that number of German aircraft had been shot down. The rough and ready tactics of the Luftwaffe general staff served to increase the casualties; too many men like the unsparing Richthofen had mercilessly wielded the sledge-hammer during the Battle of France. Adolf Galland, always in the thick of the fighting, has since commented: "Dunkirk should have been an emphatic warning to the leaders of the Luftwaffe." Unfortunately for Goering, the writing on the wall could only be read by the keenest eyes in the spring of 1940.

After the B.E.F. had returned to England, the fall of France became only a matter of time. On 3rd and 4th June the Armée de L'Air was finally knocked out by a Luftwaffe offensive code-named Operation *Paula*—a series of heavy bombing attacks on the airfields and aircraft factories around Paris. More than a hundred French aircraft were shot down and many others destroyed on the ground, for the loss of twenty-five to thirty German machines. The following day the Wehrmacht launched a tremendous offensive with all 143 divisions along the whole front from Abbeville to the Upper Rhine, and the French forces disintegrated in confusion before the overwhelming onslaught. On 10th June the French government left Paris; for three days a great silence hung over the undefended city, then the Champs

Elysées resounded to the tramp of German jackboots and the swastika flag fluttered from the Eiffel Tower. "A great day in the history of the German Army!" wrote General Halder in his diary. "German troops have been marching into Paris since nine o'clock this morning."

On the afternoon of 21st June a procession of gleaming staff cars moved through the lovely Forest of Compiegne and halted in a clearing surrounded by stately trees and pleasantly shadowed by the warm summer sunshine. From the big cars alighted Hitler, Goering, Brauchitsch, Keitel, Raeder, Ribbontrop and Hess, their immaculate uniforms glittering with decorations; they walked forward proudly, triumphantly, because this ground beneath their feet was the very same on which Marshal Foch and the German emissaries had negotiated the armistice on 11th November, 1918. Before their eyes was the symbol of Germany's former humiliation and Hitler's revenge; the old railway restaurant car in which the 1918 negotiations had taken place had been brought from its Paris museum and now awaited a second armistice. The wheel had turned full circle; the unknown corporal of the 16th Bavarian Reserve Infantry Regiment had carried the sword of vengeance into France.

Shortly after Hitler and his party had entered the railway car the French delegation arrived. Keitel commenced reading the German terms of surrender, but once the preamble was over Hitler and most of his entourage departed, leaving the negotiations in Keitel's hands. The Fuehrer strode back to his waiting Mercedes, the German band played *Deutschland über Alles*, the bright sunshine filtered through the tall elms and pines—and France had been defeated. The Austrian tax-collector's son had come a long way since those shivering, hungry days when he had roamed the streets of Vienna as an unwanted vagabond, but he would never surpass this, the greatest triumph of his career; his life had been dedicated to obliterating for ever the humiliation of 1918 and here in the Forest of Compiegne his purpose had at last been fulfilled.

It remained only for the conqueror to acknowledge that his generals had served him well. Hitler enjoyed a minor triumph over his subordinates here, for he cunningly chose to award them so lavishly with promotions that not until afterwards did they realise that he had cheapened their high military ranks and reduced their stature. In a colourful ceremony at the Kroll Opera House on 19th July no less than twelve generals were promoted to the rank of field-marshal, or Generalfeldmarschall, nineteen promotions to Generaloberst were awarded, together with seven to General and one new Generaladmiral. The highest Luftwaffe promotions were very satisfactory; three new Generalfeldmarschaelle, Milch, Kesselring and Sperrle; five new Generaloberst, Grauert, Stumpff, Keller, Weise and Udet, and five new General der Flieger, Jeschonnek, Geissler, Loerzer, Greim and Richthofen. Glittering with decorations, the long line of field marshals posed with Hitler for the photographers before the ceremony came to an end, "cheaper by the dozen"— as many junior officers commented—and rendered indistinguishable as leaders by their very profusion.

Only Hermann Goering remained secure and aloof on his lofty pinnacle of glory, for Hitler had thoughtfully created for him an entirely new rank, that of Reichsmarschall des Grossdeutschen Reiches, or Marshal of the Greater German Reich. Hailed in the official citation as "the creator of the Luftwaffe", he was also awarded the Grand Cross of the Iron Cross, the only one of its kind to be given during the entire war, and a brandnew uniform had been devised for him to mark the occasion. This unique masterpiece could be tailored either in grey-blue or white, and had crossed gold-embroidered batons backed by silver brocade on one collar tab and a golden Reich eagle, also on a silver brocade base, on the other. The brilliant uniform, together with Goering's new gigantic Marshal's baton, soon gave rise to great hilarity in Germany, but he would have requested no other reward; personal power and gleaming, useless baubles were as the breath of life to him.

In fact, the newly created Reichsmarschall was about to undertake the most responsible and unenviable task of his career. On 16th July Hitler had issued his Operational Directive No. 16, which stated: "Since England, despite her militarily hopeless situation, still shows no sign of willingness to come to terms, I have decided to prepare a landing operation against England, and if necessary to carry it out. The aim of this operation is to eliminate the English homeland as a base for the carrying on of the war against Germany, and, if it should become necessary, to occupy it completely."

The words "to prepare a landing operation against England" were of the utmost importance to Goering. In those preparations the Luftwaffe would be decisive; without overwhelming air superiority a seaborne invasion would be utterly impossible. Even General Jodl, who was convinced that Britain was already beaten to her knees, admitted that a landing could ". . . only be contemplated after Germany has gained control of the air . . ." and yet Kesselring doubted that the Luftwaffe was in good enough shape to knock the Royal Air Force out of the skies so soon after the Battle of France.

If Goering had any qualms about the forthcoming air offensive he refused to let them dismay him. "The enemy is already morally defeated . . ." he stated at a conference of high Luftwaffe commanders in The Hague. ". . . Our first objective will be the destruction of his fighter forces, partly in the air and partly on the ground, together with the destruction of his airfields. This objective will be attained within two or three days, and that will be decisive."

More than one of the men listening to Goering's boastful speech must have reflected that now, for the first time, the Luftwaffe urgently needed a strategic long-range bombing force to strike at the heart of England again and again. But the heavy four-engined bombers so often demanded by General Wever in the past had never been built, and the Luftwaffe's medium bombers, protected by a small and sadly neglected fighter force, would somehow or other have to tackle the problem. Doubt and uncertainty hung like a cloud over the conference table; only Goering seemed confident and convinced that all would be well.

The Reichsmarschall, resplendent in his new white uniform, dismissed all arguments by insisting that German air strength was far superior to that of Great Britain, and commenting that the Messerschmitt Bf 109 was a better fighter than the Supermarine Spitfire. When the conference came to an end he was in high spirits, having managed to reassure himself, if not his leaders, that the Battle of Britain was already as good as won, and the Luftwaffe could, in his own words, "not only destroy the Royal Air Force, but put the Royal Navy out of action as well."

Perhaps it was just as well for Goering that summer that he

could not look into the future and see the outcome of his latest venture. The Battle of Britain proved to be the turning point in his career; after it had ended, he would never again have any faith in his Luftwaffe, and his commanders would henceforward remember him as the man who had condemned their air weapon to complete disaster.

CHAPTER XII

A FORTRESS BESIEGED: THE BATTLE OF BRITAIN

MANY of the German operational instructions in the field for the first phase of the Battle of Britain issued, curiously enough, from an old omnibus situated on the cliffs at Cap Blanc Nez near the Bleriot statue commemorating the first cross-Channel flight in 1909. From this unusual and cramped little command post, Johannes Fink, the forty-five year old Kommodore of Kampfgeschwader 2, hoped to achieve air superiority over the English Channel and the Straits of Dover, using his own force of Dornier Do 17 bombers, two Stuka Gruppen and two Jagdgeschwader of Messerschmitt Bf 109s, one led by Werner Molders and the other by Adolf Galland. Fink therefore had at his disposal some seventy-five medium bombers, sixty or more dive-bombers and about 200 fighters, and as commander of this battle force he bore the imposing title of Kanalkampffuhrer, or Channel Battle Leader. Further down the coast near Le Havre, Wolfram von Richthofen's Fliegerkorps VIII had been assigned the task of attacking British shipping in the Channel until everything that moved on the water had been dive-bombed out of existence, notwithstanding the fact that these same Junkers Ju 87s had already taken a severe beating in the skies over Dunkirk.

The Oberkommando der Luftwaffe orders for the campaign against Britain were issued on 2nd July, 1940, and during the following weeks the four telephones in Fink's temporary headquarters jangled incessantly with activity as he directed his battle group into action. In the brilliant summer sunshine, the tiny dots high in the vast blue bowl of the heavens would tilt sharply over to port and resolve at once into ugly gull-winged Ju 87s, falling vertically out of the sky in screaming power dives towards the convoys that continued to steam placidly along in the shadow of the white cliffs of Dover. Anti-aircraft fire exploding angrily among the plunging dive-bombers; great fountains of water erupting in the midst of the ships as they took violent evasive action; then the sky over the Channel would become filled with twisting, turning fighters as the Spitfires and Hurricanes of the R.A.F. tangled with the Ju 87s and escorting Bf 109s. The attacks, initially small and spasmodic, increased in number until on 10th July Fighter Command flew no less than 609 sorties in protection of the Channel shipping and harbours and destroyed thirteen German aircraft for the loss of six British fighters. From that date, the R.A.F. and the Luftwaffe were engaged in a bitter life-or-death struggle for mastery of the air.

By 25th July the Luftwaffe had lost large numbers of Ju 87 dive-bombers and a surprising number of fighters, but Johannes Fink had achieved his purpose and gained a tactical victory by driving all British shipping out of the Channel. The attacks had shown that the British radar network found it impossible to give sufficient warning of the approach of German aircraft at such short range, and the vulnerable convoys had been forced to undergo heavy punishment before intercepting fighters could be hurled into the battles. Also, of course, both sides were still sparring warily around the ring; the Luftwaffe was using only small numbers of aircraft on each sortie, and the R.A.F. was very sensibly reluctant to commit its fighter force in strength without good reason.

The outcome of the Channel Battle should have brought little joy to Hermann Goering, for the actions during July had destroyed for ever the Stuka myth fostered within the higher ranks of the Luftwaffe for almost a decade. The Junkers Ju 87 attacks on British shipping and harbours illustrated for the first time that when opposed by a determined fighter defence the dive-bomber was seriously handicapped as a striking weapon. As Adolf Galland has commented : ". . . the slow speed of the Ju 87 turned out to be a great drawback. Owing to the speed-reducing effect of the externally-suspended bomb-load, she reached only 150 m.p.h. when diving, and as the required altitude for the dive was between 10,000 and 15,000 ft. the Stukas attracted Spitfires and Hurricanes as honey attracts flies . . . the Stukas, once they peeled out of formation to dive singly on to their targets, were practically defenceless . . ." The vulnerability of the Ju 87s to the British eight-gun fighters, apart from disconcerting the Luftwaffe high command, was a source of annoyance and frustration to the German fighter-pilots, whose Bf 109s were too fast to provide suitable close escort cover. Refusing for some time to admit that the dive-bombing policy was now a catastrophic failure, Goering openly blamed the fighter force for the high losses in Ju 87s, although by the middle of August the limitations of the Stuka type of aircraft were so obvious that all dive-bomber formations had to be withdrawn to the Pas de Calais in the hope that they would be of some use again after the R.A.F. had been destroyed.

Goering could also reflect that his vaunted Messerschmitt Bf 110 Zerstorer formations had not lived up to their reputation in this first phase of the Battle of Britain. When used as escort for dive-bombers, these twin-engined fighters could exist when attacked by Hurricanes only if they formed a tight defensive ring and devoted themselves entirely to their own protection. Admittedly the high speed of the Bf 110s was an advantage, for they were often able to escape if seriously engaged, but they lacked the armament and performance to battle with single-engined fighters, and had already proved to be hopelessly inadequate in the escort role. Yet the Heinkel He 111 and Dornier Do 17 medium bombers would undoubtedly have a hard time of it over England without strong fighter protection; and the overworked Bf 109 squadrons could not stand up indefinitely to the rigours of a long drawn out struggle for superiority.

Even to Goering it was becoming increasingly obvious that before an invasion could be attempted the British fighter force would have to be totally destroyed—and in the shortest possible time.

On 6th August Goering decided to hold an important conference at Karinhall to discuss with his senior officers the next phase of the Battle of Britain. Hitler's Operational Directive No. 17, issued three days earlier, had metaphorically brought the Reichsmarschall rigidly to attention by stating firmly : ". . . The German Air Force must with all means in their power and as quickly as possible destroy the English air force. The attacks must in the first instance be directed against flying formations, their ground organisations, and their supply organisations, and in the second against the aircraft production industry and the industries engaged in production of anti-aircraft equipment. . . ." Now, Milch, Sperrle, Stumpf and the other German air leaders were assembled to hear Goering outline the plans for Adlerangriff, or "The Attack of the Eagles", as the offensive had been named, although in fact most of them already possessed detailed knowledge of the Luftwaffe dispositions. Only the important subject of co-operation between the army, navy and air force during the actual invasion, which had been code-named *Seelowe*, or Sealion, still remained something of a mystery; indeed, Hitler's plans for the seaborne assault on England were so vague as yet that Kesselring, for one, doubted if he intended to invade at all.

The total German first-line strength deployed against Britain in August, 1940, was approximately 2,550 serviceable aircraft, including 900 bombers, 250 dive-bombers, 800 single-engined fighters and 200 twin-engined fighters. This apparently formid-able force was absorbed into three air fleets; Luftflotte 2, under the command of Generalfeldmarschall Albert Kesselring; Luft-flotte 3, under Generalfeldmarschall Hugo von Sperrle; and Luftflotte 5, under Generaloberst Stumpf. Luftflotte 5 had been based in Norway and Denmark since the Norwegian campaign, and was mainly to be directed against northern England, while the two air fleets in the west had merely extended their boundaries across Occupied France, Belgium and Holland during the Channel Battle. The main H.Q. on Luftflotte 2 was established at Brussels, with an advanced H.Q. at Cap Gris Nez, and the main H.Q of Luftflotte 3 was at Paris, with an advanced HQ at Deauville. An unusual feature of the com-mand structure for Adlerangriff was the grouping together of fighters in the air fleets into units known as Jagdfliegerfuhrer, or Jafu, which were supposed to have a measure of operational independence, but in fact seldom benefited from it because they lacked any radio close control.

As in Poland and France, the single-seater Messerschmitt Bf 109 E, the twin-engined Messerschmitt Bf 110C, the Heinkel He 111K and Dornier Do 17Z medium bombers and the Junkers Ju 87B and Ju 88C dive-bombers represented the nucleus of the attacking force. The Heinkel He 115, a twin-engined seaplane, was earmarked for use in small numbers to harass convoys in the English Channel, and a few Heinkel He 59 float biplanes had been adapted for air/sea rescue duties.

The German Intelligence system accurately assessed the

British fighter forces available in July, 1940, at fifty-two squadrons of Hurricanes, Spitfires and Defiants, a total first-line strength of some 900 aircraft. Using the same armament of eight Browning machine-guns and the same Rolls-Royce Merlin liquid-cooled vee engine, the Supermarine Spitfire and the Hawker Hurricane had been designed to fulfil the requirements of Air Ministry specification F5/34 of 1935, which called for a very fast eight-gun single-seater monoplane fighter to provide the hard core of British air defence. Nevertheless, these two types of aircraft were totally different in conception, the Spitfire's lines bearing distinct traces of its Schneider Trophy seaplane ancestry, and the Hurricane being a direct development from the Hawker Fury biplane. The Boulton and Paul Defiant two-seater fighter superficially resembled the Hurricane, but carried no forward armament and concentrated all its fire power in the rear cockpit, which held a four-gun power-operated turret.

The Supermarine Spitfire was a slim and supremely beautiful monoplane with graceful semi-elliptical wings, and such smooth lines that it seemed too ethereal for the rough and tumble of air fighting, but R. J. Mitchell, the designer, had used his Schneider Trophy experience to produce a thoroughbred; excellent handling characteristics, outstanding high-altitude manoeuvrability and a speed of over 350 m.p.h. turned the Spitfire into the epitome of the single-seater fighter. In July, 1940, there were nineteen squadrons of Spitfires in Fighter Command in readiness for the Battle of Britain.

Designed by Sidney Camm, the Hawker Hurricane marked the transition from the twin-gun fighter biplane to the eight-gun monoplane in Great Britain, and was in fact the first aircraft of that type to enter service with the R.A.F. A sturdy, robust fighter capable of taking very heavy punishment, the Hurricane featured the famous Hawker tubular girder construction covered by fabric, a method of construction used on the Fury biplane fighter in 1930 and retained on the Hurricane in preference to the more complicated stressed-skin fuselage of the Spitfire in order to get some of the new eight-gun fighters into quantity production as quickly as possible. Rather larger and heavier than the Spitfire, the Hurricane had a maximum speed of 316 m.p.h. at 17,500 ft. and an overall performance not unlike that of the Messerschmitt Bf 109, although the German fighter was more manoeuvrable and delicate to handle.

The Boulton and Paul Defiant turret fighter was a contemporary of the Messerschmitt Bf 110, and suffered from the same disadvantages : too much weight and inadequate armament. The conception of both aircraft could be traced back to various outstanding two-seater fighters in service during the period 1916-1918, but the two-seater fighter as such had died a natural death some time between the wars, and the Defiant and the Bf 110 merely emphasised the fact that a two-seater must have exceptional qualities to beat a single-seater in a general dogfight. The Defiant had a brief but remarkable success over Dunkirk, mainly against bomber formations, although on at least one occasion the Defiants of 264 Squadron were mistaken for Hurricanes by a German fighter formation, which dived on to their tails and were immediately blasted out of existence by the devastating fire from the two-seaters' four-gun turrets. If attacked from below, however, the Defiant was defenceless, and by August, 1940, losses were so high that it was obviously outmatched in every way by the German single-seater fighters. Consequently, it was about to be withdrawn from daylight operations and undergo modification as a night fighter.

At Bentley Priory, above the village of Stanmore, Middlesex, stood the headquarters of the man who faced the difficult task of breaking the German air offensive before all his fighters had been consumed in the furnace of battle. Air Marshal Sir Hugh Dowding, the brisk Commander-in-Chief of Fighter Command, so unlike his fat and jovial German opponent that he had been nicknamed "Stuffy" because of his reserved, austere nature, had no doubts about the tremendous responsibility that rested on his shoulders; he knew that in this battle there would be only the narrowest of margins between victory and defeat. Thanks to his own untiring efforts since the inception of Fighter Command in 1936, often a grim uphill struggle against superiors who preferred to bury their heads in the sands of complacency and let the future take care of itself, Britain had in four years been provided with a first-class fighter defence organisation, yet within a month Dowding had seen many of his precious Hurricane squadrons drained away during the disastrous campaign in France. When he could bear the tragic wastage of machines and men no longer, Dowding warned the War Cabinet that his fighter strength was being seriously weakened, and when this had no effect composed a characteristically outspoken letter to the Air Ministry, clearly stating the position, and ending with the following words : ". . . if the Home Defence Force is drained away in desperate attempts to remedy the situation in France, defeat in France will involve the final, complete and irremediable defeat of this country." Informed in the same letter that only thirty-six fighter squadrons remained in Britain, Winston Churchill decided that no more squadrons would be sent to France. It was a decision influenced by Dowding, and not easily made, but it was destined to affect the history of the whole world.

Now that all his fighters were back at their home bases, Dowding found that he could muster fifty-two squadrons, including twenty-five for the protection of the Southern and Western Counties; these, under 11 Group, commanded by Air Marshal Sir Keith Rodney Park, would have to bear the brunt of the battle. About a thousand trained pilots were in readiness to meet the German onslaught, the young men later to be described in the Official Short History as "the gayest company who ever fired their guns in anger" and yet who were in many cases inexperienced, over-confident or simply afraid. Come what may, Dowding felt certain that all would acquit themselves well when the storm broke; but he could not know that when it was all over many of his most irreplaceable pilots would have been killed in action.

During the conference at Karinhall, Goering had announced that the opening of the air offensive against Britain, named by him Adlertag, or "Eagle Day", would take place on 10th August, but in fact the second phase of the Battle of Britain began on 8th August, when three heavy attacks by heavily escorted Junkers Ju 87s of Fliegerkorps VIII were intercepted and repulsed by seven Spitfire and Hurricane squadrons from the south-coast aerodromes. The escorting Bf 109s fought savagely to protect the slow ungainly Stukas, and in the dogfights that raged over the Channel thirty-one German aircraft were shot down for the loss of nineteen R.A.F. fighters.

The following day was quiet, with only scattered raids, mainly because low cloud obscured the Channel, and Goering and his staff were preoccupied with the Adlertag preparations. The meteorological reports were far from promising, and it was decided to postpone Adlertag pending the arrival of more favourable weather. Nevertheless, on 12th August a series of hammer blows were delivered against the three forward fighter airfields of Manston, Lympne and Hawkinge, the naval base at Portsmouth and six of the vital radar stations along the south coast.

Lympne airfield was heavily attacked by a formation of Ju 88s soon after nine o'clock in the morning, and an hour later the radar stations near Eastbourne and Hastings were bombed, while fifteen Ju 88s dive bombed the long-range radar station at Ventnor in the Isle of Wight, putting it out of action. The raid on Manston airfield was carried out by a formation of Dornier Do 17s, which hurtled in very fast and low over the hangars while the escorting Bf 109s fought a running battle with the Spitfires of 54 Squadron. The bombs rained down as 65 Squadron's Spitfires were taxi-ing out for take-off, and the fighters rose into the air miraculously unscathed through eruptions of smoke and flying debris. Heavily engaged, the Do 17s turned for home; in five minutes they had pitted the airfield with craters and knocked out the workshops and two hangars. When the tumult of roaring engines and hammering guns had died away, Manston was out of action, and accordingly deleted from the operations maps at Luftwaffe headquarters. In fact, it had been made serviceable again by the following morning.

The attack on Portsmouth was carried out by determined Ju 88s, which plunged straight down through a solid wall of anti-aircraft fire to strike hard at the city and dock area, starting several fires which were still burning many hours later. By night-fall the German radio was rightly claiming that all the selected targets had been seriously damaged, but the British air defences had survived the onslaught, and all the attacked units except the radar station on the Isle of Wight were in operation again within a matter of hours. Also, thirty-six German aircraft had been shot down for the loss of twenty-two R.A.F. machines, a score that evened out in some measure the success on the German side.

On 13th August, despite early morning cloud and uncertain

weather, Goering decided to officially launch his Adlerangriff offensive against Britain. The main force, seventy-four Dornier Do 17s of Kampfgeschwader 2, in two formations and personally led by Johannes Fink, headed for Eastchurch; the Junkers Ju 88s of Kampfgeschwader 54 were directed against Odiham aerodrome and the Royal Aircraft Factory at Farnborough; and the Ju 87s of Stukageschwader 77 took off with orders to bomb Portland and selected airfields in Hampshire and Kent. Mass attacks were also to be made on Southampton and the Thames Estuary later in the afternoon.

Warned by his invaluable radar system, Dowding committed a large concentration of fighters, and the dogfights which developed during the day were furious cut-and-thrust battles with no quarter asked and none given, a foretaste of the struggles that lay ahead. Fink's hard-pressed Do 17s managed to retain their superb formation—and concentrated fire-power—as far as Eastchurch, and seriously damaged the airfield there before the Spitfires harrying them were joined by two Hurricane squadrons, which broke up the mass of bombers. Dodging through the clouds, the Dorniers fought their way back to the coast, leaving behind them four which would never return and another four so badly damaged that they would be lucky to reach their home bases.

The Ju 87 and Ju 88 raids met with little success, the aircraft of Kampfgeschwader 54 being so hotly engaged by fighters that they missed their targets and scattered bombs indiscriminately everywhere, and a formation of Ju 87s being intercepted and shot to pieces so effectively that nine were lost without having achieved anything. The escort of Bf 110s for the dive-bombers directed against Portland missed the rendezvous and arrived over the target still seeking their bombers, to be met instead by two Fighter Command squadrons, which destroyed six of the vulnerable two-seaters in five minutes. The attack on Southampton was carried out with only moderate success, and seven British airfields were hit without suffering anything more than minor damage, although a raid that night by Heinkel He 111s of the élite Kampfgeschwader 100 did considerable harm, eleven bombs being dropped on the Spitfire shadow factory at Castle Bromwich.

The next day, 14th August, was cloudy, and apart from a

few scattered raids by odd Ju 88s and He 111s and a few bomb-carrying Bf 110s there was a strange absence of German aircraft over England. In fact, the inauspicious opening to Adlerangriff had shown the Luftwaffe leaders that their first mass attacks had been badly organised and lacking in the perfect co-ordination of the British fighter defences. Also, the targets had been too scattered, giving negligible results for heavy casualties. With a clear weather forecast for the following day, it was therefore decided to make a concerted effort with all three Luftflotten on a wide front, concentrating against the forward airfields and radar stations, and above all encouraging the British fighters into the air all along the line, to be overwhelmed by sheer weight of numbers. In short it would bring about a climax of this phase of the battle, although neither side were able to realise as much at the time. On this day, but never again, the Luftwaffe would be able to make nearly 2,000 sorties, and the R.A.F. have to use all four fighter groups to repel the aerial armada.

The first blow on 15th August fell at 11.30 a.m. in the bright morning sunshine, when about sixty Ju 87s with an escort of fifty Bf 109s from Galland's Jagdgeschwader 26 attacked the airfields at Hawkinge and Lympne, and were intercepted by two Fighter Command squadrons. While the Spitfires were battling with the Bf 109s, the dive-bombers hit their targets, causing almost complete devastation at Lympne but only slight damage at Hawkinge. Galland attacked a Spitfire which vomited fragments and burst into flames, and then swung on to the tail of another, which escaped by turning inside the Bf 109.

At noon Luftflotte 5 from Norway and Denmark unexpectedly entered the arena by striking with about a hundred He 111s of Kampfgeschwader 26 and seventy Bf 110s of Zerstorergeschwader 76 at the north-east coast in the Newcastle and Sunderland area. Five squadrons of R.A.F. fighters met these formations and quickly broke them up; fifteen German aircraft were shot down without losing a single British machine. "The Squadron was flying at 22,000 ft. on course 020 deg, with the enemy well below," ran a typical combat report, from 72 Squadron, "flying west in many Vic formations, line abreast and line astern ... Circling the flank, I warned the rear guard of escort fighters and then ordered the Squadron to attack, leading my Blue Section in a No. 3 stern chase on (He) 111s which were flying behind and slightly above the enemy preceding Vics. I opened fire at 250 yards closing to about 30 yards, and saw smoke burst from the fuselage and port engine. Intense return fire was encountered but this was inaccurate. On diving away from He, I spotted a Me 110 circling above me, so dived straight for the clouds 900 ft. below. Before entering the cloud I could still see this Me 110 spiralling down, but this time I got the impression that it might have been out of control, though no smoke was issuing from it. . . ."

While these dogfights were raging over Sunderland and the North Sea, the Ju 88s of Kampfgeschwader 30 raced in at high speed to attack the Bomber Command aerodrome at Driffield, inflicting fairly serious damage before they were engaged by the Spitfires of 616 Squadron, which destroyed six of the raiders. By the early afternoon, as the bullet-riddled survivors of Luftflotte 5 struggled back to their Scandinavian bases, it was obvious that the sorties against northern England had proved to be a costly failure. In the final reckoning, Luftflotte 5, numerically the weakest of the three air fleets, had lost twenty-three bombers and escort fighters; unable to risk such heavy casualties again, it would take no further part in the campaign, having literally been knocked once and for all out of the Battle of Britain.

Meanwhile, in the south-east the Fighter Command operations tables were becoming alive with renewed activity as radio and telephone messages poured in again. After a minor attack on Manston airfield by twelve Bf 109s, wave after wave of escorted bombers crossed the coast near Felixstowe, Harwich and Orford Ness, and soon afterwards a force of nearly a hundred German raiders was reported coming in over Deal. Four R.A.F. fighter squadrons endeavoured to turn away the enemy formations, but by sheer weight of numbers the hard-pressed bombers fought through to their targets, heavily damaging the aero components factories at Rochester and striking again at Eastchurch and the coastal radar stations. Twenty minutes later another formation of 150 bombers approached from the Folkestone area, followed by some 250 aircraft from Luftflotte 3, which spread out over Hampshire and Wiltshire. Eight fighter squadrons from 10 and 11 Groups rose to cross swords with the raiders, the largest force Dowding had yet committed at any one time, and the vapour trails wove fantastic patterns in the skies over the southern counties as the Spitfires and Hurricanes harried the German bombers and fought desperately with the escorting Bf 109s. Guns chattered, men died and aircraft twisted and turned in a nightmare of smoke and flame high above the quiet English countryside, then suddenly the German forces were unravelling back across the coast and out to sea. The weary Fighter Command pilots returned to their bomb-cratered home bases hoping that the enemy would call it a day; but they were soon to find that Kesselring and Sperrle still had a few cards to place on the table.

At 6.15, when most of the forward fighter squadrons were refuelling and re-arming, about seventy German aircraft were detected heading for the coast between Dover and Dungeness. Four squadrons of 11 Group immediately took to the air, followed by six more as the bombers continued to battle their way inland, until at last the Luftwaffe formations were broken up and driven away from their main targets of Kenley and Biggin Hill. Instead, they succeeded in hitting West Malling airfield, putting it out of action for several days and inflicting heavy damage on the Croydon base of 111 Fighter Squadron. Other raiders, disorganised and scattered by the persistent fighter attacks, dropped their bombs at random on Kent and Surrey before turning away, while their escorting Bf 109s engaged in dogfights with Spitfires and Hurricanes all over the sky south of London.

Despite the efforts of 111 and 32 Squadrons, it turned out to be a bad day for Croydon. At the height of the battle a tight group of Messerschmitt Bf 110s converted to the fighter role and escorted by Bf 109s, came in at low level to strike hard at the Rollason and Redwing aircraft component factories, almost completely destroying both works, together with over forty training aircraft under construction, and killing or seriously injuring about eighty people. The Hurricanes of 111 Squadron fell straight out of the sky from 10,000 ft. on to the raiders, and a confused tangle of air battles took place at roof-top heights, the unfortunate Bf 110s no sooner leaving the Hurricanes behind than they were intercepted by the fighters of 32 Squadron, which hammered away at them as they raced for the coast. Four of the twin-engined fighters were shot down before the scattered formation receded into the distance over the Channel and brought to an end the last raid of a very eventful day, apart from a few scattered night attacks by some seventy medium bombers.

As darkness fell, Dowding and Park could relax and feel that Fighter Command had stood up courageously to the greatest onslaught that had yet tried to break it. Between dawn and dusk some eighteen hundred German aircraft had been sent against England, and seventy-six had been shot down, for the loss of thirty-four British fighters. One of the three German air fleets, Luftflotte 5, had been so badly mauled that it was now out of the daylight battle; a terrific strain had been imposed on the German fighter force, which had been compelled to put almost every available machine into the air; the appalling Ju 87 Stuka losses could not possibly be borne much longer; and, last but by no means least, the twin-engined Bf 110s would be useful in the future only in the fighter-bomber role, bringing Goering's so-called elite Zerstorer formations to an ignominious end. Against these important setbacks, Kesselring and Sperrle could credit themselves with negligible material success against England and an appreciable strain on the British air defence system. It was now obviously developing into a battle of attrition; but how could the Luftwaffe withstand such a high rate of losses and yet bring the R.A.F. to a standstill?

While the 15th August air struggles were at a height, Hermann Goering was again in conference at Karinhall with his senior commanders. "The fighter escort defences of our Stuka formations must be readjusted, as the enemy is concentrating his fighters against our Stuka formations," he stated. "It appears necessary to allocate three fighter Gruppen to each Stuka Gruppe. One of these fighter Gruppen remains with the Stukas and dives with them to attack; the second flies ahead of the target at medium altitude and engages fighter defences; the third protects the whole attack from above. It will also be necessary to escort Stukas returning from the attack over the Channel. . . ." While the high officers of the Luftwaffe wondered where they were going to find the vast numbers of fighters that would be required for escort tactics of the kind Goering visualised, the Reichmarschall rambled on. "Until further orders," he said, "operations are to be directed exclusively against the enemy air force, including the targets of the enemy aircraft industry. . . . We must concentrate our efforts on the destruction of the enemy air forces. . . ."

The air staff leaders listened to their commander-in-chief in silence. Much of what Goering told them that afternoon he had already said before, although he seemed to have conveniently forgotten that not so long ago he had stated that the R.A.F. would be beaten out of the skies and destroyed on the ground within three days. Then, in the closing words of his speech, he made a decisive blunder, an error of such importance that it would affect the whole course of the battle. "It is doubtful," he said, "whether there is any point in continuing the attacks on radar sites, in view of the fact that not one of those attacked has so far been put out of action." In that single sentence, the ex-fighter pilot of the First World War betrayed his total ignorance of the science and engineering of modern air defence; the forward radar stations were vital to Dowding, and without them Fighter Command would have no warning of enemy formations. Looking back, it only seems strange that not one of the men seated around the conference table tried to explain that concentrated bombing of the radar stations should be an essential part of the offensive. Air tactics, after all, merely interested Goering because they brought to light unusual little problems he believed could be solved at once by quick, unconsidered decisions. He was a typical amateur dabbling in the whirlpool of grand strategy; but most of his commanders were soldiers of the old school, with years of military experience behind them.

The conference ended, but the air battles went on. During 16th August the Luftwaffe again attacked in force, with the British fighter airfields and sector stations as the main targets, including West Malling, Manston and Tangmere. No less than twelve Fighter Command squadrons endeavoured to break up the enemy formations, but many of the bombers succeeded in getting through and the West Malling and Tangmere stations were temporarily knocked out of action. Meanwhile, heavily escorted Ju 87s and Ju 88s struck at Lee-on-Solent and Gosport, and a few raiders dropped bombs on the outskirts of London. In the evening Brize Norton aerodrome was heavily damaged, forty-six training aircraft being burned out in the hangars, and many other buildings totally destroyed. Then, suddenly, it was all over for another day, and the R.A.F. had shot down forty-five German aircraft for the loss of twenty-two fighters.

On 18th August massed formations of German bombers again crossed the Channel to hammer away at the weary fighter airfields, including Kenley, Croydon and Biggin Hill. With great courage, the Do 17s directed against Kenley came thundering in over the coast at an altitude of less than 50 ft., leaving their escorting Bf 109s to engage the intercepting R.A.F. fighters. Flying through a barrage of anti-aircraft fire from guns of all calibres, the raiders skimmed the airfield, dropping over a hundred bombs that destroyed a number of aircraft on the ground, wrecked ten hangars and turned the operations room into a shambles. The nine Do 17s of Kampfgeschwader 76 which attacked Biggin Hill also came in at low level, but here the anti-aircraft fire was so intense and accurate that only two bombers survived to reach their home base, and one of those with the flight engineer at the controls, the pilot dead at his side. The high losses later convinced Goering that low-level attacks were a failure, but in fact Dowding and Park dreaded such tactics, which gave little warning and seriously restricted their fighters in action.

In the afternoon Gosport was dive-bombed again, this time by twenty-one Ju 88s; a force from Stukageschwader 77 attacked Thorney Island in Hampshire and Ford in Sussex, losing twelve Ju 87s in damaging a few buildings; and, later, twelve Bf 109s rocketed over Manston with cannon and machine-guns blazing, destroying two Spitfires on the ground. When the now familiar night raiders began throbbing over England to seek out their scattered targets, Fighter Command had flown 766 sorties and seventy-one German aircraft had been shot down, against twenty-seven British fighters destroyed.

The following day brought an unexpected lull in the offensive. It was to last for nearly a week, a tacit admission from Goering that his all-out effort to destroy the Fighter Command airfields had proved unsuccessful and his aircrews were weary to the point of exhaustion. Calling another war conference at Karinhall, the disappointed Reichsmarschall told his fighter commanders that he had decided their forces were responsible for the bomber losses over England, because, in his opinion, the escort pilots lacked the aggressive spirit. Ignoring the crux of the problem—that the Bf 110 was utterly useless and the Bf 109 essentially a short-range fighter—Goering then outlined his scheme to improve morale in the fighter units by promoting younger men with exceptional qualities to senior rank, and thus gradually replacing the "old soldiers" he now distrusted. He began at once by placing Galland and Molders each in command of a fighter Gruppe. "The vital task is . . . the defeat of the enemy air force. Our first aim is to destroy the enemy fighters," he stated. "Until further notice the main task of Luftflotten 2 and 3 will be to inflict the utmost damage possible on the enemy fighter forces. . . ."

The direct result of this conference and the Oberkommando der Luftwaffe directive which followed was a drastic re-grouping and massing of the German fighter forces, in readiness for the third phase of the battle. All the Bf 109 squadrons of both air fleets were concentrated in the Pas de Calais area under the command of Luftflotte 2, leaving Luftflotte 3 with only Bf 110s for escort duties, reinforced by the Bf 110s of Luftflotte 5, which had been withdrawn for services in France. Not that anything startling was expected of the Bf 110 in the light of recent events; it simply remained in use because nothing better existed to replace it. Even Goering had been forced to admit at last, however, that his Ju 87 dive-bombers were too vulnerable to risk over England again in daylight, even if heavily escorted, and Richthofen's Fliegerkorps VIII received orders to take no further part in the battle. So much for that typical German air striking weapon, the vulture-like Stuka; as a Blitzkrieg spearhead it had screamed and bombed its unopposed way through Poland, France and the Low Countries, only to meet fighter resistance for the first time in the Battle of Britain and reveal itself to be merely an awkward and practically defenceless machine.

While the Luftwaffe was making preparations for another onslaught against Great Britain, Air Marshal Dowding was anxiously facing an unanswerable problem. Some twenty-five per cent of his one thousand trained pilots had now been killed or wounded in action, and it was impossible to replace the crippling losses as the situation demanded. It was true that pilots were available from the other Commands—volunteers were already being hurriedly drafted into fighter squadrons after only ten or twenty hours on Spitfires or Hurricanes—but the fact remained that the hard core of men experienced in fighter tactics was steadily being dwindled away. The remarkable efforts of Lord Beaverbrook after he had been appointed Minister of Aircraft Production had kept Dowding supplied with the aircraft he needed, but even that human dynamo could not conjure trained pilots out of thin air. The greatest crisis of Dowding's whole career was almost at hand, and during the next four weeks his determination would be tested as never before.

Ultimate victory for Fighter Command or Great Britain naked to the German sword. It was as simple as that; and Dowding bore the awful responsibilities, while the guns chattered angrily above the roar of the engines and the vapour trails twisted lazily in the bright summer sky.

During the third phase of the Battle of Britain, the German air staff leaders gradually stepped-up the pace of their main offensive in an attempt to draw Dowding's fighter forces into the air in strength and then destroy them. From 19th to 23rd August the Luftwaffe had made only light, scattered raids, using the cloudy weather between those dates as an excuse for a respite, but on 24th August over a hundred fighters and bombers of Bruno Loerzer's Fliegerkorps II crossed the coast near Dover and were intercepted by eleven R.A.F. fighter squadrons. Other German formations struck at Manston, causing such widespread damage that it had to be evacuated, except as an emergency airfield, and later in the afternoon North Weald was heavily hit by about fifty Do 17s and He 111s. The air fighting was again intense, the Spitfires and Hurricanes being so engaged in life-or-death struggles with masses of German fighters that they seldom got a chance at the bombers. Consequently, most of the raids were considered highly successful, although by the end of the day the Luftwaffe had lost thirty-eight aircraft. The British casualties were a bitter blow for Dowding, twenty-two of his fighters having been shot down.

On 25th August Warmwell aerodrome was attacked by bombers of Luftflotte 3, while the Fighter Command squadrons were fighting desperately to penetrate the escort screen of over 200 Bf 109s. A second mass raid was more successfully broken up

over the Thames Estuary, but again it was not a good day for
Dowding, who lost sixteen fighters against the German total of
twenty aircraft destroyed. After dark, the Luftwaffe was again
out in force over England, but the R.A.F. was also at work that
night with a raid by eighty-one Hampden bombers on Berlin.
This bombing of the German capital, to be repeated on a
number of subsequent nights, would within a week have an
important effect on the Battle of Britain, for it was to provide
Hitler with an excellent reason for discontinuing Goering's
latest strategy in favour of a concentrated air assault against
London.

Meanwhile, the devastating attacks on Fighter Command
went on. The sector station at Debden was heavily damaged
on 26th August, on the 27th Eastchurch was bombed again,
and on the 30th Biggin Hill suffered so badly that the airfield
was reduced to a shambles of gutted buildings and cratered
runways. The following day, thirty Do 17s arrived over Hornchurch just as 54 Squadron was taking off, and the first two
sections of Spitfires became airborne with bombs falling all
around them. The third section was not so lucky; all three
fighters had reached a height of 20ft. when they were suddenly blasted like toys across the airfield. By a miracle the pilots
escaped uninjured. To finish the job, a force of Ju 88s and
bomb-carrying Bf 110s returned to Hornchurch in the late
afternoon, increasing the vast number of craters that covered
the airfield and destroying two more Spitfires on the ground.

August was the month of attrition, and Goering was reaching
out for victory with open arms. The Fighter Command and
Luftwaffe losses were now almost in proportion, but the
Germans still had a fair number of trained pilots in reserve,
while Dowding was desperately short of replacements. Circumstances had compelled him to use his two squadrons of Defiants
and send the two-seater turret fighters of such uncertain ability
into battle against the most élite German single-seater Gruppen;
and, inevitably, they had been decimated. 141 Squadron had
been shot to pieces by the Bf 109s of Jagdgeschwader 51 the
first time it ventured into the tracer-streaked skies over the
south coast, and 264 Squadron survived only a little longer,
Adolf Galland and other experienced pilots of Jagdgeschwader

26 finally bringing to an end the brief career of the only British two-seater fighter to see action in the Battle of Britain. During those ill-fated dogfights of 28th August Galland himself shot down at least one Defiant, which came apart under his fire, great burning pieces falling away as it disintegrated. Three days later, all Defiants in service were officially relegated to a night-fighting role.

The storm continued unabated into September, resisted but seldom checked by the weary Hurricane and Spitfire squadrons, some of them by now so depreciated that they had virtually ceased to exist as fighting units. As an example, on the last day of August thirty-nine R.A.F. fighters were shot down, against German losses of forty-one miscellaneous aircraft; and, while the Luftwaffe could barely endure such heavy casualties, Fighter Command was being whittled away, with Dowding powerless to conserve his depleted forces.

Then Hitler and Goering stepped in to effect a reprieve. On 3rd September, the Reichsmarschall called a conference of his air commanders in The Hague, which brought forth the general opinion that Fighter Command was as good as finished, although von Sperrle unexpectedly disagreed, maintaining that Dowding still possessed about a thousand serviceable aircraft. Nevertheless, with many of the R.A.F. sector stations and forward airfields reduced to wreckage, Kesselring considered the time was ripe for a final assault on London, the concentration of a powerful force against a single objective that had proved so successful in Poland and Holland. Goering strongly supported this argument, and after some discussion it was decided that the attacks on the R.A.F. should cease in favour of massed bombing raids on London. When the German air staff leaders left the conference table they were confident that intensive bombing of the British capital would soon break the morale of the people, but in fact Goering had just saved Fighter Command when it was on the verge of disaster. And Fighter Command could save London.

Goering's fatal decision was undoubtedly influenced not so much by Kesselring as Hitler, who was outraged that Britain not only refused to accept defeat, but actually dared to take the offensive by sending bombers over Berlin. Just as he had halted Guderian's tanks outside Dunkirk, now he had interfered with

Goering's conduct of the air war against England, and the conference in The Hague did little more than confirm his decision
and act upon it. On 4th September Hitler gave vent to his anger
in public when he delivered an oddly nervous and uncharacteris-
tic speech from the Sportpalast in Berlin. "In England they're
filled with curiosity," he said, "and keep asking, 'Why doesn't he
come?' Be calm. Be calm. He's coming!" This was a pledge he
might not be able to honour for some time now that autumn
was at hand, but it aroused his audience to thunderous applause;
apparently a few bombs and sleepless nights were a small penalty
to pay for the conquest of Britain.

"Just now . . . Mr. Churchill is demonstrating his new brain-
child, the night air raid," continued Hitler. "Mr. Churchill is
carrying out these raids not because they promise to be highly
effective, but because his Air Force cannot fly over Germany in
daylight. . . ." Now, he stated, the R.A.F. attacks would be
answered a hundredfold "When they declare that they will
increase their attacks on our cities, then we will rase their
cities to the ground. We will stop the handiwork of these night
air pirates, so help us God!" It was not one of his best speeches,
but it made the German people feel strong and secure again, and
the women in his audience became almost hysterical with
joy as they visualised the retribution about to descend on
England.

The wheels had thus been set in motion for the fourth phase
of the Battle of Britain, which Goering considered to be of such
vital importance that it required his presence in the front line.
On 6th September his special armoured train, heavily defended
by anti-aircraft guns and so laden with rich food and wines
that it resembled a luxury hotel on wheels, arrived at the Pas
de Calais. A second train, equipped with radio, teleprinter
machines and batteries of telephones, provided the only outward and visible proof that the man who guided German air
power had, in fact, come at last to direct his offensive in the
field, drive his air fleet commanders to despair with his incompetence and listen wistfully to the exciting tales of battle
his tired pilots brought back from England. Once, his stories
would have matched any of those he now heard; but that was
a long time ago, before he became an aging fighter-pilot trying
to show the professional soldiers how to wage another war.

Two days later, with unconscious but ironic humour, the German radio announced that Reichsmarshall Goering had assumed command of operations "for the first time since the outbreak of war". So much was said, and little more; the German people could decide for themselves whether the campaign would benefit or otherwise from such tardy intervention.

CHAPTER XIII

HEINKELS OVER LONDON: SEPTEMBER 1940

THE stout man in the immaculate braided uniform stared intently out across the English Channel. Almost at his feet, the grey cliffs of Cap Gris Nez fell steeply away to the sea, and above his head the gulls swept past with shrill cries. The breeze lightly touched his face, bringing with it the unfamiliar tang of the sea; the morning was fine but misty, and across the water he could just make out the faint white outline of the English coast.

Suddenly, Hermann Goering raised the powerful naval binoculars in his hands, gazing up at the myriad gleaming dots—the vast formations of his fighters and bombers known as Valhallas—that had appeared almost overhead. The sky echoed with the thunder of mighty engines as Geschwader after Geschwader swung majestically out over the sea, a great aerial armada such as this man who watched had always dreamed of sending against London. "My bombers will darken the skies over England," he had once said, and now, his eyes on the resounding heavens, he saw the fulfilment as his Luftwaffe went forth to war.

It was a historic moment, and he could not resist the supreme joy of sharing it with the German people. The medals and decorations he wore gleaming brightly in the sunshine, he grasped the microphone before him and poured words excitedly into it, shouting that a great air assault was taking place on London, and that he, the architect of German air power, was listening to the roar of his bombers as they crossed the English Channel. The group of officers clustered around him looked at each other and listened in silence to the rambling, emotional outburst; they knew that Goering could be forceful and ruthless when he was in the mood, but only too often he embarrassed them by acting like a child.

Over 300 German bombers and 600 fighters, stepped up in solid layers of aircraft, took part in this first mass raid on London on 7th September, 1940, attacking in two waves at heights between 16,000 and 20,000 ft. Sheer weight of numbers carried the Luftwaffe formations through the aggressive, harrying Spitfires and Hurricanes of four Fighter Command squadrons and over the capital, where they dropped their bombs. Despite fighters and anti-aircraft fire the targets were hit, and hit hard. The dock area became a blazing inferno, the oil tanks at Thameshaven were set alight and dozens of houses in the East End destroyed, while more and more R.A.F. fighter squadrons rose into the air to tangle with the masses of enemy aircraft, until almost the whole of 11 Group had been committed. Poplar, Woolwich, Limehouse, Tottenham, Barking and Croydon, all were deluged with bombs before the German forces turned back, losing forty aircraft at a cost of twenty-eight R.A.F. fighters.

When darkness fell, the vast London docks were still blazing furiously, and the great beacon of fire drew a further heavy raid by over 250 bombers, which lasted until the following morning, 13,000 incendiaries lighting so many conflagrations that the sky glowed dully for miles around with the reflection. Goering was not quite correct when he reported gleefully, "London is in flames," but he could hardly be blamed for assuming the destruction of the city to be complete, with so many fires out of control. In fact, the martyrdom of London was just beginning, and would continue without respite for another fifty-nine endless nights, yet the British people, like the R.A.F., could "take it" and somehow managed to emerge battered but undefeated from the smoke and rubble each morning.

On 8th September Fighter Command put eleven squadrons into the air in good time to intercept and repulse the main daylight raid by about 100 bombers against the Kent and Essex airfields, but during the night Luftflotte 3 again successfully bombed London, causing many fires, including twelve conflagrations, and rendering every southward railway line out of the city unserviceable. The following afternoon, 11 Group again broke up the enemy formations before they reached London, and most of the raiders jettisoned their bombs in confusion. Twenty-eight German aircraft were shot down during the day for the loss of nineteen R.A.F. fighters. The same night over a hundred enemy bombers attacked London almost from dusk to dawn, heavily damaging many residential areas and causing over 1,700 casualties, their repeated successes and negligible losses indicating only too well that the capital still lacked efficient night-fighter and anti-aircraft defences.

Unsettled weather brought a welcome lull in the offensive during the next three days, although on 13th September single enemy aircraft penetrated to central London and dropped bombs on Downing Street, Whitehall and Buckingham Palace. Nevertheless, thousands of invasion barges were massed in the ports along the coast of France, and the slackening in the air assault obviously amounted to nothing more than a calm before the storm. "If this invasion is to be tried at all, it does not seem it can be long delayed ..." Winston Churchill warned the people of Britain. "Therefore we must regard the next week or so as a very important period in our history. It ranks with the days when the Spanish Armada was approaching the Channel ... or when Nelson stood between us and Napoleon's Grand Army at Boulogne. ..."

At a conference in Berlin on 14th September Hitler informed his field marshals that all naval preparations for the invasion had now been completed, and added that, in his opinion, four or five days of good weather would be sufficient for the Luftwaffe to achieve complete air superiority, and 17th September would therefore be the final date for *Sealion*. While he was speaking, three formations of German bombers and fighters were striking at London and battling furiously with no less than twenty-seven R.A.F. fighter squadrons, fourteen aircraft of each side being shot down. The Luftwaffe and Fighter Command were now suffering almost proportional losses every day, and the German air staff felt that the British air defence system had been weakened to such an extent that it was on the point of collapse; one knock-out blow should be enough to overwhelm it. Uncomfortably aware that his "lightning offensive" against England had now dragged on for nearly three months, Goering willingly agreed with the latest appraisal of the situation, and ordered the final great air assault on London to take place the following day.

In anticipation of this major daylight attack, the night raids on 14th-15th September were on a greatly reduced scale, warning Fighter Command that a second, and even more fateful Adlertag was at hand. "I see only one sure way through now—

to wit, that Hitler should attack this country, and in so doing break his air weapon," Winston Churchill had said in June, on the eve of the Battle of Britain. That air weapon had since been bruised, bent and blunted; now, it remained only to be seen if the weary British defence organisation could muster sufficient strength to snap the blade thrusting at the heart of London. Though neither Goering or Dowding realised it at the time, this was the climax of the whole battle, reached at a moment when both sides were stretched to the limit; and all the military bands in Germany blaring out the inevitable *"Wir fahren gegen England!"* and newspapers in England loudly proclaiming great enemy losses made not the slightest difference. In the final outcome, the youth of Britain faced the youth of Germany in the air, and the courage, will power and determination—or lack of it—of these so alike and yet very different men would win the day.

On 15th September, 1940, the warm Sunday ever afterwards to be remembered annually as the greatest day of the Battle of Britain, opened with misty weather that quickly cleared and gave way to brilliant sunshine. During the morning Mr. and Mrs. Churchill visited the 11 Group underground operations room at Uxbridge, and by eleven o'clock the Prime Minister was listening to the reports of many enemy formations circling over their airfields in France. "Forty plus . . . sixty plus . . . eighty plus . . ." intoned the plotters, and still it went on, until the operations table became saturated with raids as hundreds of heavily escorted German bombers set course for England. As the great armada moved across the Channel, Air Marshal Park began to commit his waiting squadrons, and soon fierce air battles were raging over Kent, with the scattered German forces breaking away in all directions, dropping their bombs anywhere and everywhere. Soon, Park had ordered nearly the whole of his 11 Group into the air, and as more Do 17s and Ju 88s thundered in across the Channel the five squadrons of 12 group, built up into a massive wing formation, rose to engage them. Smoke and flame and gunfire mingled in an inferno of sound and fury, and soon aircraft were falling everywhere; a Do 17 in the station yard at Victoria; a Spitfire and another Do 17 locked together in tangled wreckage over Kent; and a Hurricane pilot who baled out ending his descent in a Chelsea dustbin. Then, suddenly, the shattered German formations were streaming back to the coast, utterly defeated by the combined efforts of 11 Group and the five squadrons of 12 Group—the famous Duxford wing.

In the operations room at 11 Group headquarters, the staff worked quickly and efficiently to land their squadrons for re-fuelling and rearming, keenly aware that at any moment another mass raid could explode in at low level from the Channel. "How many fighters have you left?" asked Mr. Churchill, meaning, of course, at instant readiness for just such an emergency. "None, sir," replied Air Marshal Park; the whole of 11 Group, the breastplate of Fighter Command, lay naked and defenceless on the ground. Then slowly but surely the bulbs began to glow again on the totalisator as one squadron after another completed refuelling and rearming, and Churchill and Park—and England—could breathe again.

Two hours later, the second Luftwaffe assault came in from the sea in three waves, some hundred and fifty aircraft, with more on the way. They were intercepted at once by twenty-three squadrons from 11 Group and the five squadrons of the Duxford wing, and savage, running battles unreeled all over the sky on the way to London. Two of the enemy formations were broken up by the 11 Group fighters before they reached the capital, and the bombers that did manage to fight their way through were met and hammered mercilessly over the target by the Duxford wing. Again there came that desperate, whirling tumult of tracer, burning aircraft, sweating hands and thudding hearts, every second of time vivid with the brilliance of violent death, then another ten minutes snatched out of eternity were over and the German forces had scattered once more.

Thanks to the perfect teamwork and sheer determination of Fighter Command, the Luftwaffe had failed completely to repeat its success on 7th September over London, bombs being jettisoned over a wide area and causing comparatively little damage. Fifty-six German aircraft had been shot down, and the remainder were straggling back to their bases, some with cock-pits running in blood and dead or wounded men lying among the empty ammunition drums and spent shell cases that littered their interiors, others with bullet-starred windscreens or smoking engines, all bearing the unmistakable signs of a savage battle. *"Listen to the engine singing—get on to the foe! Listen, in your ears it's ringing—get on to the foe!"* had thundered the Luftwaffe marching song against England, but to no avail. Disillusioned and bewildered, the German airmen were left to contemplate an apparently endless future battering away at a fighter force that had already been destroyed on paper, yet continued to rise like a phoenix from the ashes of defeat.

So ended what came to be known as the greatest day of the Battle of Britain, save for an unsuccessful raid by about twenty bomb-carrying Bf 110s of Kampfgruppe 210 on the Supermarine works at Woolston in the late afternoon. It has sometimes been said that a fighter-pilot is privileged to select his opponent and kill gracefully, with all the skill and artistry of a modern Lancelot, but such chivalrous combats were uncommonly rare on 15th September, 1940. Too many of the air battles that day were fought at high speeds and close quarters, with more than a hint about them of the axe and sword work of war in the Middle Ages, a bloody butchering business, with every man fighting for himself and devil take the hindmost. Some Fighter Command pilots attacked at such point-blank range that their victims literally exploded right in front of their windscreens, and they found themselves hurtling through the black smoke and flying wreckage. German bombers trying to retain a tight formation were knocked out of control by the concussion when one of their number blew up under fire, and men who baled out were fortunate to tumble unscathed through the confused mêlée of roaring, gun-flashing aircraft. At least one Hurricane pilot returned to base with blood spattered on his engine cowling and pieces of human flesh in his radiator, grim evidence that air fighting could not always remain cold and impersonal when eight Browning guns were used at close range. It had been a great and yet tragic day memorable not only as a victory, but because so many individual acts of courage and determination shone brightly through the ugliness of war.

Hermann Goering was in despair, a ridiculous, sweating figure in a now crumpled uniform, mopping the perspiration from his brow with a handkerchief as he listened to the gloomy reports of scattered formations, bullet-riddled aircraft and heavy casualties. Turning like a dog at bay on the weary fighter arm of the Luftwaffe he again accused his pilots of unwillingness to get at grips with the enemy, and ordered them to provide an even closer escort for the bombers. In future, he said, the mass formations, or Valhallas, would only be used on rare occasions, and maximum fighter escort would have to be provided at all times. London remained an important target, but it was obvious that both Luftflotten must again concentrate on the Fighter Command bases and aircraft production centres. Goering admitted that his airmen were tiring and that the offensive was "very exhausting", yet he still refused to look facts squarely in the face and stated that the R.A.F. fighter force could be finished off "in four to five days". Gaining confidence from the sound of his own voice, Goering added that the Luftwaffe could crush Britain unaided, without the benefit of a seaborne invasion; a statement unlikely to amuse Hitler, who had massed thousands of barges in the Channel ports, with two army groups patiently awaiting embarkation orders.

In fact, the Fuehrer no longer had any illusions about the immediate chances of success for Operation *Sealion*. Until 15th September he had been fairly satisfied with the air offensive, and at a conference with his Service advisers in Berlin on the 14th still had sufficient confidence in Goering to comment : ". . . the operations of the Luftwaffe are above all praise. Four or five days of good weather are required to achieve decisive results. . . ." The following day, with its violent air battles and heavy German losses, completely changed Hitler's attitude to the invasion. Autumn was at hand, and yet, in his own words : ". . . the prerequisite conditions for Operation *Sealion* (had) not yet been realised," and the British fighter defence seemed revived and more aggressive than ever. Taking everything into consideration, Hitler decided that *Sealion*, if attempted at once, would be a very risky business.

On the afternoon of 17th September, the diarist of the German Naval Staff recorded the Fuehrer's decision. "The enemy air force is by no means defeated; on the contrary it shows increasing activity. . . . The weather situation as a whole does not permit us to expect a period of calm. . . . For these reasons, the Fuehrer therefore decides to postpone Operation *Sealion* indefinitely. . . ." However, the Naval Staff carefully pointed out that the postponement did not mean that *Sealion* had been abandoned. "The Fuehrer still wishes to be able to carry out a landing in England even in October," recorded the diarist, "if the air war and the weather conditions develop favourably." Goering was thus committed to the unenviable task of continuing the air offensive until further notice, regardless of casualties, and against an increasingly more powerful Fighter Command.

During the last fortnight in September the now smaller German bomber formations and their massive fighter escorts continued to hammer away with a weary indifference at the south-coast aerodromes and factories, and the air still trembled to the brittle chatter of machine-gun fire, but it soon became apparent that the immediate danger to England had been averted. It continued as a strange battle that seemed unending, and became history while it still raged and men died high up in the late summer skies. A Spitfire gutted by gunfire, inverted and burning; a Heinkel in a spin, one engine on fire, the rear gunner hanging half in and half out of his cupola; a Hurricane seeming to hang motionless in the air, shaken by the recoil of its wing-mounted Brownings; and, beyond, a Bf 109 quickly flicking wing over wing, out of control, trailing a ribbon of flame and that long, high-pitched whine that is the last cry of a dying air-craft—these were the brush strokes, the vivid details, that completed the great sprawling canvas of the Battle of Britain. And all for nothing; because the Luftwaffe had already been beaten, and was merely wasting itself away.

On 27th September, as if shaken by a sudden outburst of childish temper, Goering hurled a last major daylight assault against England. In the early morning, a wave of bomb carrying Bf 110s with a heavy single-seater fighter escort came in over Dungeness, were hammered mercilessly by Dowding's waiting squadrons all the way to London, and finally retreated in confusion, scattering their bombs anywhere. They were immediately followed by two strong formations of Do 17s and Ju 88s, which were also broken up and dispersed by the Spitfires and Hurri-canes of 11 Group; and later by a further 300 raiders that struggled manfully across Kent and were turned back, shot to pieces, within sight of London. The only success for the Luft-waffe during the whole day, and that a moderate one, was achieved at Bristol, where the survivors of some eighty bombers directed against that city managed to hit their targets. Fifty-five

Above, the Fokker Dr 1 triplane was used extensively during the later part of the First World War. This particular machine is being flown by fighter ace Manfred von Richthofen; *below*, a squadron of Albatros fighters lined up at Taulis in 1916

Above, von Richthofen was killed in action in 1918 after recording eighty victories in the air; *below*, General von Hoeppner, Chief of the Imperial Air Force, talking with von Richthofen beside the latter's machine

Right, Oswald Boelcke, one of the first German fighter aces . . . killed in a collision during a dog-fight in 1916; *below*, left to right, Bruno Loerzer, who became a general in Goering's Luftwaffe; Anthony Fokker, the designer, and Hermann Goering, who commanded the Richthofen Circus late in the First World War after Richthofen's death

Peter Strasser, Commander of Naval Zeppelins until he was killed in action in 1918

Zeppelin ace Heinrich Mathy successfully bombed London on several occasions

Right, Hugo Eckener, who developed the German airship fleet and pioneered the trans-Atlantic crossing; *below* Ernst Udet, fighter ace during World War 1, stunt pilot and Luftwaffe general

Above, the Heinkel He45, produced in 1933; *below*, Henschel Hs123s appeared in the 'thirties as a ground-attack aircraft and were used during the early part of the Second World War. Goering later resurrected a squadron for service on the Russian Front

Right, Hugo Junkers . . . inventor of the first all-metal aircraft; *below,* the Junkers Ju52/3m, an airliner version of the Junkers transport

Above, the last of the German airships: the *Hindenberg*. She is seen here in 1936 on her moorings at Lakehurst, N.J., above which she caught fire and was destroyed; *below*, the Focke-Wulf Fw200, produced as an airliner in the 'thirties

Above, reviewing the Richthofen Squadron at Staaken in 1935: Goering talks to Hitler with Erhardt Milch, then Secretary for Air, looking on (second from right); *below*, the twin-engined Dornier Do217, used throughout the Second World War as a medium bomber

Two "Wonder Weapons" produced late in the Second World War: *above*, a tandem-engined Dornier Do335, used as a day fighter; *below*, a Junkers Ju88, mounted with an Fw190. The pilotless Junkers was filled with explosives and released over the target by the Focke-Wulf pilot

The Focke-Wulf 190, first German fighter to be designed with a radial engine. With the Messerschmitt Bf109, often called the Me109, below, it was one of the outstanding Luftwaffe aircraft of World War Two

Above, the Bf109E, an effective fighter-bomber in the Battle of Britain; *below*, another Battle of Britain fighter, the two-seater Me110. After the Battle, in which it proved slow in manoeuvre, it became a night-fighter

Above, two Heinkel He111s joined together and given a fifth engine. Intended as a glider tug, it did not live up to expectation and was never used to a great extent; *below*, the Junkers Ju87, or Stuka. One of the most successful dive-bombers in the early part of the war, it later proved unable to combat fighter opposition

The first-ever operational jet fighter, the Me262, was produced in 1944 as a fighter, but Hitler destroyed its potential by using it as a bomber; *below*, first used as a military bomber in the Spanish Civil War the He111 saw service during the whole of the Second World War

General Hans Jesch-onnek, Chief of Air Staff, right, with Field Marshal Kesselring centre

Adolf Galland, who became General of Fighters but was relieved of the position after a dispute with Hitler over the use of the Me262

Above, the end of the Luftwaffe: a graveyard for German machines at Bad Abling; *below*, the end of Goering: seen here with an interpreter after the capitulation in 1945

German aircraft had been shot down by nightfall for the loss of twenty-eight British fighters, a conclusive R.A.F. victory that prompted Winston Churchill to signal the Secretary of State for Air in characteristic words the following morning : "Pray congratulate the Fighter Command on the results of yesterday. The scale and intensity of the fighting and the heavy losses of the enemy . . . make 27th September rank with 15th September and 15th August, as the third great and victorious day of the Fighter Command during the course of the Battle of Britain."

The last mass daylight attack in any strength on London took place on 30th September, although the night Blitz against the capital—and also Liverpool, Birmingham, Coventry and many other cities continued without respite. The fifth, and last, phase of the Battle thus began on 1st October with a series of raids by bomb-carrying Bf 109s and 110s, leading inevitably to the first of the fighter-versus-fighter battles at great heights which typified the activities over England during the autumn of 1940. About a third of the German fighter force—some 250 aircraft— had been hurriedly converted to the fighter-bomber role in order to reserve the medium-bomber squadrons for night operations, but the fighter-pilots had little heart for undertaking a new task in what was obviously a "dead" offensive, with raids that, in the words of Adolf Galland, ". . . had no more than nuisance value."

Galland, and also his contemporary Werner Molders, who had shot down forty-five enemy aircraft by early October, 1940, showed no hesitation in criticising Goering's latest policy of using their fighter Gruppen as a makeshift bomber unit. Both these rising young aces had already incurred the displeasure of the Reichsmarschall more than once during the course of the Battle, Galland on a notable occasion when he had tried to point out the problems peculiar to the fighter arm, and Goering demanded at last to hear what he needed to solve them. "A Gruppe of Spitfires," Galland had replied calmly, a request the downright impudence of which it is not hard to believe "made even Goering speechless". Now the arguments of Galland and Molders fell on deaf ears, the vast Reichsmarschall commenting angrily that the fighter arm had failed adequately to protect the bomber formations during the summer offensive, and if it was proving reluctant to undertake the fighter-bomber role it might as well be disbanded. He attempted to pour a little oil on the troubled waters by decorating both fighter leaders with Germany's highest military award, the Oak Leaves to the Knights Cross, and conducting a stag hunt for their benefit at Karinhall, but they returned to their units in an unhappy frame of mind, comforted only by the knowledge that their daylight "nuisance" raids were enabling the night offensive to continue without respite.

On 12th October Hitler finally decided to bring the fiasco *Sealion* had become to an end. His invasion fleet had remained a priority target for Bomber Command during the late summer, with the result that much of the original assemblage had been dispersed and 214 barges and twenty-one transporters sunk in harbour, yet Hitler had insisted that a vast number of ships, men and equipment be kept at immediate readiness. At last, repeated pressure by Admiral Raeder and other commanders had its effect, and the Fuehrer gave permission for *Sealion* to be abandoned. "The Fuehrer has decided that from now until the spring," wrote Generalfeldmarschall Keitel, "preparation for *Sealion* shall be continued solely for the purpose of maintaining political and military pressure on England...." This decision was followed by a vague statement about reconsideration of the invasion in the spring or early summer of 1941, but it was agreed that shipping should in the meantime continue to be released for other tasks, with only about a thousand barges to remain in the Channel ports for possible future use. Later, Hitler would disparage the importance of *Sealion* and comment that in his opinion the war against England was won in any case, but in fact he knew quite well that the moment for invasion had come and gone, and the opportunity would almost certainly never occur again. And yet, without a seaborne invasion England remained an impregnable island unable to be totally defeated.

The Battle of Britain thus drifted rather wearily to a close, an anti-climax that almost passed unheeded in the thunder of bombs falling night after night on London. In one of the last fighter battles of the year, on 28th November, Helmuth Wick, with fifty-six victories and then commander of the Richthofen Jagdgeschwader, was shot down and killed, probably by Flight Lieutenant J. C. Dundas of 609 Squadron, who also failed to return that day. Hauptmann Balthazar, a born leader and gifted fighter-pilot with over thirty victories, took over command of the Richthofen Geschwader, which by that time had accumulated a total score of five hundred enemy aircraft shot down since the outbreak of war. Despite heavy casualties in the Battle of Britain, morale remained high in the Geschwader; indeed, with so many brilliant pilots serving in the same unit it was unlikely to be otherwise, but some of the old confidence in an easy victory had gone, never to return again.

On the night of 29th-30th December, 1940, Hermann Goering brought the year to a blazing end with his heaviest attack to date on London during the hours of darkness. After an initial incendiary raid by Kampfgeschwader 100, which had gained considerable experience and notoriety as a "pathfinder" unit, large numbers of incendiaries, high-explosive bombs and parachute mines were dropped on the city by wave after wave of twin-engined bombers, causing no less than 1,500 simultaneous and uncontrollable fires. Insufficient water supplies and a lack of trained fire watchers seriously hindered the task of checking the inferno, and before morning the centre of London was a great heaving sea of flame, with the dome of St. Paul's Cathedral rising like an island out of the smoke and gleaming like burnished gold against the crimson sky. If the Luftwaffe could have repeated its success that night with a series of similar raids, London, despite its famous slogan, would no longer have been able to "take it" but with the night blitz as with the day-light offensive there existed no definite plan. The smouldering capital staggered up from her knees to face the new year bloody but unbeaten, and grasped at the welcome opportunity to recover while Goering sat in Karinhall and debated on the best method of striking against England in the future.

For both sides, it had been a hard and bitter struggle. Between 10th July and 31st October the Luftwaffe had lost a total of 1,733 aircraft of all types, against 915 R.A.F. machines shot down. These could be replaced; but Germany and Great Britain had also lost many of their best airmen, most of them under the age of twenty-five, and these were irreplaceable. More often than not, they had been in service before the outbreak of war, and therefore were not "born into battle" like so many who followed, but entered it already grown to full stature. Only on the German side could it be said they had died in vain; they had come that summer in their hundreds, and in their hundreds they had been destroyed; the mightiest aerial army the world had ever seen broken by a thousand men who did not want war, but having had it thrust upon them willingly gave their young lives to end it.

Much has been said and written about those warm August and September days in 1940, but perhaps only one man was capable of summing up in a few words the great achievement that turned the bulky files so carefully compiled on Operation *Sealion* into so much useless paper, and in his wisdom he had chosen to utter them at the height of the Battle. "Never in the field of human conflict," said Winston Churchill in the House of Commons on 20th August, "was so much owed by so many to so few."

CHAPTER XIV

SUNSHINE AND SLAUGHTER: CRETE, 1941

ON a bleak October evening in 1940, Generaloberst Ernst Udet, then chief of the Reichsluftfahrtministerium Technical Department, returned to his secluded villa on the outskirts of Berlin. Pouring himself a stiff brandy at the little cocktail bar in the lounge, Udet carried his glass into the gun-room and selected a revolver from the long rack of gleaming weapons there. Slowly he raised his arm, aiming carefully at the target on the opposite wall, and a moment later the room shook to the thunder of the revolver as shot after shot crashed home. Blue smoke drifted gently around Udet in the angry silence; he stood quite still for a long moment, gazing sadly at the widely scattered bullet holes that told him his old skill, even in this, was no longer there. Then, wearily, he dropped the gun and sank heavily into a chair, staring moodily into space. Again and again, his thoughts returned to the fateful news Goering had confided to him less than an hour before; that Adolf Hitler intended to attack Russia within a year. To Udet, the quiet night outside his home seemed suddenly filled with grim shadows, the accusing figures of Milch, Jeschonnek and the rest, all closing inexorably in to surround him.

Udet was ill and disillusioned, a man broken in spirit by the failure of his Stukas in the Battle of Britain and the unceasing struggle to avoid the intrigue woven around him by his opponents. Always, he longed desperately for those carefree pre-war days when he was free to do and say what he liked: the man who had demonstrated the prototype Messerschmitt Bf 109 and later broken the world speed record in a Heinkel He 100 at a speed of 397 m.p.h., the great ace of 1918 who loved to talk over old times with his former enemies; and above all, never needed to worry about tomorrow, because every new day was an adventure. But Udet knew that he was his own executioner. He had destroyed his freedom for an idea that was now tumbling like a pack of cards around his ears, and he was slowly being strangled by red tape and stupidity, becoming the scapegoat that Goering needed to appease Hitler.

Yet Udet had tried hard to shoulder the responsibilities of his office during the first year of war. More than once, he protested that there was a serious shortage in the aircraft industry of skilled workers and vital materials, such as aluminium, but Goering cheerfully waved all his arguments aside. Germany would soon need fighters and still more fighters to defend the homeland, warned Udet, after the first British bombing raids on Berlin; what did fighters matter when the war would soon be over? smiled Goering, unmoved. Finally, Udet gave up the hopeless battle against such overwhelming complacency and ignorance and simply made his own decisions, unfortunately all too often plunging out of his depth into matters quite beyond him. Meanwhile, he eased his conscience by too much hard drinking and excused his inadequacy by saying, in effect, "I'm doing the best I can in this job, but don't expect too much from me."

The dive-bomber fiasco was the real beginning of the end for Udet; if he had never returned from America so filled with enthusiasm for such a daring venture his life would have remained as careless and untroubled as that of any other cosmopolitan playboy in the 'thirties. But he infected the Luftwaffe with "Stuka madness" and for that he alone was to blame. Now, he faced the results of his own, and Jeschonnek's, thoughtless implementation of the dive-bomber policy; the Ju 87 condemned as a complete failure; the twin-engined Ju 88—the so-called Wonder Bomber—just coming into quantity production as dive-bombing was revealed to be a costly and useless procedure; the new Do 217 being fitted with a complicated, troublesome and totally unnecessary dive brake; and the four-engined He 177 still under development three years after acceptance because it was proving impossible to turn such a huge machine into a dive-bomber.

More than any other single type of German aircraft, the Heinkel He 177 typified the short-sighted policy of the Luftwaffe leaders in refusing to prepare for anything except a localised war. It could have been a decisive answer to the American B-17 Flying Fortress and the mainstay of German air power, for the specification that gave birth to this aircraft called for a four-engined long-range heavy bomber, and resulted directly from the theories propounded by General Wever. Unfortunately, on Wever's death the development of the Dornier Do 19 and Junkers Ju 89 heavy bombers was abandoned, and the He 177 only allowed to continue in development because it was considered a suitable maritime reconnaissance and anti-shipping bomber. At this time, the He 177 was still on the drawing-board, and had a rival in its new role, the Focke-Wulf Fw 200 Condor, but the Heinkel team, headed by Walter Gunther, nevertheless persisted with the design, which was finalised by 1938, the prototype He 177 flying for the first time in November, 1939.

The He 177 was unusual in employing twin "double-motors" or coupled units, each comprising a pair of inverted vee liquid-cooled engines mounted side by side and geared together, an arrangement successfully tested on the record-breaking Heinkel He 119 prototype fast bomber. The first He 177 was powered by two Daimler-Benz DB 606 units, which each comprised two DB 601 engines and provided 2,700 h.p. for take-off, but many teething troubles were soon experienced with these coupled motors, including frequent engine fires. While these problems, and also certain structural failures, had still to be overcome, Udet reminded Ernst Heinkel that the four-engined bomber, as such, was dead, and the He 177 must be able to dive before it could enter Luftwaffe service.

"A giant plane like that can't be a dive-bomber!" objected Heinkel, according to his autobiography, but Udet disagreed. "In practice the machine is twin-engined," he said, "and if the twin-engined Ju 88 can be a dive-bomber, why not the He 177?"

"Because it's nearly twice as heavy," replied Heinkel. Nevertheless, Udet had his way, and the five prototype He 177s were fitted with dive brakes above and below the outer wings, a modification causing further delays in development. Time passed, and the design dragged wearily through 1939 and on into 1940, mainly because the diving characteristics not unnaturally proved to be extremely dangerous in an aircraft weighing over twenty tons. Also, the innumerable troubles with the coupled engines led Ernst Heinkel to request authority for the construction of two prototypes as normal four-engined bombers, with four single Junkers Jumo 211 motors. This proposal was rejected at once, on the grounds that the efficiency of the He 177 depended upon it being used with two power units, as the normal four-engined aircraft could not be used as a dive-bomber! This was the kind of curious reasoning that came to be taken for granted by many German aircraft designers—although Heinkel for one tried to argue against it—and eventually led to the disintegration of the industry as a whole.

When the Battle of Britain came to an end, the He177 was the only new bomber Udet could consider almost ready for squadron service—and this at a time when the He 111, Do 17 and even the Ju 88 had revealed so many operational short-comings that they needed extensive modifications as to armour and defensive armament. The fighter situation had at first sight a rather brighter outlook, the Messerschmitt Bf 109E compar-ing favourably with the Spitfire, and the first production batch of an excellent new radial-engined fighter, the Focke-Wulf Fw 190, almost ready to leave the Hamburg and Bremen assembly lines. Also just coming into production was the ill-fated Messerschmitt Me 210, envisaged as a more powerful successor to the inadequate Bf 110. Unfortunately, literally dozens of new fighter and bomber designs were scattered through the German aircraft industry, varying from the conventional to the down-right ridiculous, and facing Udet with the unenviable prospect of a bottleneck in the future caused by the arrival of too many different designs at the same time. This was the problem that neither Udet or Milch succeeded in solving; a serious shortage of new types when they were badly needed, and the promise of all kinds of wonderful aircraft just out of reach over the horizon.

Not for the first time, Udet endeavoured to bring about a simplification of types to be produced and thus increase the flow of aircraft into the Luftwaffe; he introduced a plan known as Elk, which was intended to discard all aircraft that had failed under operational conditions and concentrate the industry on the manufacture of a few carefully selected models. Elk could have been a first-class scheme, but, regrettably, Udet chose two types of aircraft destined to remain dogged by ill fortune—the He 177 and the Me 210—as the mainstay of the Luftwaffe bomber arm, with production of the Ju 87 and He 111 to be abandoned. In the event, Plan Elk had in many ways to be turned completely upside down, the He 177 and the Me 210 never fulfilling Udet's hopes, and output of the He 111K having to be stepped-up despite its obsolescence, for the simple reason that no suitable replacement existed.

In that winter of 1940, Udet had good cause to ponder gloomily on the future of the Luftwaffe; and before Christmas his worst fears had been realised. On 13th December, Hitler issued his Directive No. 20 for the invasion of Greece, code-named *Marita*, supposedly ". . . to foil British attempts to create air bases under the protection of a Balkan front . . . for this would be dangerous above all to Italy as well as to the Rumanian oil fields. . . ." Five days later Directive No 21 confirmed the Fuehrer's intention to undertake *Barbarossa*, the invasion of Russia, for it stated : "The German Armed Forces must be prepared to crush Soviet Russia in a quick campaign even before the end of the war against England. . . . Preparations are to be begun now—if this has not yet been done—and are to be completed by 15th May, 1941. . . ." A further Directive ordered the establishment of a Luftwaffe striking force in Sicily and the transfer of German troops—the nucleus of Rommel's Afrika Korps—to Tripolitania.

Already weakened by the Battle of Britain, and constantly beset by many internal problems, the Luftwaffe was thus being committed to one full-scale offensive after another in the year ahead; and the R.A.F. bombers continued to roam night after night over an anxious Germany, small in numbers, but always leaving behind them the unspoken question : "When is Hitler going to do something about England?" But the slight, insignificant man roaming restlessly from room to room in his Obersalzburg mountain retreat had for the moment lost interest in Great Britain. He hoped to earn undying fame for himself in the vast wastes of Russia, and it was true he was destined to become a second Napoleon; but in a way that he had never dreamed.

At dawn on 6th April, 1941, as the armoured columns of the Wehrmacht thundered into the Balkans, bomber squadrons of Luftflotte 4 took off from their Rumanian airfields on yet another of those operations that Hugo von Sperrle liked to consider "an act of force"—the systematic destruction of

Belgrade by aerial bombardment. For three days the bombs rained down on the stricken city, the unopposed German aircraft skimming the rooftops to make absolutely certain that the centre of Belgrade was destroyed, and when the martyrdom came to an end more than 17,000 people had been killed. "Yugoslavia, despite her protestations of loyalty, must be considered as an enemy and crushed as swiftly as possible," Hitler had declared, when the pro-German government of that country was overthrown, and Belgrade died as a result of his decision. On 17th April, Yugoslavia capitulated.

Meanwhile, masses of German infantry and armour were flooding into Carinthia and Hungary, Sofia had been occupied, and the Greek Army, which had successfully resisted the Italians for six months, was on the brink of capitulation. Again, this was Hitler's tried and tested Blitzkrieg technique, carried out so efficiently that on 24th April—a week after hostilities came to an end in Yugoslavia—the Greek government surrendered. For Great Britain, Greece had proved to be another Norway; a punitive expeditionary force of some 60,000 men hopelessly overwhelmed, stunned by sheer weight of metal, and finally evacuated after suffering heavy losses in men and material. The eight R.A.F. squadrons of Blenheims, Hurricanes and Gladiators available were inadequate in numbers if not in courage against the might of Luftflotte 4, and were nearly all destroyed in the air or on the ground, the handful of aircraft that remained being flown to Crete as the campaign in Greece disintegrated into an Allied nightmare.

The island of Crete, a bulwark for the Balkans and Asia Minor, and of vital strategic importance as a Mediterranean base, remained in British hands, the garrison of 8,600 men now reinforced by some 20,000 battle-worn troops evacuated from Greece. Although Crete had four excellent harbours on the north coast—Canea, Rethimnon, Iraklion and also Suda Bay, used as a naval refuelling base—and airfields at Maleme, Iraklion and Rethimnon, Hitler had not, in fact, planned to launch an operation against the island when he attacked Greece. However, Generaloberst Lohr, the commander of Luftflotte 4, considered that Crete could be captured solely by airborne and parachute troops, and suggested as much to Goering. The Reichsmarschall was only too anxious to throw himself and the

Luftwaffe back into the limelight of conquest after so many set-backs over England, while Hitler, whose agile brain was teeming with the preparations for *Barbarossa*, needed very little per-suasion before giving his official agreement. Accordingly, on 25th April, 1941, the Fuehrer issued his Directive No. 28, which stated: "An operation to occupy the island of Crete, Operation *Merkur*, is to be prepared, with the object of using Crete as an air base against Britain in the eastern Mediter-ranean." All responsibility for the success of the attack on Crete was slyly delegated to Hermann Goering, who took the burden quite happily on his broad shoulders, secure in the knowledge that the island was defended from air attack by only fifty anti-aircraft guns and some thirty obsolescent fighters.

The initial assault on Crete was to be carried out by the air-borne and parachute troops of Fliegerkorps XI, under the command of General Kurt Student, supported by the ground attack aircraft of Fliegerkorps VIII, commanded by Baron Wolfram von Richthofen. Using over 500 three-engined Junkers Ju 52 transport aircraft and D.F.S. 230 gliders, it was estimated that Fliegerkorps XI would be able to drop or land from the air about 16,000 men, and it was hoped to land a further 7,000 from the sea. Assembled in the ground support squadrons of Fliegerkorps VIII was a striking force of more then 400 medium bombers and dive-bombers and 250 fighters and reconnaissance aircraft; many of these were in action from 1st May, attacking British naval units, dive-bombing harbour installations in Suda Bay, and finally striking at the unprotected airfields of Maleme and Iraklion. Within a fortnight, twenty-three German aircraft had been shot down, but the R.A.F. suffered such heavy losses during the same period that by 19th May only three Hurricanes and three Gladiators remained un-damaged, and the same day they were withdrawn from the island.

On the early morning of 20th May, 1941, the dawn of a warm, fine day, hundreds of Messerschmitt Bf 109 and 110 fighters rocketed in from the sea in wave after wave of blazing guns and indescribable noise to attack the defences on Crete, followed almost at once by formations of Ju 87 and He 111 bombers, which saturated the airfields at Maleme and Iraklion with a deluge of high explosive comparable only to the bombardment that preceded the Battle of the Somme in 1916. Oddly enough, the infantry cowering in their slit trenches sustained only a scattering of casualties, although the more exposed artillery positions were largely knocked out or rendered ineffective by the smoke and confusion. At last, there came a brief lull in the onslaught; then the alarm whistles were sounding again, and the huge, ponderous Ju 52s were swaying overhead.

Line after line, the lumbering troop carriers throbbed slowly in over Crete at a height of only 300 ft., many of them releasing their towed gliders which drifted gently down to the beach and disgorged armed men, or, with less good fortune, fell into the sea or crashed into olive groves in tangled wreckage. Simultaneously, the sky became filled with hundreds of multi-coloured parachutes, men dropping apparently everywhere, but actually in three main concentrations, over Maleme aerodrome, in Prison Valley near Canea, and on the Akrotiri peninsula. They fell through a hail of rifle fire, and many tumbled through the trees to hang there, riddled with bullets, while others, hurling stick grenades and spraying bursts from their Schmeisser machine pistols, were nevertheless killed before they struck the ground. Time passed, and as the defensive fire slackened more and more of the paratroopers were landing unscathed; although General Meindl, commanding in the Maleme area, was seriously wounded in the initial fighting, and General Sussmann, who had been ordered to take command in the Canea area, was killed when his glider crashed on the island of Aegina. Confusion reigned everywhere, with the airborne troops pinned down by a surprisingly heavy British fire and the parachute troops fighting for their lives as they sought to link up and form their widely scattered groups into a disciplined force.

By nightfall on 20th May General Student had a critical situation on his hands. The airborne troops had to a great extent captured their objectives, but only at the cost of many gliders and an appalling wastage in men. On the other hand, the parachute troops had been handled so fiercely on landing that all timing arrangements had been ruined, and their only success of the day was a precarious hold on Maleme airfield, which immediately came under heavy British artillery fire. Also, during the night a German convoy of assorted small vessels attempting to land troops on Crete was totally destroyed by British warships off Suda Bay, with the loss of some 1,500 men; not a very promising beginning for an operation supposedly depending entirely on close co-operation between the air and sea borne forces.

On 22nd May, Maleme airfield was still in German hands, but under such intense artillery fire that it was still considered impossible to disembark troops from the air, although a few Ju 52s had managed to crash-land on the beaches east and west of Maleme. Hundreds of the big three-engined aircraft continued to drone in monotonously over the sea from Greece, dropping their parachutists with an utter disregard for casualties. Many of the transports were shot down in flames and plunged to earth, tumbling men and equipment into space all the way down; paratroopers fell like stones, trailing long streamers of fire; British machine-gun fire riddled the corrugated fuselages of the slow Ju 52s as they passed overhead; and still the armada would not be repulsed. However, despite their undiminished efforts, the Germans failed to achieve complete success, and the vital airfields remained almost within their grasp but uncaptured.

Many miles away in Berlin, Hans Jeschonnek, with Goering's approval, decided to save the situation in Crete, a feat he accomplished very simply by ordering the airborne landing of a mountain infantry division on Maleme airfield—ignoring the artillery fire !—or, if the airfield was no longer in German hands, on the open ground to the west of Maleme. Wolfram von Richthofen's already overworked Fliegerkorps VIII was required to protect the landings at Maleme, and also support further paratroop attacks on Canea and Suda Bay. It was an admission from Luftwaffe headquarters that the whole operation was in jeopardy, and nothing mattered any longer except success; everyone and everything on Crete was committed and expendable.

On the morning of 22nd May, the troop-carrying Ju 52s again arrived over Maleme, this time to circle slowly and purposefully over the airfield. As they swung in to land, the British artillery fire increased in intensity, but one by one the transports touched down, hurriedly unloaded forty infantrymen into the inferno of shellfire, and then took off again. Rifle and machine-gun bullets swept the airfield, mowing the exposed German troops down like corn before the scythe, but reinforcements continued to arrive in an apparently endless stream. Many aircraft were hit, and crashed heavily, engines and bits of wings and tailplanes flying into the air; within a few hours Maleme airfield became a shambles of tangled debris and burning wreckage. All the time, more and more Ju 52s brought in men and equipment and then rumbled away through the smoke and confusion to fly back to Greece and load up once more, returning with a machine-like determination and disregard for human life that appalled the New Zealand defenders.

While the battle at Maleme raged on into the hot afternoon, General Student learned that the parachute landings to the west had met with little success, and his troops were fighting their way forward only very slowly, against strong resistance. However, by nightfall the New Zealand forces were running desperately short of ammunition, and without air support they could not hope to survive much longer. In fact, General Freyberg, the officer responsible for the defence of Crete, had planned a counter-attack the same night, but with the arrival of such heavy German reinforcements during the day the move was first delayed for some hours and finally abandoned.

What happened to air support for the defenders in the Battle of Crete? On 23rd May, after four days without a British aircraft on or anywhere near the besieged island, six Hurricanes and a few obsolete Blenheims were sent from North Africa, with the remarkable orders to use Iraklion as a base and attempt to disorganise the German airborne landings at Maleme. They survived the unceasing attentions of Fliegerkorps VIII for exactly twenty-four hours; in that time they found Iraklion airfield so pitted with craters that even to land or take off safely amounted to a miracle, the sky overhead was filled with enemy aircraft and the strip itself surrounded by paratroopers who raked everything that moved with automatic fire. Indeed, the only purpose served by this futile gesture from Cairo was a completely negative one, for the unexpected arrival of British fighters immediately brought German reinforcements to the Iraklion area and increased the pressure there.

By 26th May, all the defending forces on Crete were on the point of exhaustion. In the Suda Bay area, the Imperial troops were being pushed relentlessly into the sea, and the men at

Rethimnon and Iraklion had been almost completely surrounded during the last two days. Some 20,000 German airborne and parachute troops now swarmed all over the island,
and in the face of such overwhelming opposition General Freyberg faced a hopeless situation. The following day, his weary
forces were ordered to withdraw, while Freyberg urgently
requested permission for an immediate evacuation. The living
conditions under which the New Zealand and British defenders
were existing at this time was beyond description; but without
sleep, food or water, they continued to resist the élite and well-
equipped German parachute and mountain troops to the bitter
end, retreating in good order, carrying their wounded, and
even dragging their remaining ammunition along in hand carts.
Human endurance could do no more; and two days later the
Mediterranean Fleet was despatched to Crete to save those who
still survived.

During the night of 29th May the British warships embarked
some 6,000 men, on 31st May another 1,500 were lifted from
the Sphakia beaches, and the following day a further 4,000
were evacuated. The three cruisers and six destroyers that embarked the Iraklion garrison at first light were attacked re-
peatedly by German bombers during the return journey to
Alexandria, the cruisers *Ajax* and *Orion* being heavily damaged
and the destroyer *Hereward* so crippled that it sank during the
afternoon. The Battle of Crete thus ended on a note of complete
tragedy, for a fifth of the men lifted that morning had been
either killed or wounded in the stricken ships, but a total of some
16,500 had been evacuated by the Mediterranean Fleet and
brought safely to Egypt; an everlasting tribute to the naval forces
based at Alexandria, in view of the severe losses already incurred
by the Royal Navy in operations off Crete and Greece.

From the German point of view, a costly and indecisive
victory had been achieved, that even to Goering must have
seemed scarcely worth the expenditure in men and material.
Over 3,600 highly trained airborne troops had been killed, not
including 320 men of the Luftwaffe who had also been lost, and
some 200 transport aircraft—nearly half the attacking force—
lay scattered in wreckage on Crete, together with an untold
number of gliders and assorted light aeroplanes. It was all very
well for the German High Command to beat the big drum over

Crete and emphasise that the invasion had been a dress rehearsal for other operations of a similar nature, with vague references to England, but that in itself did not justify the wholesale destruction of Fliegerkorps XI, Goering's crack parachute division. Crete was a strategic pearl beyond price; it guarded the whole Balkan peninsula, brought Cyprus, Alexandria, Cairo and Suez within German medium bomber range and threatened Turkey and the Dardanelles. After his success in Greece, Hitler should have realised the importance of Crete; it only remained to be seen if he had the sense to exploit such outstanding possibilities.

In the event, Hitler showed his approval of the victory by boasting that "there are no more unconquerable islands", and promptly withdrew most of his troops and aircraft from Crete to take part in the forthcoming campaign in Russia. Within a few weeks, only a handful of German and Italian air squadrons were left on the island, and without the bombers which could have struck at the heart of the Middle East, Crete became just another little piece of territory in German hands, a conquest that had served no purpose. So, the wastage of Fliegerkorps XI did not increase Goering's prestige after all; and yet never before had there been a greater need for him to prove his value to the Fuehrer.

The friendship between Hitler and Goering, already weakened after the failure of the Luftwaffe in the Battle of Britain, had cooled visibly when the Fuehrer declared his intention to attack Russia. For once, Goering decided to speak his mind, and reminded Hitler that Germany would be taking a fearful risk in attempting to wage a war on two fronts. The dictum of *Mein Kampf* had stressed that very danger, he said; why was the Fuehrer prepared to abandon his own logic now? "There will be no war on two fronts," replied Hitler, calmly. "The Atlantic Wall will protect us in the west while we quickly overcome Russia." A lengthy argument ensued, but when it came to an end Hitler was as convinced as ever that Russia should be attacked in the near future, and Goering had gained nothing except the Fuehrer's unmistakable displeasure.

Then, on 10th May, 1941, occurred the strange incident that severed another link in the relationship between Hitler and the Commander-in-Chief of his Air Force, a thunderbolt out of the blue for both leaders that surprised the Allies and rocked the so-called invincible Third Reich to its very foundations.

That memorable Sunday evening, Hitler was sitting in his spacious study at the Berghof when the arrival of a courier bearing an important letter for the personal attention of the Fuehrer was announced. Hitler glanced at the contents of the letter, there was a moment of awful silence, then the storm burst over the unsuspecting heads of those around him. "Hess has flown to England!" he shouted. "He must be crazy . . . he has gone to England . . . call Ribbentrop. I must talk to Goering right away!" He slumped into a chair, mumbling that Hess was crazy, and from time to time shouting that he wanted to see Goering at once. "The Luftwaffe, the damned Luftwaffe again!" he roared at Karl Bodenschatz, Goering's only representative in the Berghof that night, who was already urgently telephoning his Berlin headquarters.

It was incredible, almost unbelievable. Rudolf Hess was the deputy leader of the party, Hitler's closest friend for over twenty years, the man who had helped him to write *Mein Kampf* while they languished together in Landsberg prison after the 1923 Putsch, and ever since accepted as a fanatically loyal member of the Third Reich. What Hitler did not know was that the dark, beetle-browed Hess had for some time been frustrated by the growing power within the Nazi hierarchy of that mysterious, shadowy figure, Martin Bormann, and his muddled reasoning finally convinced him that only by some sensational act of devotion could his former position be regained. Slowly, he became certain that he was the only man in the Third Reich who could bring the war to an end by negotiating a peace between Germany and England. On 10th May, 1941, Hess became Hitler's unofficial envoy, to gain the notoriety he craved, and surprise the world.

When Goering arrived at the Berghof after a reckless four-hour drive from Veldenstein, Bodenschatz quickly placed the known facts about the Hess affair before him. A first-class pilot, the deputy Fuehrer had taken off alone from the Messerschmitt factory aerodrome at Augsburg in a twin-engined Bf 110 fighter which had later been sighted passing over Oldenburg, flying in the direction of the North Sea. Goering immediately telephoned a surprised Adolf Galland and ordered his whole Geschwader into the air. "The deputy Fuehrer has gone mad and is flying to England in a Bf 110," he shouted. "He must be brought down!" Then he slammed the receiver into place, leaving Galland to wonder how one particular Bf 110 could be successfully intercepted at an hour when many aircraft of the same type were flying, and within ten minutes of darkness.

The Berghof was in pandemonium, with everyone talking at once and Goering wilting under the barrage of questions Hitler directed at him. "Can he make it? You are an airman, tell me, can he get there alone?" he snapped, but Goering was at a loss for an answer. Finally, Galland called to report that his fighters had failed to sight the missing aircraft, and another argument exploded in the Berghof when Goering suggested that Hess had at least "a fifty-fifty chance" of reaching England, and a statement declaring his insanity should therefore be issued at once. "What if he has fallen into the sea, and nobody knows anything about it?" demanded Hitler, and decided to await British confirmation that Hess had arrived. Meanwhile, he contented himself by ordering the arrest of those nearest and dearest to the deputy Fuehrer, including his wife, his personal staff, and even Willy Messerschmitt, who had so regrettably supplied the new aircraft he would never see again.

Some hours before the agitated men at the Berghof dispersed in the grey light of dawn, Rudolf Hess had reached Scotland, where shortage of fuel brought his flight to an abrupt end. Nevertheless, he baled out within twelve miles of his destination, the home of the Duke of Hamilton, and was arrested by a farmer, identifying himself as a Luftwaffe pilot, Alfred Horn. Later, Hess revealed his correct name, stating that he was "on a special mission of humanity" and requesting an interview with the Duke of Hamilton, to whom he had been introduced during the Berlin Olympic Games in 1936.

After an inconclusive meeting with the Duke of Hamilton, subsequent conversations between Hess and Ivone Kirkpatrick, the former First Secretary of the British Embassy in Berlin, soon proved that the muddled deputy Fuehrer was almost certainly sincere, but also the victim of his own confused delusions. His "peace proposals" included such curious conditions as a free hand for Germany in Europe, the satisfying of certain German demands in Russia, and a reminder that negotiations could not under any circumstances be entered into with the existing British government, which contained Mr. Churchill and his colleagues: ". . . who had lent themselves to his war policy. . ." Hess insisted that he had flown to Britain because he felt that England could come to an understanding with Germany without loss of prestige on either side, and warned that a rejection of his proposals would entitle the Fuehrer to destroy Britain utterly without further delay

On 12th May, after Hess's arrival on British soil had been confirmed, the Goebbels propaganda machine surpassed itself with an official communique which stated: "The party member Rudolf Hess recently managed to obtain an aircraft against the Fuehrer's strict orders forbidding him to fly on account of an illness which has been growing worse for some time. On 10th May, at about 6.0 p.m., Hess took off from Augsburg on a flight from which so far he has not returned. . . . It seems that party member Hess lived in a state of hallucination, as a result of which he felt he could bring about an understanding between England and Germany. . . . This, however, will have no effect on the continuance of the war. . . ."

So ended the political career of Rudolf Hess. The shock of his remarkable flight soon subsided, and he became a forgotten man, remaining a prisoner of war until October, 1945, when he was released to stand trial at Nuremberg. Hitler was only too pleased to find the affair had come to such a quiet conclusion, and after giving orders to have Hess shot at once if he should return to Germany the Fuehrer decided to forget the whole embarrassing business. However, his wrath was still kindled resentfully against Goering, whose position was not improved by the Hess episode and its aftermath—the appointment as deputy Fuehrer of his old enemy, Martin Bormann. Udet, Milch and Messerschmitt had also been affected by the latest upheaval in the Nazi hierarchy; they could not be accused either of conspiring to assist Hess or professing faith in his convictions, but all three were forced to endure the Fuehrer's ravings at their ineptitude and returned from Berchtesgaden shaken by the unpleasant experience.

Fortunately for Goering, so many military preparations for the conquest of Russia absorbed Hitler during the spring of

1941 that he found little time to worry about the shortcomings of his air leaders. The Wehrmacht generals had again proved troublesome, displaying their opposition to the *Barbarossa* plan by quietly raising doubts about the German Intelligence assessment of Soviet strength; they had finally been won over by Hitler's argument that nothing could be accomplished against England or in the Middle East until Russia was eliminated. "When *Barbarossa* commences," he told them, "the world will hold its breath and make no comment!" Yet he had already lost four valuable weeks in conquering Yugoslavia and Greece—a delay the German generals would later assert made the difference between victory and defeat when they were faced with the bitter Russian winter—and the launching of *Barbarossa,* originally planned for 15th May, was postponed until 22nd June.

Conference followed conference with Hitler reassuring his leaders by telling them that the campaign would be over and done with before the autumn; a few sharp Russian defeats in the early days would lead to the overthrow of the Stalin régime. The most inveterate gambler in history thus committed his greatest blunder of the war in refusing, against all advice to the contrary, to make any preparations for an extended, winter campaign in Russia. Aware that the Soviet forces were numerically superior in men and material, but confident that the weaknesses of the Bolshevik political system were on his side, he assured General Jodl: "We have only to kick in the door and the whole rotten structure will come crashing down."

In National Socialist Germany the Fuehrer was always right. But Ernst Udet, pondering gloomily amid his gleaming collection of rifles and revolvers, had never been a dedicated party member; and he was beginning to doubt if Hitler and Goering would ever be right again.

CHAPTER XV

RED STAR BURNING: RUSSIA, 1941

THE German High Command estimated Russian military strength in June, 1941, at 160 infantry divisions, thirty cavalry divisions and thirty-five motorised and armoured brigades. Soviet security had always ensured that information about the Red Air Force would be defective, and it remained difficult to form a clear picture regarding operational efficiency; but the total Russian air strength was considered to be about 8,000 aircraft, including some 3,000 fighters, about 2,500 ground attack, medium and light bombers and 500 reconnaissance and liaison aircraft. Some 1,500 obsolete large bomber/transport machines were also known to be available. However, the obvious numerical superiority enjoyed by the Soviet Air Force—twice the number of aircraft about to be deployed by Goering against Russia—was thought, with some justification, to be largely offset by its lack of operational experience and modern machines.

It was true that many Soviet units were still equipped with obsolescent aircraft in 1941. The history of the Russian Air Force had followed a pattern not unlike that of the Luftwaffe, and it would soon reveal very similar deficiencies. The collection of antiquated foreign aeroplanes that passed for a Soviet air arm in the 'twenties had grown during the 'thirties into a rather unwieldy Air Force, which remained an integral part of the Red Army, and therefore consisted mainly of short-range, lightly armed bombers for support of the ground forces. It had no effective long-range bomber arm capable of striking at the industrial heart of a potential enemy, and lacked an adequate fighter defence and ground and air transport facilities. Radar had never been developed, and there was no satisfactory early warning system in operation, weaknesses that still existed in 1941 and contributed to the element of surprise that brought so many initial German successes. Even so, the Luftwaffe was to find that in many ways the Russian Air Force had improved enormously during the years 1936-1940.

The Spanish Civil War, which had afforded such a fortuitous opportunity for the Luftwaffe to try out its strength under actual battle conditions, served just as useful a purpose for the Soviet Air Force, and soon awakened the Red aircraft industry to the plain fact that it was falling badly behind the times. The standard Russian fighters sent to Spain, mainly I-15 and I-153 biplanes and I-16 monoplanes, held their own against the Heinkel He 51s initially supplied to the Legion Kondor, but proved to be outclassed in every way by the Messerschmitt Bf 109s later sent to oppose them. The Russian SB-2 aircraft, the so-called "fast bombers" needing no fighter escort, turned out to have all the disadvantages of the Dornier Do 17s in the same class with none of the advantages of the German machines, and for reconnaissance the Russians could provide nothing better than archaic R-5 biplanes. No dive-bombing ground support aircraft comparable to the German Henschel Hs 123 or Junkers Ju 87 were available.

By 1939, the Russian aircraft designers were showing the world that the lessons of the Spanish Civil War had been heeded. Lavochkin was introducing the first of his highly successful LA series of single-seater fighters, soon to be followed by the even more famous LAGG series; Petlyakov's twin-engined PE-2 was about to enter service, and subsequently become one of the outstanding medium bombers of the Second World War; and Ilyushin had just designed the IL-2 Sturmovik ground-support aircraft later to prove unequalled in its class anywhere in the world. By concentrating almost entirely on the production of these types of aircraft, Russia was able to modernise her air arm during the period 1939-1941 considerably, although when the German attack came many Soviet fighter units were still equipped with the obsolescent I-15s and I-16s, just as many bomber units retained SB-3s and the massive four-engined TB-3 aircraft classified as bombers but actually suitable only for transport duties.

The Luftwaffe deployed a strength of about 3,000 aircraft in the summer of 1941, including 1,000 twin-engined medium bombers, some 350 dive-bombers, 600 single-engined fighters, 700 reconnaissance aircraft and over 350 twin-engined fighters and transport aircraft. Each of the three Army Groups to be launched against Russia had an air fleet assigned to its support, these being Luftflotte 4 under General Lohr, Luftflotte 2 under Kesselring, and Luftflotte 1 under General Keller. The three Luftflotten counted in all some 1,300 machines, including many fighters of the latest Messerschmitt Bf 109F type, with a top speed of 380 m.p.h., and large numbers of Dornier Do 17 and Heinkel He 111 long-range reconnaissance aircraft. Nearly all the seventeen armoured divisions on their way to the Eastern Front in June, 1941, had the added advantage of special short-range reconnaissance Staffeln equipped with Henschel Hs 126 or Focke-Wulf Fw 189 aircraft, flown by experienced crews well trained in the art of providing "eyes" for the ground forces. The Junkers Ju 87 dive-bombers of Fliegerkorps VIII had managed to justify their continued existence in the campaigns in Greece and Crete, and von Richthofen correctly assumed that the offensive against Russia would provide similarly ideal conditions for Stuka operations; although even closer support was to be given the Wehrmacht by a Schlachtflieger unit of Henschel Hs 123 biplanes, and, of course, ground strafing fighters.

The stage was thus set for the Battle of the Titans, a military campaign such as the world had never before seen, to be fought on a front of over 2,000 miles from the Danube to the Baltic and north to Leningrad. At 11 o'clock on 21st June, 1941, the final code message implementing *Barbarossa*—"Dortmund, Mohn, Kresse, Aster, Aster"—hummed over the wires to the commanders of the three German Army Groups, and soon after midnight hundreds of Luftwaffe pilots were climbing into their cockpits. Lights flickered in the darkness, airscrews spun and blue flames flickered from exhausts as the powerful engines thundered into life, then the swift fighters and heavily laden bombers were speeding away into the dawn, receding until they were almost indiscernible dots against the lightening eastern sky.

Zero hour for the Wehrmacht offensive in the east was 03.30 hours on 22nd June, 1941, and exactly at that time the preliminary artillery bombardment crashed out along the whole front. Then, with the terrifying, mathematical air of efficiency that characterised the German military machine, the three army groups taking part thrust wedges of steel into Soviet Russia; Army Group Centre, commanded by von Bock, driving a spearhead in the direction of Moscow; Army Group South, under von Runstedt, taking as its objective the rich grain lands of the Ukraine; and Army Group North, under von Leeb, heading for Leningrad. To the surprise of their commanders, the armoured columns and motorised units were soon racing almost unchecked across the flat, open country, leaving the frail, insufficiently manned frontier defences far behind them, although Army Group South came up against the stiffening resistance in the days that followed. Amid the sunflowers and the cornfields, the yellow thatched cottages and the cold, grey towns, the soldiers of the Red Army fought and died, seeking in vain to stem the merciless tide of war. Overhead, the Luftwaffe roared through the heavens unhindered and unchallenged, spreading death and destruction along the roads to the east.

In the main, the Russian forces were taken entirely by surprise. Ahead of the advancing German armour, the Stukas hammered airfields and troop concentrations ruthlessly into dust and rubble; beneath their wings the empty land seemed to stretch away to eternity on every side. Overwhelmed, awed by the vastness of this strange, savage country, the airmen gazed down at the waves of tanks thrusting ever onwards—and wondered. Could the lightning war succeed even here? Or was this the fatal error? In fact, they were seeing the Blitzkrieg technique in action for the last time, and Hitler's unchanging strategy would never bring success again.

In the early days of the campaign, the Russian Air Force was unprepared, not co-ordinated and thrown recklessly into the battle, with the result that large numbers of Soviet aircraft were destroyed, both in the air and on the ground. Dazzled by so many easy victories, German pilots reported that the Russians were poor airmen and hampered by inferior equipment, and the illusion of a speedy end to the campaign was quickly born. The Oberkommando der Luftwaffe claimed that over 3,000 Russian aircraft had been shot down during the first week of *Barbarossa,* and although this remains a doubtful figure—Luftflotte 2 alone destroyed twice the estimated total Soviet air strength before the end of the year, on paper—the Red Air Force was indeed almost knocked out in the first three months of the campaign.

Obsolete fighters and bombers from the Far Eastern Air Armies, training planes and Aeroflot air liners were hurriedly thrown into the Smolensk, Leningrad and Kiev battles, but German air superiority, for the first time since the Battle of France, had been gained before the Soviet reinforcements arrived and remained unchallenged until winter laid its icy hand on the face of Russia.

Unfortunately for Goering and his air fleet commanders, the Soviet Air Force was never completely annihilated during that decisive summer of 1941, and even by the autumn there were indications that it retained a spark of life. Meanwhile, the German fighter aces reaped a record number of victories; Werner Molders, for instance, passed the hundred mark, excluding the score he had achieved during the Spanish Civil War. In July, 1941, he was decorated with the Jewels to the Oak Leaves with Swords to the Knight's Cross, thus becoming the first soldier of the Reich, and about the same time left the Eastern Front to take up the appointment of Inspector of Fighter Aircraft at Luftwaffe Headquarters. Reluctant as the pilots of his beloved Jagdgeschwader were to say farewell to "Daddy" Molders, they realised that such an outstanding officer was wasted on active service; his type of young, keen brain was badly needed to blow fresh air through the musty corridors of the hidebound Luftwaffe.

Along the dusty, uneven Russian roads, far below the great air umbrella, rumbled the apparently endless armoured columns of the Wehrmacht, followed by all the vast impedimenta of modern war, swinging out in the pincer movements that brought bitter encirclement battles at Bialystok, Minsk, Kiev and Vyasma and finally trapped millions of Russian troops within their steel jaws, with an astounding haul in prisoners and tanks, guns and other equipment. In July the German tanks crossed the Beresina not far from the spot where Napoleon's Grand Army had met with disaster during the appalling winter of 1812, in the August von Kliest's armour reached Smolensk and entered Kiev in the September. Somehow, the weary infantry and horse-drawn transport kept the marathon pace, and the tanks rolled on to Orel, Odessa and finally Kharkov, while the long, hot summer passed away and the first cold breezes of winter began to sweep across the endless plains of Russia.

By October, the campaign seemed virtually at an end, and Hitler reduced the flow of munitions and replacements to the front. The whole of Army Group Centre was now thundering eastwards at full spate, and the capture of Moscow was so imminent that a special engineer unit had been formed to undertake the demolition of the Kremlin. In Berlin, the Goebbels propaganda machine joyfully trumpeted out the news that the war in the East was over and the Soviet forces destroyed; Goering congratulated himself on wiping out another enemy air force with his glorious Luftwaffe and the exhausted German troops in sight of Moscow began to believe that Hitler's greatest gamble had succeeded after all.

Then everything began to go wrong at the same time. To the surprise of the German commanders, Russian resistance unexpectedly stiffened along the whole front, and during the Battle of Vyasma a powerful new Soviet tank, the T-34, came into action. So heavily armoured that they could resist the standard Wehrmacht 37-mm. and 50-mm. anti-tank weapons with ease, the T-34s broke the back of the German advance, scattering the forward infantry, running over the artillery turned against them and spreading confusion and chaos everywhere. The approach of winter turned the Russian roads and fields into a sea of mud, and soon the unfortunate German troops were floundering and fighting under conditions reminiscent of Passchendaele in 1917. Heavy artillery sank to the axles and could not be moved, horses had to be dragged out of the slime with tractors, and many aircraft crashed while trying to land or take off from the swampy forward landing fields. To add to the German troubles, the Soviet Air Force showed increasing activity, and the great air battles that developed in the Leningrad area so weakened Fliegerkorps I that it had to be reinforced by elements of the ubiquitous Fliegerkorps VIII under von Richthofen.

The last offensive against Moscow in 1941 was launched by the armoured divisions of von Kluge, and had the misfortune to begin just as the autumn mud and slime abruptly changed to winter snow and ice, preceded by intense cold and great blizzards of sleet and blinding rain. Without proper winter clothing and equipment—often wearing their summer uniforms —the German troops struggled forward, and even managed to reach the outskirts of Moscow, but could go no further. The mechanism of many artillery and automatic weapons froze; tank engines would freeze and burst if they were stopped for only a few moments. Tyred vehicles skidded on the ice and overturned. Water in the boilers of railway locomotives froze and rendered them useless. Mobile artillery pieces that had stuck in the mud solidified there and could not be towed out; aircraft engines had to be kept ticking over, and landing or taking off became even more of a hazardous adventure.

By December, the Wehrmacht forces in Russia were at a standstill, in temperatures of 40 deg. C. below zero, patiently waiting the arrival of the furs and other winter clothing being collected for them in the Fatherland that now seemed so very far away. They did not spend a very cheerful Christmas; even the wine despatched by a thoughtful Fuehrer to his troops on the Eastern front had frozen and exploded its bottles en route, and arrived as unappetising red ice. More than one commander in the field wondered what curious logic had prompted the High Command to send his unit wine instead of the ammunition it desperately needed, and reflected sadly that 1942 was going to be a very difficult year for the German armies in Russia.

On 17th November, 1941, Ernst Udet made the last and greatest decision of his life. For over a year he had been an ill and broken man, hopelessly adrift in the sea of confusion that flooded his office and buffeted this way and that by the negligence of Goering and the intrigue of others. The Elk plan, Udet's attempt to reorganise the German aircraft industry, was already coming apart at the seams, with the Heinkel He 177 proving so inadequate that it had temporarily been taken out of production again, and the Messerschmitt Me 210 suffering the first of the many disasters that would soon turn it into a dismal failure. "Why must all this happen to the He 177? Everything is against me," complained Udet to his friend, Ernst Heinkel, but to no avail; he had lost control of his department. and the ponderous bureaucratic machinery of the Reichsluftfahrtministerium was running away with him.

Always, behind the scenes, lurked his enemies. "Udet is responsible for the failure of the Luftwaffe over England," they said. Supplies of new aircraft to the Russian front had almost broken down during the summer; "Udet is responsible," they reiterated. Dozens of He 177s were crashing in flames when the engines caught fire in flight; "Udet is to blame," was the cry—and Hitler believed them. By August, 1941, Udet was at the end of his tether, quarrelling with his staff, fighting verbal battles every day with the aircraft industrialists trying to satisfy his hazy requirements, and ready to resign in favour of Milch or anyone else who wanted the job. In desperation, he said as much to Goering, in a private interview with the Reichsmarschall at Karinhall.

He was beating his head against a stone wall. Goering, pacing heavily up and down the great baronial hall in his medieval hunting costume with buckled shoes, shook his head when Udet spoke of resignation. "If I let you go," he said, "the people will draw their own conclusions. The whole façade will crumble." Udet would have to try and co-operate with Milch; the outside world must be shielded from the internal problems of the Luftwaffe. "A few weeks' rest and everything will seem different again," Goering went on, cheerfully. "Go away and get well; forget your troubles." But Udet knew he was listening to a jovial hypocrite; the issue at stake had been cunningly avoided, and he was still caught between the hammer of Milch and the anvil of his conscience. Feeling betrayed and abandoned, he left Karinhall having achieved nothing of any consequence, his last hope gone, an empty future of arguments, mistakes and chaos stretching endlessly before him.

Sick in body and spirit, Udet rested for over a month in Goering's hunting lodge on the Rominter Heide, but he was too depressed by the nightmare war Hitler had unleashed on Europe to take any part in the stag hunts he had once enjoyed; his old love of shooting had gone for ever. In his absence there were changes, including the dismissal of the head of his planning department, General Tschersich, and later his chief of staff, General Floch, who was summarily posted to the Russian front. Slowly but surely, other changes were made, until the time came for Udet to return to Berlin. He found himself a stranger in his own office, his most faithful henchmen spirited away and only a sprinkling of men left who might—or might not—support him.

It was the end. On the morning of 17th November, 1941, Udet awoke after another restless night, donned his vivid red dressing-gown, and walked down the stairs to his gun room. For a moment he studied the row of shining black weapons, then selected a revolver, broke it with practised fingers, and slid a single round of ammunition into the breech. Slowly, he returned to his bedroom, holding the gun loosely in his hand; poured out a glass of brandy, drank it, and lay down on the bed. He closed his eyes, and time seemed to stand still, the faint noises from the world outside his window seeming very far away, as if they no longer concerned him.

"I have no one to fear now. No longer." He had spoken those words to his dearest friend, Frau Bleier, after Goering had deserted him, and it was true that in this final irrevocable act the last enemy was himself. It remained only for the weary raising of an arm, the gentle pressure on a trigger, the hurtling take-off on the flight to oblivion. But he would be free; unshackled from the ambitious, envious ghosts crowding around him; there was everything to gain now and nothing to lose.

The report of the Mexican Colt revolver echoed and re-echoed in the confined space of the room.

His brow heavy with many cares, the Propaganda Minister of the Third Reich limped up and down before his desk, his agile brain juggling with the startling item of news he had just received from Karinhall. It was not so much the sudden death of Ernst Udet that troubled Dr. Goebbels; tears of pity came easily to him in public, but his heart had seldom been moved by genuine sorrow. However, the German people had to be given a reason for this particular tragedy, and the responsibility for that task rested oppressively on Goebbels' shoulders. The Hess affair had already struck his propaganda machine a hard blow, forcing it to take the drastic step of revealing at least a measure of the truth, but that was a risk not worth taking again. Yet Goebbels had both hands full explaining away the stalemate in Russia; and Udet had been a popular figure. Life should not hold so many nasty surprises in quick succession for anyone, but for Goebbels the year 1941 was proving the exception to the rule.

By the afternoon of 17th November, Goebbels' genius for distortion of the truth had proved equal to the occasion. "The General in charge of Luftwaffe Supplies, Generaloberst Ernst

Udet, has been killed testing a new weapon," stated the official announcement that evening. "He died of his injuries on the way to hospital. The Fuehrer has ordered a state funeral for this officer who died in so tragic a manner, while in the performance of his duty. In recognition of his magnificent achievements in the war, of his fifty-two fighter victories and of the great services he rendered in building up the Luftwaffe, the Fuehrer has perpetuated Generaloberst Udet's name by bestowing it upon Jagdgeschwader No. 3." Later, Erhard Milch received Udet's mother at the Kaiserhof Hotel in Berlin and blandly gave his version of the "accident" involving a weapon so secret that details could not be revealed.

Then, with due ceremony, all that remained of Ernst Udet was laid to rest. The coffin stood on a catafalque in the Reichsluftfahrtministerium that Friday morning, the guard of honour of outstanding Luftwaffe aces—Galland, Lutzow, Oesau and Pelz—standing at attention in steel helmets and jackboots, with drawn swords. The strains of Wagner's Funeral March from *Götterdämmerung*, played by a section of the Berlin Philharmonic Orchestra, drifted over the assembled company in the great hall; Goering, in a light grey uniform with chestnut boots and spurs; Goebbels, in a brown leather cloak; Jeschonnek, looking thoughtful and depressed; and many other Luftwaffe, Wehrmacht and party leaders. At last, all were seated, and as the solemn music died away the Commander-in-Chief of the Luftwaffe, the man who had fought and flown beside Udet in 1918, ascended the dais to deliver the funeral oration.

"Now we must take leave of you," said Hermann Goering sadly, while the press cameras hummed gently behind him. "The thought that you are no longer with us, my dear Udet, is inconceivable. . . . It is not my task to praise your services, for by your deeds you have become immortal. . . . By your wartime operations you gave our brave young pilots confidence in their weapons, for what you conceived and flew they took for granted. You must have been inordinately proud when I was always able to say to you that our aircraft, which were the best, would always remain so thanks to your work. . . ." Like Mark Anthony grieving over the body of Caesar, the Reichsmarschall had to pause for a moment, overcome with emotion. Then he concluded: "We do not know how we shall fill the gap that you have left behind. You were such a vital character that we almost feel you are still among us. We must go on living with the self-assurance and confidence in victory which you have always shown. Your death will strengthen us. And now I can only say, Farewell, my best friend."

In the cold, grey November mist the long procession moved off through the crowded streets to the Invaliden Cemetery in the north of Berlin. It was a very sad and impressive cortège: the standard bearers marching with impassive faces, the solemn music of the band; the wreaths brilliant with colour, the adjutants carrying Udet's orders and decorations; the gun carriage drawn by horses. Then Goering, walking alone with bowed head, followed by the cloaked and booted generals, the relatives and other mourners. Many of those who had known Ernst Udet must have reflected that in life so much empty ceremony would have amused him intensely; and who can say his ghost was not there that morning, shaking with silent laughter to see Goering tramp heavily past with clanking spurs?

But unexpected tragedy greeted the tired Reichsmarschall when he returned from the Invaliden Cemetery at noon. From Dresden came the news that General Wilberg had been killed when the Messerschmitt Taifun flying him to Udet's funeral crashed in appalling weather conditions. Then, from Breslau, Goering heard that fate had struck the Luftwaffe yet another blow; the fighter ace of aces, Werner Molders, would also never reach Berlin. He had been a worthy successor to the legendary Oswald Boelcke; and, like Boelcke, his life had been claimed in a simple accident that could not be avoided.

Molders had been directing air operations in the Crimea when the telegram arrived summoning him to join the guard of honour at Udet's lying in state. He had taken off at once in a Heinkel He 111 bomber hastily converted for transport purposes. Flying through thick cloud and heavy rain, the aircraft had been forced to land at Lemberg, but Molders fretted at the delay—he was obeying a personal order from Goering—and insisted on continuing the flight against the advice of his pilot. One engine had to be cut when the oil pressure dropped, and Molders reluctantly agreed to a landing at Breslau. Slowly, the He 111 dropped through the fog and rain—the blind approach dreaded by every airman. Abruptly, the wires of a cable railway leapt into view before the windscreen. Too late, the pilot hauled back on his control column; and at once the remaining engine failed. The He 111 stalled, one wing struck a factory chimney, and the aircraft spun in from a few hundred feet. Molders, in the big perspex nose of the bomber, was killed outright, and the pilot and flight engineer of the He 111 were also fatally injured, the radio operator and Molders' aide-de-camp being the sole survivors.

It was a sombre period for the Luftwaffe. In Adolf Galland's own words, "Eight days after Udet's state funeral we were standing once more beside an open grave; once more members of the fighter arm wearing the Knight's Cross stood the last guard of honour; once more Goering exhorted a comrade: 'Arise to Valhalla'...." After the ceremony, the Reichsmarschall beckoned Galland from his place in the guard of honour, and taking him aside, said: "Now it is your turn; I name you herewith as Molders' successor, to be General of the Fighter Arm."

Galland has admitted that he accepted his new post with mixed feelings. He loved flying, and he had all the dislike—even contempt—of the average fighting man for the mysterious body of dull, pompous beings known as "the staff"; but he realised that at last he might be able to cut some of the red tape throttling the Luftwaffe, for in matters relating to the fighter arm he would be subordinate only to Goering and Hitler. And Galland had no intention of suffering in silence. "I wanted to fight and swear at the Command," he states in his memoirs. "Nothing else! In any case, I had the firm intention of never losing contact with the men, of becoming just 'Staff' or of giving up combat flying."

Molders and Galland have often been compared with the leading German air aces of the 1914-1918 War, Boelcke and von Richthofen, and it is true there are certain similarities. Just as Boelcke had shown himself not only to be an accomplished fighter pilot, but also a brilliant tactician, so Molders worried less over his personal score than the efficiency of his squadron as a whole. Galland, too, was an outstanding air fighter, but, like Richthofen, he was an organiser, who liked to take up the gauntlet on his own terms. Both Molders and Boelcke were men who remained quietly devoted to duty, never demanding more of their pilots than they were prepared to

undertake themselves; von Richthofen, though not as flamboyant and rebellious against authority as Galland, had the same
liking for publicity and personal glory.

Undoubtedly the fighter arm of the Luftwaffe needed a man
like Galland to knock it into shape. Before the end of the year,
he was crossing swords with Jeschonnek, who had been ordered
by Hitler to mobilise every available aircraft for a proposed
spring offensive in the east, and was even considering calling
upon his training reserve units to make up the required
numbers. Galland's objections were overruled, but he was undismayed; a beginning had been made, and sooner or later Jeschonnek would listen to the voice of experience.

On 8th December, 1941, another of Hermann Goering's
private nightmares came true. At 12.20 p.m. that day, in
Washington, D.C., a fleet of ten shining black limousines entered
the Capitol grounds and slid smoothly to a halt at the south
entrance. From the leading car stepped President Franklin D.
Roosevelt, assisted by his son Jimmy; he smiled and waved
cheerfully at the inevitable crowd waiting in the pale, wintry
sunshine, then disappeared into the Capitol building. In the
House Chamber at that moment Senators and military leaders
were taking their places, followed by the Supreme Court and
members of the cabinet. A strange air of urgency, almost of
anger, hung over the gathering—a sense that the days of
complacency were over, and now the time had come for hard
work.

At 12.30 p.m. President Roosevelt, dressed in formal morning
attire, mounted the rostrum, waited until the thunderous
applause had died away, then prepared to address the Senate.
"Yesterday," he began, "7th December, 1941—a date which
will live in infamy—the United States of America was suddenly
and deliberately attacked. . . ." Within the hour, the President
had departed, the Senate had voted, and America was officially
at war with Imperial Japan.

Unfortunately for the Nazi hierarchy, Germany was tied to
Japan by the Axis pact Hitler had hoped would serve as a deter-
rent to keep the United States out of his "limited" European
war. Now, without any warning to her western allies, Japan had
decided to strike a blow on her own account, and overnight

Hitler found that the flames of war were out of control and encircling the world.

For three days, the worried Fuehrer tried to wriggle out of the binding agreement of the Tripartite Pact, but if he wanted to save any face at all there was no way out. On 11th December, an icy von Ribbentrop received Leland Morris, the American charge d'affaires in Berlin, and handed him Germany's formal declaration of war on the United States. The Third Reich, already heavily committed against Great Britain and the Soviet Union, henceforward would also have to reckon with another enemy—the most powerful industrial nation in the world. The year 1941 had been overshadowed by dark days for Germany; but darker and far more terrible days lay ahead.

CHAPTER XVI

THE UNCONQUERABLE ISLAND: MALTA, 1942

ON 27th September, 1941, several Spitfire pilots of the Royal Air Force returned from a Fighter Command sweep over Amiens and reported that they had encountered an entirely new type of German fighter, described as a radial-engined aircraft not unlike the Curtiss Hawk 75A used by the French Air Force in 1940. At the same time, the British pilots insisted that the phenomenal performance of the unusual enemy fighter ruled out any possibility of it being the Curtiss Hawk, although a few of the obsolescent American-built fighters were known to be in Luftwaffe service. Royal Air Force Intelligence finally squashed all arguments by stating firmly that Germany possessed no modern radial-engined fighters; the Spitfire pilots had either seen captured Curtiss Hawks or been confused by the outline of the Messerschmitt Bf 109 in the heat of action.

Within a month, camera-gun photographs of the radial-engined German fighter had been brought back for study on the ground. They proved beyond any doubt that a new type of German single-seater fighter—the remarkable Focke-Wulf Fw 190—was indeed coming into operational service. For the next twelve months, it would be a consistent problem to the squadrons of Fighter Command, far out-classing the Spitfire V and Hawker Typhoon in general performance and reigning supreme in the skies over France and the English Channel.

The Focke-Wulf Fw 190, designed by Kurt Tank, originated from a request by the Reichsluftfahrtministerium in 1937 for a single-seater fighter to supplement the Bf 109 then just entering service with the Luftwaffe. From the beginning, the Fw 190 was an excellent aircraft, achieving a maximum speed of nearly 400 m.p.h. and displaying such an outstanding ability to zoom, climb or dive in combat at high speed that in many ways it was better than the Bf 109. However, the Messerschmitt fighter had attracted more favourable attention, and been rushed into mass production as first-line equipment for the Luftwaffe, with the result that the Fw 190 remained nothing more than another iron in the fire. Also, the Reichsluftfahrtministerium tended to distrust air-cooled radial engines; even Tank was surprised when Ernst Udet supported his decision to build Germany's first radial-engined monoplane fighter.

It is true that Tank radically altered the German policy of designing all new fighters around in-line engines by powering his Fw 190 with a BMW 801 air-cooled radial engine of 1,800 h.p. with an engine-driven fan to improve the cooling, ingeniously blending this bulky power arrangement into the neat, clean lines of the fuselage. Five prototypes were built, undergoing very successful flight trials, but progress with the new fighter still tended to be slow but sure until Goering decided to inspect the Fw 190 in 1940 and was so impressed that he told Tank he must turn out the new machines "like so many hot rolls!"

Armed with four MG 17 machine-guns, two in the wing roots and two in the upper fuselage decking, all firing through the airscrew arc, the first production Fw 190s appeared over the Channel coast in July, 1941, replacing the Bf 109Es in service with Jagdgeschwaden 2 and 26. By the end of the year they had established almost complete superiority over the Spitfire Vs then in use by Fighter Command, and maintained that superiority for nearly two years. The most successful version of the Fw 190, the 190A-3, came to be regarded by both sides as the best fighter which Germany produced during the Second World War. It was fitted with a more powerful BMW radial engine with a rating of 2,100 h.p., had a maximum speed of 408 m.p.h. and carried four 20-mm. MG 151 cannon and two 13-mm. MG 131 machine-guns.

Early in 1942 the new Fw 190s of Jagdgeschwaden 2 and 26 were earmarked to take part in one of Hitler's most daring ventures—the transfer of the German battle fleet from Brest through the Straits of Dover to the sanctuary of home waters. During 1941, the fast, powerful 30,000-ton battle cruisers *Scharnhorst* and *Gneisenau* had ranged the Atlantic, sinking over 100,000 tons of Allied shipping before at last taking refuge in Brest, where they remained a potential menace to the already depleted convoys from the United States and Canada. In both London and Berlin it was realised that the next move of the two battle cruisers could be decisive in the war at sea; the recent exploits of the *Bismarck* had taught both sides a bitter lesson.

The new German battleship *Bismarck*—the most powerful warship in the world—had simply sailed from Bergen one night in company with the heavy cruiser *Prinz Eugen* and vanished into the Atlantic, throwing the Admiralty into confusion. Three days later the German ships were intercepted by the Home Fleet and brought to action by the veteran battle cruiser *Hood* and the brand-new battleship *Prince of Wales*, hurriedly rushed to sea when barely completed. The superb gunnery of the *Bismarck* destroyed *Hood* and so badly damaged the *Prince of Wales* that she had to break off the engagement, then the German battleship set course for Brest, her high speed apparently making further interception by the Royal Navy impossible. But later that day Swordfish torpedo bombers from the aircraft carrier *Victorious* damaged *Bismarck*, forcing her to drastically reduce speed, and a second Swordfish attack from *Ark Royal* finally sealed the fate of the German ship. She was brought to action by the Home Fleet and sunk, long after *Prinz Eugen* had slipped away to find safety in Brest. The fate of *Bismarck* would almost certainly overtake *Scharnhorst* and *Gneisenau* if they ventured out again; but that knowledge provided little consolation for the Admiralty, compelled in the meantime to thin down the Mediterranean and Home Fleets in finding capital ships for the convoy routes.

While Admiral Raeder hesitated to send his battle cruisers into the lion's mouth of the wild Atlantic again, and the Royal Air Force deluged Brest with bombs—299 attacks, with a loss of forty-three aircraft failed to put the warships out of action— Hitler came to the conclusion that the Allies were about to invade Norway. He therefore decided that the *Scharnhorst* and *Gneisenau* be transferred from Brest to home waters and undergo refitting for the defence of Scandinavia; also, he insisted that the Channel route should be used. Appalled at the idea of sending German capital ships through the Dover Straits within eighteen miles of the English south coast, Raeder pointed out the fearful risk they would be taking, but the Fuehrer remained adamant. "You can count on this," he said. "From my previous experience I do not believe the British capable of the conception and execution of lightning decisions such as will be required for the transfer of their air and sea forces to meet the boldness of our operation."

Despite Raeder and his naval staff, the decision was made. Adolf Galland was ordered to provide a continuous air umbrella over the German fleet, and for this purpose Jagdgeschwaden 2 and 26 were each increased in establishment to some ninety Bf 109s and Fw 190s. These were reinforced for Operation *Cerberus*, as the Channel venture was code-named, by twelve Bf 109s from a fighter training school and a further sixty Bf 109s from Jagdgeschwader 1, making some 252 aircraft available to provide air cover. For obvious reasons, a much smaller number of fighters was bound to be over the warships at one time; an elaborate "shuttle" service had to be organised during the whole day. In Galland's own words: "A continuous escort at high altitude and low level could not be carried out by more than sixteen fighter planes, the single waves of sixteen aircraft each remaining approximately thirty-five minutes over the ships. This varied according to distance from base to object. . . . The relieving wave arrived according to a precisely fixed schedule ten minutes before the time was up for the first escort to return. . . ." For possible action against attacking British naval forces, a single bomber Geschwader was placed in readiness on the Channel coast.

On the evening of 11th February, 1942, the port of Brest shook to the concussion of the inevitable British air raid. Just before 10 p.m., as the "all-clear" sirens wailed over the town, the *Scharnhorst, Gneisenau* and *Prinz Eugen*, surrounded by seven destroyers, slid quietly away from their harbour moorings and headed out into the open sea. Engine-room telegraphs clanged, and white foam broke away from the bows of the warships as they gathered speed. Vice-Admiral Ciliax, flying his flag in *Scharnhorst*, stood on the bridge, surrounded by the velvet darkness of the night, and waited for the dawn—and the British reconnaissance aircraft he was certain would appear at first light.

But for once Hitler's intuition had served him well. A grey, misty dawn came to the English Channel and found the German battle fleet still undetected after being at sea for just over ten hours, and already 250 miles nearer its objective. At 8.30 a.m. the first batch of Galland's day fighters joined the night fighters that had been patiently circling over the warships during the hours of darkness. The arrival of German aircraft somewhere in the Le Havre area was duly plotted by Newhaven radar station and reported to 11 Group of Fighter Command without comment. No action was taken.

Fifteen minutes later, the British early morning reconnaissance patrol of two Spitfires appeared over the Channel. By great misfortune, one fighter flew directly to Boulogne and turned for home after sighting E-boats leaving the harbour, and the other Spitfire covered only the area between Cap Gris Nez and Ostend before also returning to report E-boat activity east of Zeebrugge. The reinforcements moving to join the German fleet had thus been seen without being recognised for what they were, and the early morning mist still enshrouded the battle cruisers long after they should have been discovered.

Admiral Ciliax could scarcely credit his good luck. At 10 a.m. the German fleet was approaching the narrowest part of the Channel, between Dover and Calais—and still it remained undetected. The Bf 110 night fighters were now withdrawn until the evening and the day fighter cover increased, activity that brought reports from various radar stations along the English south-east coast of enemy aircraft circling, yet in a curious orbit that was moving up the Channel at more than 20 knots. Despite frequent interference—thought to be caused by atmospherics, but in reality due to German jamming of the radar system— every plot clearly indicated that surface vessels were steaming up the Channel at high speed under air cover. Nevertheless, Fighter Command assumed that the unusual German air activity amounted to nothing more than an exercise or air-sea rescue operation, and the radar reports aroused only mild interest.

At 10.20 a.m. another pair of Spitfires took off on the second Channel reconnaissance patrol of the day. Ten minutes later, two Battle of Britain veterans, Group Captain Beamish and Wing Commander Boyd, out in their Spitfires for an unofficial jaunt over the Channel, sighted two enemy fighters and joyfully dived to the attack. The German pilots immediately turned back for the safety of Galland's "umbrella" and Beamish and Boyd, thundering in pursuit, abruptly found themselves hurtling across the bows of the battle cruisers they thought were still at anchor in Brest. Bound by Fighter Command standing orders

to maintain strict radio silence at all times, the startled Battle
of Britain aces could only bank steeply away and race back to
base. The same rule of silence hampered the two reconnaissance
pilots, who sighted the German fleet five minutes later, protected by what appeared to be masses of Bf 109s and Fw 190s;
too much valuable time was lost while they were returning to
Hawkinge. The flick of a switch and a few quick words might
have made all the difference; but Hitler had judged the British
reaction correctly, and the "lightning decision" was never
made.

By 11.0 a.m. the secret was out—after the German ships had
been at sea for nearly fourteen hours. But the vague British plan
to counteract a "Channel dash" by the enemy was based entirely
on the assumption that he would only dare to attempt a night
passage, and another vital hour passed before any direct action
was taken against the battle cruisers steaming majestically
through the Straits of Dover. When the dazed Commands of the
R.A.F. had sorted out the situation, the lack of any proper
attacking force for a daylight operation became appallingly
clear; apart from a squadron of Beaufort torpedo bombers just
transferred from Leuchars to Coltishall, barely landed and
therefore not at readiness, only six antiquated Swordfish torpedo aircraft and the Dover motor-torpedo boats were immediately available. Too late, the Coast Artillery batteries at Dover
opened fire, and the great fountains of water erupted more than
a mile to port of the nearest German ships. Within half an hour,
they were out of range.

Lieutenant-Commander Eugene Esmond, a young Irishman,
was destined to lead the six Fleet Air Arm Swordfish into action
against the German armada that morning, the hopeless, suicidal
attack from which few, if any, could possibly return. He was
promised five fighter squadrons for top cover and close escort;
when the Swordfish squadron took off from Manston at 12.25
p.m., not a single fighter had arrived. In that omission lay the
tragedy of Eugene Esmond. Acknowledged by the Admiralty to
be "a wise and brave captain with too much integrity to waste
either their (his crews) lives or his own in an attack which held
no hope of success," he accepted the inevitable dangers of his
job—and found himself faced with the supreme sacrifice.

Over Ramsgate, the six Swordfish biplanes were met by ten

Spitfires, and with this pathetic little escort they dropped to a height of 50 ft. and headed out to sea. Almost at once, the fighters became tangled in running dogfights with two flights of Galland's Bf 109s. Occasionally, a black-crossed machine would hurtle through the Swordfish formation, hammering cannon and machine-gun fire into the big, unwieldy biplanes as they throbbed relentlessly through the mist towards their target. With wingtips almost touching the water, the rear gunners standing up in their open cockpits to spray first one attacking fighter and then another, fuselages trailing torn fabric, the Swordfish presented a curious sight; they could—and did—absorb tremendous punishment, but they were no match for the might of the German fleet. And no man knew that better than Eugene Esmond.

Then the German battle fleet was looming up ahead, and simultaneously the full weight of Galland's fighter cover fell on the lumbering Swordfish. Attacking in waves, the Focke-Wulf Fw 190s of Jagdgeschwaden 2 and 26 swept in to rake the biplanes with devastating bursts of cannon fire before banking steeply around to fire again. Beyond, the destroyer escort surrounding the battle cruisers became wreathed in smoke and flame as hundreds of rapid-firing anti-aircraft guns crashed into action. Into this reeking hell flew the first three Swordfish, swaying to the concussion of shells bursting all around them, great holes appearing in the tattered wings and fuselages.

As if indestructible, Esmond calmly led his sub-flight through the awful flak barrage from the destroyers, ignoring the flame-stabbing cowlings of Fw 190s hurtling past on either side. At two thousand yards, the battle cruisers opened fire on him with every gun that could be brought to bear, including the main 11-inch armament, which belched out broadside after broadside with clockwork precision. The huge shells hit the sea in front of the sub-flight, sending up a great wall of water which cascaded down on the staggering biplanes. Abruptly, the lower port wing of Esmond's Swordfish was shot clean away by a direct hit; the skeleton of what had been an aircraft wavered dangerously then flew on, heading relentlessly for the vast bulk of *Scharnhorst*. A dozen German fighters, with undercarriages and flaps fully lowered to try and reduce their speed to the pitiful 90 knots of the Swordfish, hung on behind, riddling it with point-blank fire.

Dying, with two dead men huddled in the cockpits behind him, Eugene Esmond released his torpedo. Then the stricken Swordfish crashed into the sea; just as the second biplane, taking terrible punishment from the concentrated anti-aircraft fire, came in to attack *Gneisenau*. Its torpedo released at last, it flew right into the flaming muzzles of the battle cruiser's guns in a desperate attempt to gain height, barely clearing the super-structure of the German ship before belly-landing heavily on the water. The third Swordfish of that ill-fated yet glorious sub-flight, streaming sheets of flame from the engine and port wings, also managed to drop its torpedo—aimed at *Prinz Eugen*—before plunging into the sea.

While the great battle cruisers were still altering course to evade the streaking torpedoes, the second sub-flight of Sword-fish, in impeccable Vee formation, struggled through the awful holocaust of steel surrounding the German ships. Gutted by fighter cannon fire, manned by dead and dying crews, they entered the mighty flak barrage and deluging water around the battle cruisers and vanished into the furnace; three Swordfish and nine fragments of humanity simply consumed like moths in the heat of a candle. Officially, they were presumed to have released their torpedoes, but the truth of what actually happened in that moment of destruction will never be known.

So ended perhaps the most gallant sortie ever to be flown in the splendid history of the Fleet Air Arm. The German ships had not been halted or even damaged, and therefore the operation had failed in its purpose; but the failure of Esmond and his squadron was more bright with glory than many a victory. Aptly described in the German War Diary as "the moth-ball attack of a handful of ancient planes piloted by men whose bravery surpasses any other action by either side that day", the sortie had clutched vainly at the chance of success. But success that day was a straw in the wind, beyond the grasp of even a man like Eugene Esmond; he could do no more than accept the great sacrifice. Later, he was posthumously awarded the Victoria Cross.

Other men were fated to die on that grey February afternoon. Fighter Command was soon heavily committed, and innumerable air battles reeled back and forth over the German battle fleet as it surged on at top speed. Again, valuable time was lost before a second torpedo attack could be mounted. When it did come, at 3.45 p.m., the two or three Beauforts involved could not penetrate the appalling flak barrage thrown up by the warships. A second, more organised Coastal Command attack, this time by fourteen Beauforts, also met with little success, although at least six aircraft managed to break through and release their torpedoes. Against this display of determination, three Beauforts became lost in the rising mist and finally dropped their torpedoes against "three large ships" which turned out to be British destroyers racing to intercept the German fleet. In this atmosphere of confusion and chaos, Coastal Command activities came to an end. Three Beauforts and two Lockheed Hudsons had been shot down; and still the enemy ships had not been halted.

However, Admiral Ciliax was also having a difficult time. At about 2.30 p.m.—when Coastal Command was hurriedly assembling a striking force of Beauforts—the flagship *Scharnhorst* was abruptly shaken from stem to stern by a tremendous explosion. By great misfortune from the German point of view, she had struck a mine, and, with both propeller shafts damaged, was soon wallowing heavily to a standstill. Haunted by the fear of air attacks which were expected to hit the battle fleet at any moment, Ciliax decided to transfer his command to the destroyer Z-29, which was ordered alongside. As the two ships closed, the Admiral, his staff and the vital Luftwaffe fighter liaison staff leapt across the gap, and within minutes the destroyer was heading after the main fleet at full speed. However, *Scharnhorst* soon managed to repair her damage sufficiently to get under way again, despite repeated attacks during the afternoon by aircraft of Bomber Command.

Nearly four hours had elapsed after first sighting of the enemy ships before Bomber Command struck against them in any force, mainly because many of the aircraft supposedly at immediate readiness were armed only with armour-piercing bombs. When the alarm was given, high-altitude bombing with armour-piercing bombs was obviously impossible in the heavy cloud and deteriorating visibility of early afternoon, and most of these had therefore to be switched for general purpose bombs fused to explode on impact. Bomber Command thus accepted that it had little hope of crippling the German battle cruisers; it compromised by endeavouring to damage the lightly armoured upper decks and superstructures.

These final air attacks of the day were all courageously pressed home despite the fearful German flak barrage, yet none proved effective. At 2.30 p.m. the first wave of Bomber Command aircraft—seventy-three assorted bombers—struck at the enemy ships. Of the second wave of 134 bombers, only a few found the targets in the thickening mist, and those that survived the blanket of anti-aircraft fire had no success. A third wave, which went in through rain and mist in the early evening, failed to contact the enemy fleet at all. In the final assessment, fifteen bombers had been lost out of 242 committed—and again nothing had been achieved.

The fighter battles raged on without respite until nightfall. Cannon-firing Hurricanes and twin-engined Whirlwinds of Fighter Command fought through the flak and Galland's air cover to attack the German destroyer escort and E-boat screen; dozens of Bf 109s and Fw 190s strove to intercept them. "Conscious that everything was at stake on that day, no scruples about safety existed," comments Galland in his memoirs. "The fighter pilots had done more than their duty. They were carried away by the grandeur of the operation and showed an enthusiasm I did not think could be possible after the long, hard struggle the squadron had waged on the Channel. . . ."

Nevertheless, the scales of fortune were still heavily weighted against Admiral Ciliax. In the late afternoon, the destroyer Z-29 developed engine trouble, and again the German commander and his staff had to be transferred, this time to the destroyer *Hermann Schoemann*. However, the vast bulk of *Scharnhorst* soon loomed out of the mist, having at last caught up with the main fleet, to the great relief of Ciliax. Having beaten off destroyer and M.T.B. attacks and repulsed determined air attacks for hour after hour, the German flotilla was still intact and running at maximum speed up the Dutch coast, beyond the range of British fighters and medium bombers. From Le Touquet, Adolf Galland withdrew his air cover and signalled his congratulations to the exhausted Luftwaffe crews, many of whom had scarcely been out of their machines since dawn.

Then, off the Friesian Islands and almost in German home waters, *Gneisenau* trembled to a violent explosion; she, in her turn, had struck a mine. An hour later, she was again limping slowly along, and just after midnight reached the sanctuary of Heligoland Bight. Shortly before dawn *Prinz Eugen* reached the mouth of the Elbe and dropped anchor alongside *Gneisenau*, to the accompaniment of cheering from the tired crews of both ships.

But misfortune still dogged the flagship *Scharnhorst*. At 9.30 p.m., just inside home waters, she again hit a mine and shuddered to a standstill. Although now badly damaged, by midnight she was able to continue and proceeded independently to Wilhelmshaven. Thankfully, Admiral Ciliax despatched a signal to Berlin : "It is my duty to inform you that Operation *Cerberus* has been successfully completed. . . ." The next day, in his personal report to Hitler, he wrote : "Now that the three ships have put into German estuaries the operation *Cerberus* is ended. With it closes one day of the war at sea, a day which will probably go down as one of the most daring in the naval history of the war. . . ."

Undoubtedly, the Channel dash, as such, had been a remarkable achievement, and a hard blow to British prestige. That enemy warships could pass unscathed through the Straits of Dover was incredible; yet the impossible had taken place, and in broad daylight. Expressing all the indignation of the British people, *The Times* stated bluntly in an editorial : "Vice-Admiral Ciliax has succeeded where the Duke of Medina Sidonia failed. Nothing more mortifying to the pride of sea power has happened since the seventeenth century." Like Winston Churchill, when told that the German ships had safely reached home waters, Britons were reading their newspapers in amazement and asking, the simple question, "Why?"

Yet the Channel dash proved to be of little value to Hitler, for the very good reason that the Allies had never intended to invade Norway. The Fuehrer was left with yet another indecisive German victory, gained without any real purpose. The *Scharnhorst* was so badly damaged that she was out of action for over six months : *Prinz Eugen* was fated to rust away in German waters until crippled for good by a torpedo from a British submarine; and *Gneisenau* would soon be knocked out by aircraft of Bomber Command while still in dry dock. Also, within a year, Hitler, like a capricious child, would have decided that capital ships were out of date and suitable only for breaking up or filling with concrete as sunken fortresses. The Channel dash amounted, therefore, in Admiral Raeder's words, to "a tactical victory and a strategic defeat" which, like so many of Hitler's gambles with fortune, was scarcely worth the cost; and in the spring of 1942 the Luftwaffe could ill afford its heavy fighter losses over the Channel.

"There are no more unconquerable islands," Hitler had declared after the fall of Crete, conveniently forgetting that Operation *Sealion* still remained in abeyance. He also apparently forgot that the most important base in the Mediterranean was still in British hands; and that particular island—Malta—was fast becoming a thorn in the flesh of the Axis forces in North Africa. But in 1941 the Fuehrer had ignored the opportunity to use Crete as an air base against Alexandria, and in 1942 he was just as reluctant to take any action against Malta. Unfortunately for the inhabitants of that gallant little island, events in the Western Desert soon took such a turn for the worse that Hitler had to entrust the overworked Luftwaffe with yet another task. Thus began the operation that would decimate the German bomber force in the Mediterranean theatre and earn Malta the award of the George Cross.

Italy's declaration of war against Great Britain and France in 1940, had, of course, made the Mediterranean an operation theatre in the first place. The small British army in Somaliland, initially driven back by the Italians, had been hurriedly reinforced by the men—General Wavell's famous "30,000"—who later in the year drove the Italian army headlong out of Egypt, taking 38,000 prisoners. Bardia, Tobruk and Benghazi were occupied in quick succession, until at last Hitler began to wonder if it would be worth his while to save the situation in Tripoli. As he explained to his Army staff, "the loss of North Africa could be withstood in the military sense but must have a strong psychological effect on Italy. . . . The British forces in the Mediterranean would not be tied down. . . ."

Therefore, on 15th February, 1941, a little-known German officer named Erwin Rommel, who had served with distinction on the Western Front, was promoted General-Leutnant and appointed to command a small German force in North Africa. From this small beginning emerged the Deutsche Afrika Korps, the powerful army that under Rommel's superb leadership would in 1942 throw the British Eighth Army back to Alamein and the very gates of Alexandria.

Rommel arrived in Tripoli like a thunderbolt. Without waiting for the promised reinforcements of the 15th Panzer Division, he attacked almost at once and within a week had recaptured Benghazi and was surging on to hammer at the fortress of Tobruk. But two attempts to take Tobruk were unsuccessful, although Rommel stood fast there, repulsing the counter-offensive by General Wavell code-named *Battleaxe* and supposedly mounted in sufficient strength to destroy the German forces in Africa. The summer passed quietly enough, but a powerful attack in November, this time by General Auchinleck, caught Rommel off balance. His armour squarely beaten at Sidi Rezegh, his cunning attempt to turn the tables with a violent, unexpected breakthrough towards the Egyptian frontier foiled by Auchinleck, the German commander was forced to withdraw, and within a month the Afrika Korps was in full retreat. At El Agheila Rommel made a stand, and in the lull that followed he took stock of the situation. For the Afrika Korps it was disastrous; 33,000 men and over 300 tanks had been lost. Two-thirds of the Axis armies in North Africa had been destroyed, due in no small part to Allied air supremacy; for Rommel could muster at the height of the battle only 350 German and Italian aircraft, against a Desert Air Force of over a thousand.

During 1941, Hitler's whole attention had been riveted on the eastern front. Too late, he was persuaded to take his gaze from the map of Russia and heed Rommel's urgent requests for increased air support in Africa. Since February the inadequate Fliegerkorps X, operating from Sicilian bases, had given token air support to the Afrika Korps until so worn down by the excessive demands placed upon it that it had later been replaced by Fliegerkorps II, under the command of Bruno Loerzer. In the November, as Rommel's forces reeled back to Cyrenaica, Hitler recalled Generalfeldmarschall Albert Kesselring from the east and ordered him to take over air operations in the Mediterranean theatre. The full strength of Luftflotte 2, under Kesselring, was to be used initially to break the crisis in North Africa and thereafter undertake an air offensive against Malta, a double task which Kesselring realised only too well would incur heavy losses in men and machines. The proposed attack on Malta seemed all the more pointless when Hitler revealed that he had no plans for capturing the island in the near future, partly because he considered that it could be rendered innocuous by bombing, but also because he had no parachute or airborne troops available after the Pyrrhic victory in Crete.

Nevertheless, with Rommel depending almost entirely on supplies from Europe, and Malta serving as the main British base from which transports carrying these supplies could be sunk, an attempt would have to be made to destroy the airfields and harbour installations there. And British air and sea action from Malta had undoubtedly greatly contributed to the defeat of the Afrika Korps; by the end of 1941 over seventy-five per cent of the German and Italian ships running the gauntlet to North Africa had been sunk. Rommel, at a standstill at El Agheila, was urgently requesting the petrol and other supplies he needed to rebuild his shattered forces, and Malta stood like a dagger, threatening to cut the pipe line that could feed him victory.

Weary after the months of hard fighting in Russia, Luftflotte 2 went into action over North Africa. Due largely to this reinforcement of the Luftwaffe forces in Sicily, on 21st January, 1942, Rommel was able to attack again, and by the end of the month had driven the Eighth Army back to Gazala. After an uneasy lull, while both sides hesitated to take the offensive, Rommel made a new drive on 27th May which met and destroyed the Allied armour and then thundered on at breakneck speed. The Gazala positions were quickly overrun, Tobruk fell, then Sidi Barrani and Mersa Matruh. But the men of the Afrika Korps could not be expected to keep such a pace. Exhausted by the headlong advance, they came to a halt on 30th June at El Alamein, only sixty-five miles from Alexandria. Reluctantly, the tireless Rommel decided that he could not risk trying to push on to Cairo. The great, glittering jewel of Egypt was almost within his grasp, but the frailty of the human body and the perilous supply problem had, for the moment, beaten him. Again, the Afrika Korps was forced to rest and wait until it had the strength to undertake the final offensive that would throw the Eighth Army out of Egypt.

Meanwhile, Kesselring had turned his attention to Malta. His object was to destroy the three airfields on the island, render the harbour installations useless and sink any ships in or outside the harbour. As Malta was within easy range of the Luftwaffe air bases in Sicily, Kesselring's strategy consisted of little more than saturating the island with bombs from dawn to dusk, with the advantage that there would be no lack of fighter cover. Heavily escorted Ju 87 and Ju 88 dive-bombers were to be used for pin-point bombing of vital targets, as in Crete.

Against the massed attacks Kesselring was able to hurl against Malta, the Royal Air Force could put into the air some ninety aircraft of all types, including two squadrons of Spitfires and one of Hurricanes. These fighters and a few scattered anti-aircraft guns had successfully repulsed bombing raids by the Italians since 1940, but the island defences were quite inadequate when faced with a determined offensive; and reinforcements could, of course, only be brought from Great Britain by aircraft carriers, with the risk of heavy losses. But in spite of its apparent vulnerability to air attack Malta could be defended, for the simple reason that it was a natural fortress, honeycombed with underground barracks, stores and even hangars. It was possible for Kesselring to put the island out of action, but only if he had sufficient time—and aircraft—to crack the hard outer shell.

The Malta Blitz began on 2nd April, 1942. Day after day, waves of bombers escorted by fighters took off from their Sicilian bases and within minutes were over Malta; day after day the bombs rained down. The defending fighters were in the air from morning until night, often only ten or twelve at a time being available to intercept the raiders. The airfields became pitted with hundreds of craters, diving Stukas turned the harbour into a shambles of wrecked and sunken ships, but Malta never failed to take its toll of German and Italian bombers, until Kesselring found that his offensive was fast becoming another Battle of Britain on a smaller scale. He could inflict serious damage on Malta—perhaps put the island out of action for good—but in the attempt he was allowing Luftflotte 2 to waste itself away. The bombardment continued without respite, but Kesselring doubted if success was going to be worth the cost.

He pressed Hitler to take the opportunity of following his air assault with an invasion by airborne forces.

By 8th April Malta had endured 2,000 air raids. Far beneath the chalky surface that erupted daily to the explosions of hundreds of bombs, many of the defenders and inhabitants of the island lived an unreal, troglodyte existence, tending the wounded overcrowding the hospital wards, working night and day to keep the scanty fighter force in action, hurrying ammunition forward to the overworked anti-aircraft guns. All refuelling of aircraft had to be tediously carried out by hand from Jerricans, there was a scarcity of spare parts and an acute shortage of ammunition. Supplies of food soon became so short that Lord Gort, remembered as commander of the B.E.F. at Dunkirk, and Governor of Malta at the height of the bombardment, had been compelled to impose severe rationing; the defenders were obliged to work and fight on a few olives and figs, a portion of bully beef and a quarter of a pound of bread a day. And still the martyrdom of Malta went on, while the bombs rained down, the flat-roofed houses of picturesque Valetta crumbled into ruins and the fighters rocked and swayed over the cratered runways to take the air against the masses of enemy aircraft darkening the Mediterranean skies.

Then, on 26th May, Rommel called for a heavy air assault to support his attack on Tobruk, thus bringing a temporary relief to Malta. Kesselring hurriedly transferred every available dive-bomber from Greece and Crete to North Africa, and for good measure threw in all the Sicilian-based aircraft that could be spared. Following the tried and trusted Blitzkrieg technique, the Stukas blasted a passage through the Tobruk defences and within hours the Afrika Korps armour was rumbling into the fortress. Rommel pressed eagerly on to Sidi Barrani and then El Alamein, where he came to a standstill with only thirty tanks left fit for action; Kesselring returned to his exhausting offensive against the rhinoceros-like hide of Malta and more wastage of men and machines.

Unexpectedly, Hitler was persuaded to agree that an invasion of Malta should be at least attempted. Code-named *Hercules*, it was to be undertaken by a joint force of German and Italian parachute troops, supported by three divisions of Italian infantry flown in by gliders and large transport aircraft. A month later, when the island was obviously reeling and ripe for capture, Hitler changed his mind and postponed *Hercules*, saying that the transports were more urgently needed in Russia. To the despair of Kesselring, a few weeks later the Fuehrer postponed the invasion of Malta again, this time with the explanation that it would have to wait until after Rommel had conquered Egypt.

But there was little prospect of an early German victory on the Nile. After taking Tobruk, Rommel had been rewarded for his success with a field-marshal's baton, but he would have been happier to receive the supplies and reinforcements he so urgently needed. The British forces in Egypt were rapidly gaining in strength, thanks to the flow of tanks and guns beginning to pour in from America. Also, an eccentric but brilliant new commander named Sir Bernard Law Montgomery had arrived in the desert, full of confidence that he would soon "knock Rommel for six" and then "tidy up the battlefield". Montgomery, a man who could be greatly admired and intensely disliked at one and the same time, surprised the tired Eighth Army with his self-assurance and boundless energy; he firmly repulsed Rommel's probing attacks with the minimum of casualties, while briskly informing his troops that they would never again have to attack without the adequate means to do so. He could afford to wait until he had a vastly superior army to the Afrika Korps in both quality and quantity, but when he was certain of his strength he would strike, and when that day came Rommel would not reign long in Africa.

With a heavy heart, Kesselring resumed his air offensive against Malta. In the August, a determined effort was made to relieve the besieged island by a large convoy from Britain, escorted by the battleships *Nelson* and *Rodney*, seven cruisers, thirty-two destroyers and four aircraft carriers. All the available Luftwaffe forces in the Mediterranean were hurled against this vital fleet; after four days and nights of continuous bombing the aircraft carrier *Eagle*, two cruisers and seven merchant ships had been sunk and two other cruisers and the oil tanker *Ohio* badly damaged. Despite unceasing air and E-boat attacks, three cargo ships laden with precious supplies of food and ammunition fought through to Malta, and the battered *Ohio* was later towed into Valetta. Also, as Kesselring soon discovered, the carriers had succeeded in flying off their Spitfire squadrons, which were soon operating from Malta. Thereafter, the Luftwaffe air superiority in the Mediterranean theatre began to decline, and most of Rommel's supply ships were sunk during September. When he complained that he could do nothing without petrol, Hitler merely assured him that all would be well. "Don't worry," said the Fuehrer, confidently. "I mean to give Africa all the support needed. Never fear, we are going to get to Alexandria all right."

The air offensive against Malta had to be suspended in the late summer of 1942 because of heavy losses and the necessity to provide increased air support for Rommel in North Africa. Hermann Goering, who had passed away most of the winter enjoying the Italian sunshine and carefully avoided taking any part in the Malta Blitz, arrived in Sicily to blame the Luftwaffe fighter force for failing to protect the bombers, just as he had done during the Battle of Britain; any criticism, any excuse, sufficed for the bemedalled Reichsmarschall provided it lifted the responsibility from his own shoulders. In fact, he had not bothered to follow the Mediterranean air operations with more than a casual interest, and knew next to nothing about the conditions under which the weary Luftwaffe was struggling to remain in action.

One man, Hans Joachim Marseille, was a shining example of the German fighter force in North Africa. Acknowledged by Adolf Galland to be "the unrivalled virtuoso among the fighter pilots of the Second World War", Marseille had joined Jagdeschwader 27 in late 1940, and within months of the group landing in Africa in April, 1941, became prominent in despatches for shooting down large numbers of enemy aircraft. By the time Rommel's armour had reached El Alamein, Marseille—at the age of twenty-two—had over 100 confirmed victories and been awarded the highest German and Italian decorations, including the Knight's Cross with Oak Leaves and Swords and the Italian Gold Medal for Bravery. With the exception of Rommel, at the height of his fame Marseille was probably the most discussed and publicised figure in the desert; to the German press he was known as the "Star of the Desert", the unequalled, invincible "African Eagle".

On 30th September, 1942, Marseille was returning from a sweep in the Cairo area when he was heard to say over the radio: "There is smoke in my cockpit!" The pilots flying on either side saw him slide back his ventilator, releasing a cloud of white vapour; as the Bf 109s flew on, the vapour thickened into black smoke, tinged with red flame. "I can't see," Marseille kept saying, then, later "I can't hold out any more." He was seen to roll the aircraft over on its back and attempt to bale out, but he was too late. All the time, the Bf 109 had been rapidly losing height, and Marseille was killed instantly when it crashed four miles inside the German lines. In the year of his glory, he had flown no less than 388 sorties and destroyed 158 enemy aircraft; when he died he was worn out by too much fighting against increasing odds, physically and mentally exhausted—but undefeated. Joachim Marseille was an ace of aces in the true spirit of Boelcke and Richthofen, but he was also a typical fighter pilot in the desert war; one of those whom Goering, in his sublime ignorance, dared to criticise for inefficiency.

General Montgomery opened his mighty counter-offensive at El Alamein on 23rd October, after a tremendous artillery barrage by over a thousand guns. For eight days the Afrika Korps resisted the great weight of men and material, then Rommel decided to withdraw before his armour was destroyed piecemeal. He needed a free hand to retreat as he liked, make a stand when he could, and let the Afrika Korps live to fight another day. Rommel therefore sent his aide, Hauptmann Berndt, to Hitler's headquarters two thousand miles away in East Prussia, with a summary of the critical situation and an urgent request for "complete freedom of movement"—beginning with a tactical withdrawal into the Fuka positions to the west. "Make our position quite clear to the Fuehrer; tell him that the African theatre of war is probably lost for us," said Rommel, then left Berndt and drove back at high speed to the front line.

Hitler's answer arrived the following day in a memorable radio message. "In the situation in which you now find yourself," it stated, "there can be no other consideration save that of holding fast, of not retreating one step, of throwing every gun and every man into the battle. . . . It would not be the first time in history that the stronger will has prevailed against the stronger battalions of the enemy. You can show your troops no other way than that which leads to victory or death." Without making any attempt to find out exactly what was happening in the desert, Hitler thus immobilised Rommel as a commander and condemned the Afrika Korps to complete destruction. "It will be the end of our army," Rommel's Chief of Staff, Oberst Westphal, told his commander.

Westphal proved to be a true prophet of disaster. A soldier born and bred to unqualified obedience like Erwin Rommel could not ignore the Fuehrer's order, and so the British offensive at El Alamein, crowned by Hitler's "victory or death" command, broke up the German forces in North Africa. On 8th November an Allied Expeditionary Force of 140,000 men under General Dwight Eisenhower landed in Morocco and Algiers, and within seventy-six hours controlled 1,300 miles of coastline. From the main Luftwaffe bases in Sicily—Catania, Comiso, Trapani, and Gerbini—the German fighter and bomber arms tried vainly to stem the great avalanche of Allied ships and aircraft, pressing home attack after attack regardless of losses. Luftflotte 2, already wasted away over Malta, was reduced to a skeleton of its former self by the end of the year; Fliegerkorps II was often forced to operate with Geschwader of only ten or twelve aircraft left in action; and Fliegerkorps X, decimated during the summer months, had to be thrown into the furnace again, flying at extreme range from airfields in Crete.

With Montgomery advancing from the east against Rommel, and Eisenhower's Anglo-American army pressing slowly but surely forward on the road to Tunis, the Afrika Korps became caught in the closing pincers, a helpless target for the unopposed British bomber squadrons ranging far and wide over the open desert. The "carpet bombing" technique practised with such success by the Luftwaffe during the Spanish civil war proved no less successful when used against German targets six years later. Casualties were heavy, many vehicles were destroyed and even Rommel and his staff occasionally had to jump for cover into slit trenches. "What can we do in face of this order from Hitler?" was the question asked of Rommel again and again. "I cannot order you to disobey it," he would reply wearily; the iron hand of the Fuehrer lay heavily on the German desert headquarters.

But Hitler or no Hitler, the Afrika Korps was relentlessly pushed back; by 13th November the defeated army had retreated six hundred and fifty miles. Fighting a losing battle, Rommel continued to plead urgently for petrol—the petrol denied to him because Malta remained in British hands and Allied air and sea supremacy in the Mediterranean was complete. From Kesselring, designated Commander-in-Chief South and therefore Rommel's nominal superior, came only vague promises of assistance; he was committed to establishing a strong bridgehead in Tunis and thus preventing that city with its important harbour from falling into Allied hands. In fact, against such overwhelming Allied opposition the Tunis bridgehead was a hopeless undertaking from the beginning, and it irked Rommel to find that a quarter of a million German and Italian troops, equipped with the most modern weapons, were being thrown into the Tunis area to try and recover a battle already lost.

At the end of November, Rommel flew back to Germany and told Hitler that the situation in North Africa was hopeless; it was time to evacuate the Afrika Korps and save it to fight again in Italy. As Rommel had feared, his suggestion exploded Hitler into a violent rage. He shouted that Rommel was a defeatist, and his troops cowards who deserved to be "put up against a wall and shot". Then, unexpectedly, the Fuehrer calmed down, apologised, and sent for Goering. "Do anything you like," he told the Reichsmarschall, "but see that Rommel is supplied with all he needs."

Taking Rommel with him, Goering returned to Rome. Three days passed before Rommel realised that the vast, flamboyant chief of the Luftwaffe had nothing to offer him, no interest in North Africa, or indeed anything except statues and paintings. Rommel talked of supplies and the desperate need for air reinforcements in the desert; Goering boasted that he had a special train filled with valuable sculpture and pictures. His tie secured by a large emerald, his fat fingers sparkling with enormous diamonds, the Reichsmarschall was a grotesque, horrifying figure to the soldierly, austere Rommel, who finally flew back to Africa in disgust, a sickened and sadly disillusioned man.

"The abuse of greatness is when it disjoins remorse from power!" says Brutus in Shakespeare's *Julius Caesar*. Certainly there was no remorse in the heart of Adolf Hitler; no remorse for the dying Afrika Korps, no compassion for the men who had fought for him in the burning sands of the Western Desert. He cared nothing for Germany, the German people or the German armies; to Hitler, human life was expendable. The Fuehrer had an answer to every problem. Rommel was proving troublesome and the Afrika Korps almost decimated? Then let Goering deal with Rommel in his own inimitable way and forget the Afrika Korps. Malta seemed to be too hard a nut for the Luftwaffe to crack? Then let the British keep Malta. The Tunis bridgehead could not be held? Then let it be held until not a man remained alive. And so on and so on, question and answer in the strange, twilight mind of Adolf Hitler.

Unfortunately, in that winter of 1942 Hitler had one problem that refused to be solved, a grey spectre that night and day haunted the bleak headquarters in East Prussia. Far away in Russia, the greatest defeat in German history was at hand; the Fuehrer had ordered another German army to stand fast, and thousands of men were dying in the snow. "Not one step back!"—the whim of a megalomaniac who had convinced a whole nation that he was always right. "No retreat!" And the place of this great disaster—the cemetery of the living dead ever to remain a monument to the strategy of Adolf Hitler—was a doomed, encircled city on the Volga.

Stalingrad.

CHAPTER XVII

AIRLIFT TO DISASTER: STALINGRAD, 1943

THE German summer offensive on the Eastern Front in 1942 was initially crowned with success because the average Wehrmacht soldier possessed the ability to endure appalling hardships and see his comrades killed in hundreds all around him without losing his own unswerving faith in Fuehrer and Fatherland. The German forces in Russia had not only survived the fearful winter of 1941 without adequate equipment or clothing, but also managed to resist the Red Army until the spring mud brought a measure of rest and peace to the battlefield. Two great armies had met, suffered terrible losses for nearly twelve months, held fast, and with the approach of another summer were completely exhausted. Hitler, forced at last to face grim reality and accept the fact that he could not conquer Russia with a single Blitzkrieg campaign, decided that in 1942 he would mount a less ambitious offensive; concentrating most of his forces in the south, he aimed to capture Stalingrad on the Volga and also the vital Caucasus oil fields.

To swell out the ranks sadly thinned by 1,168,000 casualties suffered the previous year, the Fuehrer demanded fresh troops from Germany's so-called allies, and by the spring of 1942 he had managed to round up as cannon fodder for his summer offensive no less than fifty-two non-German divisions, including ten Hungarian, six Italian and five Rumanian divisions for the southern sector of the front. As always, Hitler easily became intoxicated by numbers and refused to listen to his generals when they argued that the fate of the offensive was being staked on too many "foreign" divisions with obsolete equipment and questionable fighting abilities. He could not afford to be selective with the troops at his disposal. German divisions would be used to spearhead the attack and Hitler reasoned that, good or bad, the armies of the satellite countries should at least be able to hold the ground already taken for them.

The German weakness in the air on the Eastern Front was a

very different problem. Early in 1942, Luftflotte 2 had been transferred to the Mediterranean theatre of operations, and a number of day and night squadrons had been withdrawn to reinforce the scanty defences of the Third Reich. Against this heavy depletion of Luftwaffe forces, the Soviet air strength was increasing by leaps and bounds; in 1942 over 2,000 Hurricane, Tomahawk and Airacobra fighters arrived in Russia from the United States and Great Britain. Also, the latest Soviet-built aircraft were of greatly improved design and performance, the new Lavochkin LA-5 and Yakovlev YAK-9 fighters achieving parity with the Messerschmitt Bf 109G, and the IL-2 Sturmovik, in its modernised version featuring heavy armament and rocket-firing equipment, far superior to the Ju 87 as a tactical air-support weapon. Thus, at a time when the Luftwaffe on the Eastern Front was already operating at an intensity beyond its resources, Goering had to provide air support for a full-scale offensive; this he managed to do only by scraping the bottom of the barrel and finally raising a concentration of some 1,000 aircraft of all types—about half the total Luftwaffe resources in Russia.

Hitler's 1942 summer offensive on the eastern front was launched at the end of June, and for a time sheer weight of numbers did, in fact, bring a series of victories, troops of von Paulus' Sixth Army reaching the Volga just north of Stalingrad on 23rd August, only two days after the swastika flag had been triumphantly hoisted on Mount Elbrus, the highest peak in the Caucasus mountains. But having reached those objectives the German resources in men and material proved to be stretched to the limit, and, inevitably, within a week the advance was creaking to a standstill. The air operations were intensive but to little purpose, neither side achieving local ascendancy. The Soviet Air Force remained largely concentrated in the Moscow area, mistakenly expecting a new offensive in the direction of the Russian capital; and the Luftwaffe forces lacked the strength to exploit their temporary advantage to the full.

Hitler, enraged that his offensive was petering out before the winter, reacted with characteristic violence. He dismissed Feldmarschall List, the commander of Army Group A, and later also sacked General Halder, Chief of the General Staff, replacing that unfortunate officer with a comparatively unknown general named Kurt Zeitzler. With the troops of the Sixth Army soon fighting in the streets of Stalingrad—nearly three hundred miles from the original front line in the spring of 1942— Zeitzler realised at once that the sweeping, thinly held flank would be broken if the Red Army mounted a counter-offensive, resulting in the encirclement of the Sixth Army. He therefore suggested that the Stalingrad front be withdrawn westwards to eliminate the highly dangerous situation that had arisen, reminding the Fuehrer that the perilous sector was largely held by unreliable Rumanian, Italian and Hungarian divisions. Hitler had only one answer : "I will not leave the Volga!"

October came, and with it increasing Soviet resistance in the Caucasus and also on the Stalingrad front. The city itself was an inferno, the Germans suffering staggering losses in the bitter street fighting that raged without respite. Again and again Hitler was pressed to withdraw the Sixth Army before it was too late, but he was determined not to give ground. "Where the German soldier sets foot, there he remains!" he stated in a speech to the German people. Even Mussolini, pleading for the transfer of Wehrmacht divisions from Russia to the Mediterranean, could not move the Fuehrer; he had no intention of relinquishing either Tunisia or Stalingrad.

On 19th and 20th November, as the Russian winter began to close in on the Sixth Army, three powerful Soviet armoured spearheads broke through the Rumanian line on a huge front north and south of Stalingrad, and within five days twenty-two German divisions were surrounded. From Stalingrad, von Paulus wirelessed the grave news, adding that all his supply lines had been cut and he was desperately short of winter clothing, food, petrol and ammunition. Hitler radioed back a direct order to hold Stalingrad at all costs; he hoped to supply the Sixth Army by air until it could be relieved. At the same time, the Fuehrer directed a powerful new formation—Army Group Don, under von Manstein—to strike from the south-west against the Russian forces encircling Stalingrad. But he refused to allow any attempt by von Paulus to break out of the city to the west and link up with Army Group Don; instead, he declared Stalingrad to be a hedgehog, a so-called fortress. Kurt Zeitzler, backed by von Manstein, again begged Hitler to authorise a break-out by the Sixth Army. Again that harsh voice hurled back the same unyielding answer : "I will not with-draw from the Volga !"

The stage was thus set for the entrance of Hermann Goering and his once powerful Luftwaffe. On 24th November the Reichsmarschall was present at a situation conference at Hitler's headquarters when Zeitzler stated that the Sixth Army had requested a minimum of 750 tons of supplies a day flown into the Stalingrad ring. It was realised that such a figure was beyond the capacity of the Luftwaffe or any other air force, and the General Staff had decided on a minimum of 300 tons a day. Zeitzler doubted if the Luftwaffe could raise sufficient transport aircraft to undertake the job; what had Goering to say about it ?

"Well ?" demanded Hitler, looking directly at Goering.

It is doubtful if Goering knew anything about the state of the Luftwaffe in Russia. For over a year, he had drifted lazily between Berlin and Rome; occasionally amusing himself in Vienna, always seeking refuge from the grim reality of a world at war. His star had waned in the Nazi hierarchy; he no longer had any friends, only associates who treated him with contempt or openly ignored him. He was a worried, lonely and dispirited man, hiding behind the inevitable mask of joviality and wanting desperately to be left alone with his jewels and art treasures. But the shackles of responsibility still weighed heavily upon him. He was Hermann Goering, Commander-in-Chief of the Luft-waffe.

"The task is a difficult one," said Goering. "Nevertheless, the Luftwaffe will carry it out."

Hitler turned to his Chief of Staff. "You see, Zeitzler? It can be done."

Zeitzler shook his head. "It would need at least 200 planes a day," he commented.

"The Luftwaffe can do it !" insisted Goering, flushing crimson with anger. He had spoken with scarcely a moment for thought, and, as always, had immediately convinced himself that he was right. In retrospect, one can only feel surprise that Hitler, after so many disappointments, was still willing to believe him.

Kurt Zeitzler remained certain in his belief that it would be impossible to supply the Sixth Army from the air. Even

Jeschonnek, that faithful disciple of the Fuehrer, doubted if it could be done and said as much to Goering. Airily, the Reichsmarschall waved all objections aside. Had not the Luftwaffe already succeeded in supplying 100,000 men from the air at Demiansk? Jeschonnek reminded Goering that even so heavy losses had been incurred, and pointed out that since the Demiansk operation much of the depleted Luftwaffe transport fleet had been committed in Africa—a fact apparently overlooked by his superior. Angrily, Goering snapped back, "In the discussions with the Fuehrer I order you to say that Stalingrad can and will be supplied from the air."

A worried and bewildered man, Jeschonnek made a last attempt to ease his troubled conscience. To Hitler, he said: "The Reichsmarschall has instructed me to say that the Luftwaffe will fly in the Stalingrad supplies, but—"

Impatiently, the Fuehrer interrupted him. "Very good. I'm glad to hear it. Of late, Jeschonnek, you seem to think of nothing but ifs and buts."

Hans Jeschonnek was silent. The oracle of the Third Reich had spoken; and the word of the oracle was law.

The machinery of the Luftwaffe General Staff ground into action, suitably encouraged by the assurances of Goering and the confidence of Hitler. Wolfram von Richthofen, commander of Luftflotte 4 and the man entrusted with the task of organising the great Stalingrad airlift had selected two main supply bases, one in Tazinskaya and the other in Morosovskaya, and stores of all kinds were soon pouring in to these two airfields. Transport aircraft followed: 200 of the ubiquitous old Junkers Ju 52s; about 100 converted Heinkel He 111 bombers; and twenty obsolete Junkers Ju 86s. Later, a few four-engined Focke-Wulf Fw 200 maritime reconnaissance aircraft were transferred from the Atlantic to swell the numbers, and even the double-motored Heinkel He 177s that had haunted Udet's dreams turned up in Russia as supply planes. Thus, on paper Richthofen had at his disposal nearly 400 transport aircraft. In fact, the terrible Russian winter ensured that only about half that number were serviceable at any one time.

The Stalingrad airlift got under way in December, 1942, flying into the four airfields available inside the ring, Pitomnik,

Bassargine, Cumrak and Goroditsche. As these were defended only by the Luftwaffe remnants that had survived the great Stalingrad air battles of the autumn—two Gruppen of fighters and a decimated Stuka Gruppe—many of the heavily laden Ju 52s and He 111s fell victim to the Red Air Force. Others crashed when attempting to land on the icy runways. Still others were lost while trying to plough through heavy snow-storms. Returning laden with wounded to their bases, the survivors often found that the depot airfields had been bombed into a shambles of burning stores and cratered runways in their absence. Engines refused to start in the bitter cold; windscreens froze over and thick ice formations on wings and tailplanes frequently brought disaster. Aircraft after aircraft crashed on arrival in the Stalingrad ring, and the receiving airfields soon became littered with derelict machines. The big Fw 200s and He 177s proved particularly unsuitable for operations in Russia, due to maintenance problems and the lack of experienced crews.

Defeated by the weather, the great flying distances involved and Russian air superiority, the Stalingrad airlift never had even a remote chance of success. The promised 300 tons of supplies a day was never achieved; only once did von Richthofen's transport fleet approach the target, when 154 aircraft flew in 289 tons of food and ammunition. Between 22nd November, 1942 and 16th January, 1943, some 5,300 tons of supplies were flown into the Stalingrad ring, a daily average of 100 tons which amounted to nothing more than starvation rations for the besieged Sixth Army. Before the end of 1942 the German troops in the gutted city were existing on two slices of bread and a mess tin of watery soup a day; by 10th January, 1943, over 140,000 men had been killed in action or died of hunger, cold and disease.

That same day, the Red Army opened a final offensive against the German forces in the Stalingrad ring with an artillery bombardment from five thousand guns. Richthofen did his best to keep the airlift going at full spate, but it was an impossible task, despite a direct order from Hitler to Erhard Milch that 300 tons of supplies must be flown in to Stalingrad every day regardless of losses. Milch arrived in Russia aglow with confidence, his agile brain teeming with the imposing figures of transport aircraft supposedly available, only to find that barely a third of the numbers were serviceable. Aghast at the state of Richthofen's fleet—only about a hundred aircraft were in flying condition—Milch returned to Berlin, and, surprisingly, managed to find another 300 machines. But his efforts made no difference to the outcome; the Russian climate and the Red Air Force continued to exact a terrible toll.

By 24th January the Soviet forces had driven through the Stalingrad ring and captured the receiving airfields, which had been under artillery fire for over a week. An emergency airstrip at Stalingradski was used for a few days, but finally this also had to be abandoned. Under fire from Russian tanks, the last two Ju 52s, packed with wounded, began to move; propellers which had never stopped turning spun faster and then vanished into misty blurs as the throttles were opened out to full revolutions. Tattered, skeleton-like men crowded around the big machines, fighting like mad beasts to grasp at the last chance of escape from the graveyard of Stalingrad. Rising ponderously, the first overloaded aircraft struck the ground, bounced, then struggled at last into the air. The second Ju 52 swung around, ragged figures rolling into the snow beneath the wings, the three engines filling the air with the thunder of their power. Imploring arms stretched out desperately towards the aircraft as it sped along the ground, discarding those who could no longer retain a hold. Then, abruptly, a ragged line of bullet holes jumped along the fuselage of the Ju 52; it staggered, struck the ground, and burst into flames. Like a funeral pyre for the doomed Sixth Army, a tower of greasy black smoke wreathed slowly towards the sky.

Mercilessly, Hitler prolonged the agony to the bitter end. Von Paulus radioed desperately : "Troops without ammunition or food ... Effective command no longer possible ... 18,000 wounded without any supplies or dressings or drugs ... Further defence senseless. Collapse inevitable. Army requests immediate permission to surrender in order to save lives of remaining troops." To this appeal, as to all others, the Fuehrer gave the same answer. "Surrender is forbidden," he replied. "Sixth Army will hold their positions to the last man and the last round and by their heroic endurance will make an unforgettable contribution towards the establishment of a defensive front and the salvation of the Western world."

No retreat. The Sixth Army had been abandoned; it was accepted as dead, and about to be buried. A few Ju 52s were still flying over Stalingrad, dropping supplies by parachute, a gallant, wasted gesture by the decimated transport crews of the Luftwaffe. On 28th January, their Commander-in-Chief sent his own radio message to the living corpses huddled in the ruins of Stalingrad. "The fight put up by the Sixth Army will go down in history," declared the Reichsmarschall, "and future generations will speak proudly of a Langemarck of daredevilry, an Alcazar of tenacity, a Narvik of courage and a Stalingrad of self-sacrifice."

Two days later, von Paulus wirelessed Hitler: "Final collapse cannot be delayed more than twenty-four hours." The same evening, Goering again took the opportunity to display his skill as an orator. Broadcasting to the German people, he said: "A thousand years hence Germans will speak of this battle with reverence and awe, and that in spite of everything Germany's ultimate victory was decided there. . . . In years to come it will be said of the heroic battle on the Volga : When you come to Germany, say you have seen us lying at Stalingrad, as our honour and our leaders ordained that we should, for the greater glory of Germany. . . ."

To Hitler, actions apparently spoke louder than words. He bestowed promotions and decorations with unexpected generosity on the officers in encircled Stalingrad; and, greatest honour of all, a field-marshal's baton was symbolically handed to von Paulus. If Hitler could not have a victory, he was determined to have a glorious defeat. He wanted to invoke another Teutonic legend : an army dying to the last man for the Fatherland : a monument to German youth in the snows of Russia; a dead field-marshal on the Volga. "There is no record in military history of a German Field Marshal being taken prisoner," he remarked drily to General Jodl. In Berlin, Goebbels was hard at work supervising the Wagnerian "funeral ceremony" for the Sixth Army, the mounting of a symbolic catafalque, the hanging of black velvet mourning banners for the men who were not yet dead.

When the moment came for the last act of the Battle of Stalingrad, von Paulus ruined everything, like a temperamental star who refuses to play his part. On the last day of January the

Russians reached the cellar used as German headquarters—and Paulus and his staff surrendered. Hitler's anger knew no bounds. "What is life?" he shouted. "Life is the Nation. The individual must die anyway. Beyond the life of the individual is the Nation. But how can anyone be afraid of this moment of death, with which he can free himself from this misery, if his duty doesn't chain him to this Vale of Tears . . . ? So many people have to die, and then a man like that besmirches the heroism of so many others at the last minute. He could have freed himself from all sorrow and ascended into eternity and national immortality, but he prefers to go to Moscow !"

The muffled drums rolled in Berlin and all theatres and cinemas were closed for four days of national mourning. And for a good and sufficient reason. Of the 285,000 men of the doomed Sixth Army, some 90,000 had been taken prisoner, including twenty-four generals; the remainder lay for ever amid the ruins of Stalingrad. The Luftwaffe had lost 536 transport aircraft, over a hundred fighters and 2,200 aircrew. Nearly half of the machines scraped together for the German summer offensive in Russia—a quarter of the total Luftwaffe resources on the Eastern Front or almost the strength of an entire Luftflotte— had been destroyed. Not since the Battle of Britain had German air power suffered such a disastrous defeat.

In the air and on the ground, Stalingrad had been the turning point of the war in Russia, just as Alamein had ended the German dream of conquest in Africa. Slowly but surely, the edifice of the Third Reich was crumbling around the heads of those who had tried to build on sand, and, having failed, were unwilling to admit their failure. Only Goering, idly fingering his jewels in the solitude of Karinhall, knew very well that after Stalingrad he would always be Hitler's scapegoat; twenty years association in a common struggle could not be expected to survive such a travesty of leadership in time of war.

By March, 1943, the end was in sight for the German forces in Tunisia. Trapped between the Allied First and Eighth Armies, the Afrika Korps faced piecemeal destruction; and still Rommel was pleading desperately for petrol and other supplies. Despite overwhelming Allied air superiority in the Mediterranean, the Luftwaffe again had to fly in supplies to encircled troops—the agony of Stalingrad repeated on a smaller scale in North Africa. Day after weary day, the laden Junkers Ju 52s and huge Messerschmitt Me 323s struggled out over the sea from their bomb-ravaged Sicilian airfields and met destruction. Comments Adolf Galland: ". . . The performance of the transport crews is beyond praise. Even if they succeeded in getting their planes with the urgently required load safely into the cauldron, they were exposed to uninterrupted bombing and low-level attacks while refuelling and unloading. . . . The devastating decimation of the Luftwaffe on such forced missions was nothing new, but here, because of the extended duration, we used up the very substance of our air force."

The wholesale slaughter of German transport aircraft reached staggering proportions. In a single month 200 machines were shot down, destroyed because they lacked adequate fighter cover. Jeschonnek and Milch cast their eyes around desperately for the fighters they needed in every theatre of operations, but they did not exist; in Tunisia only two fighter Gruppen had survived the Allied deluge, and these were on the verge of being swallowed up in the inferno. Oddly enough, some new types of aircraft for the Luftwaffe turned up during the final stages of the North African campaign, such as the Henschel Hs 129 close-support bomber and the Messerschmitt Me 323 troop carrier, but they met with only limited success in their particular roles and affected the scarcity of fighters not at all.

Limited success; the epitaph of so many new German aircraft in the Second World War. The heavily armoured Henschel Hs 129, with a nose battery of forward-firing cannon and machine-guns, was supposedly to replace the outdated Ju 87 Stuka as a dive-bomber and tank destroyer, but in North Africa it suffered from extensive teething troubles and proved to be only about 20 m.p.h. faster than the Ju 87. Indeed, the Hs 129 soon had to be withdrawn from service and replaced by the improved Ju 87G-1, mounting twin 37 mm. guns under the wings; it eventually was used in some numbers on the Russian front.

Typically German in conception, the Messerschmitt Me 323 transport was one of the largest aeroplanes ever built, with a wing span of 181 ft., six radial engines and a ten-wheel outrigged undercarriage. A development of the Me 321 glider, the Me 323 could carry up to 130 troops or 21,500 lb. of freight—

three times the capacity of the Ju 52—and with adequate fighter protection would have been a valuable asset in any air force. However, the great size and slow speed of the unescorted Me 323s flying supplies to Tunisia made them easy victims for the Allied fighters, and on one occasion eighteen out of a force of twenty of the gigantic machines were shot down.

On 7th May, 1943, after the back of the Luftwaffe transport fleet in the Mediterranean had been broken, the desert war came to an end when troops of the British 7th Armoured Division entered Tunis. "Europe is being defended at Tunis!" Hitler had stated. "There will be no evacuation!" Too late, much too late; General von Arnim capitulated, with what remained of the shattered Afrika Korps. Over 250,000 men were captured, the strength of four divisions. As for the Luftwaffe, it had been knocked out of the skies in the Mediterranean theatre. Of 200 bombers available at the beginning of the campaign, only about forty remained in action, and these were soon to be wasted away on unescorted suicide attacks on Malta and other heavily defended targets.

Within days, hundreds of bombs were raining down on Sicily. Adolf Galland arrived on the island to try and breathe fresh life into his exhausted fighter units, but in the face of such over-whelming Allied air supremacy there was little he could do. New fighters arrived and were blasted into fragments before they could take to the air; replacement pilots were killed without a chance to open fire at an enemy machine. From Kesselring down to the infantryman cowering in his foxhole, every German soldier knew that the Battle of Sicily was at hand. And Sicily was but the stepping stone to the Italian mainland.

On 10th July, Galland returned to Berlin for an interview with Hermann Goering. The Reichsmarschall greeted him without enthusiasm. "You must return immediately," he said. "The Allies landed today in Sicily."

The last phase in the Mediterranean war had begun.

CHAPTER XVIII

"YOU CAN CALL ME MEIER!" COLOGNE, 1943

CLUSTERED amid the tall pines of East Prussia, the gloomy buildings of Hitler's headquarters at Rastenburg seemed as cheerless and forbidding as ever in the faint sunlight that filtered through the trees. In the conference bunker since noon on that last day of May, 1942, the Fuehrer had listened to the latest situation reports from his naval and military spokesmen. Now Hitler faced the Chief of Staff of the Luftwaffe. "The Luftwaffe, General Jeschonnek?" he asked quietly, and sat back to hear the daily report of German air operations in every theatre of war.

Hans Jeschonnek fiddled uneasily with his papers. "Cologne, my Fuehrer," he said hesitantly, "there was an R.A.F. attack on Cologne last night."

Hitler said nothing. "A fairly heavy attack," added Jeschonnek.

"How heavy?" The familiar harsh voice rasped out the question as if it were an insult.

"According to preliminary reports, we estimate that two hundred enemy aircraft penetrated our defences," replied Jeschonnek, nervously. "The damage is heavy. We are still waiting for final estimates."

Hitler shook in his seat with sudden fury. "You are still waiting for final estimates?" he shouted. "And the Luftwaffe thinks that there were two hundred enemy aircraft? The Luftwaffe was probably asleep last night! But I have not been asleep. I stay awake when one of my cities is under fire!" Rising to his feet, he screamed, "And I thank the Almighty that I can rely on my Gauleiter, even if the Luftwaffe deceives me! Let me tell you what Gauleiter Grohe has to say! There were a thousand or more English aircraft—do you hear? A thousand, twelve hundred, maybe more!"

Jeschonnek stood unmoving, the storm breaking over him. "Goering is not here; of course not," went on Hitler, with biting sarcasm. But when the Reichsmarschall, hurriedly summoned by Bodenschatz, did arrive, his pitiable, sweating presence made no difference; indeed, Hitler refused to shake his hand and pointedly ignored him. The Fuehrer knew, and Goering and Jeschonnek knew, that an attack on a German city by two hundred bombers would have been a serious matter. An air raid by a thousand bombers constituted disaster.

The first 1,000-bomber attack by the Royal Air Force on a German city, carried out on the night of 30th-31st May, 1942, and directed against Cologne, rang up the curtain on a new phase of the air war over Europe—systematic area bombing on a large scale. Three possible targets had originally been selected —Cologne, Essen and Hamburg—and it was the misfortune of Cologne that favourable weather over the city on the decisive night marked it for destruction. In order to mount the massive attack, every available aircraft in R.A.F. Bomber Command had been used, together with machines borrowed from Coastal Command and the Fleet Air Arm; a total of 1,047 aircraft flying from fifty-two different airfields. The raid lasted ninety minutes, and in that time 1,455 tons of bombs were dropped, turning the centre of Cologne into a waste of rubble. Some 450 people were killed and 45,000 rendered homeless, against a Bomber Command loss of thirty-nine aircraft.

The area bombing of Cologne by a thousand aircraft laid down an important milestone on the long, tragic road that had begun with the destruction of Guernica in 1937 and would end when Dresden was burned to ashes in 1945. Blow for blow, wholesale slaughter matched by wholesale slaughter; thus the hard path for R.A.F. Bomber Command and the Luftwaffe. Yet, during the early months of the war—and despite the air bombardment of Warsaw—R.A.F. bombing attacks were confined to military targets. Losses were heavy, particularly in the daylight raids on such heavily defended objectives as Wilhelmshaven and Heligoland, and results seldom of any importance. In comparison to what followed, most of these attacks amounted to little more than pin-pricks, being carried out in the main by twin-engined Blenheim, Wellington or Hampden medium bombers with a negligible bomb load and limited range. The larger Whitley bombers were restricted to so-called "nickelling" operations—the dropping of propaganda leaflets on the Third

Reich. With such small achievements Bomber Command had to rest content; Mr. Chamberlain had declared ". . . His Majesty's Government will never resort to the deliberate attacking of women and children, and other civilians, for purposes of mere terrorism."

Then came May, 1940, the end of the Chamberlain government and the swift rise to power of Winston Churchill. Three days of war in the Netherlands ended when the Heinkels of Kampfgeschwader 54 destroyed Rotterdam. The R.A.F. attacks increased in reprisal; German bombs fell on London during the Battle of Britain; and in return Bomber Command struck again and again at Berlin. The German pathfinder technique developed by Kampfgeschwader 100—the lightening of a city by incendiaries to guide the main force of bombers—brought a night of death and devastation to Coventry in November, 1940, when 400 people lost their lives, but Goering's Blitz on Britain was coming to an end. On 10th May, 1941, London was attacked in what proved to be the last great raid on the capital by the Luftwaffe; some 2,000 fires were started and 3,000 people killed or injured. Soon afterwards, most of Germany's bomber and fighter aircraft were withdrawn for service on the Russian and Mediterranean fronts.

During 1941, the R.A.F. night attacks on the Third Reich continued, but still with only moderate success. In fact, at that time Bomber Command lacked the technical equipment and the heavy bombers needed to mount a large-scale air offensive against Germany, though steady progress was being made in the right direction. The development of four-engined strategic bombers had been encouraged since 1935, and in due course three types emerged as a result of Air Ministry specification B12/36, which called for a monoplane bomber powered by four 1,500 h.p. radial engines. However, Bomber Command remained sadly neglected while Dowding's fighters strove for ascendancy in the Battle of Britain, and not until nearly seven years later did the ungainly Short Stirling and the Handley Page Halifax enter operational service. These aircraft, with a bomb load of 18,000 lb. and 14,500 lb. respectively, were later followed—and to some extent superseded—by the remarkable Avro Lancaster, easily the best heavy bomber to appear during the Second World War.

Evolved by way of the unsuccessful twin-engined Avro Manchester, the Lancaster was powered by four Rolls-Royce Merlin engines and could carry a bomb load of 14,000 lb. for over 1,000 miles. Fitted with special, bulged bomb doors, it could carry the 12,000 lb. "Tall-boy" bomb, and without doors the amazing 22,000 lb. "Grand Slam" invented by Barnes Neville Wallis. Undoubtedly a magnificent aircraft, the Lancaster symbolised the might of Bomber Command from 1942 to 1945 and more than any other British bomber was responsible for the air bombardment of the Third Reich. It was the epitome of the heavy bomber, ideal for use in major saturation attacks or striking at selected targets of vital importance. Lancasters won the battle of the Ruhr and brought the reality of air war to Berlin; but Lancasters were also used for the memorable Augsburg daylight raid, the breaching of the Mohne and Eder dams, and the sinking of the great battleship *Tirpitz* in Alten Fjord.

All these successes lay in the future when the first two Lancaster squadrons, Nos. 44 and 97, became operational on 2nd March, 1942. The British War Cabinet had already decided to launch an intensive air offensive against Germany's industrial towns, and appointed a new Commander-in-Chief of Bomber Command to carry out the task. A highly controversial figure even to this day, Air Marshal Arthur T. Harris was not alone in accepting responsibility for the area bombing directive, but he was a dedicated advocate of mass aerial bombardment as a method of waging war. Harris believed that area bombing would break civilian morale and so destroy Germany's capacity and will to resist. He knew that almost all Germany's towns were old, with narrow streets and wooden buildings and therefore highly inflammable; incendiary attack seemed to be the solution. Thus it was that Harris became a maker of German destruction, an exponent of total war, but whether he succeeded in breaking the spirit of the German civilian population is, on all the evidence, extremely doubtful.

In April, 1942, the new Lancasters were tested on a precision attack against the M.A.N. Diesel Works at Augsburg, carried out in daylight in the face of murderous heavy and light anti-aircraft fire. The twelve Lancasters flew in at low level, so low that the flak batteries were firing at point-blank range and hitting bombers and factory buildings with equal discrimination. The accurate bombing extensively damaged the vital diesel assembly shops, but seven Lancasters were lost to flak and fighter opposition; acceptable casualties for an occasional important attack, or so Churchill and Harris considered. Nevertheless, Bomber Command never attempted a repetition of the Augsburg daylight raid until 1945, when the Luftwaffe had been shot out of the German skies.

Meanwhile, the night area bombing offensive had been launched against the Third Reich with an attack on Lubeck by 234 aircraft. On the night of 28th-29th March, 1942, 144 tons of incendiaries and 160 tons of high explosive were dropped on this old Hanseatic port of doubtful military importance, destroying at least half of the town; over 1,000 houses, the famous cathedral, the art museum and twenty other public buildings were consumed in the sea of flames. Thirteen Bomber Command aircraft were lost, but the Lubeck raid proved conclusively that even a small force of bombers carrying a high proportion of incendiaries could lay waste a city of moderate size.

The immediate reaction of Hitler to the Lubeck attack resulted in the sharp series of reprisal raids on similar British cities—"as listed in Baedeker"—that surprised R.A.F. Fighter Command during 1942. On 23rd-24th April, Exeter was attacked with little success; on succeeding nights Norwich and York were the targets; Norwich again; then Exeter for a second time. This reprisal attack, carried out by some ninety bombers withdrawn from Sicily, gutted the centre of the city, destroyed nine churches and killed or injured over 300 people. Nevertheless, Hitler's terrorangriffe against Britain petered out in the usual manner, for the simple reason that the Luftwaffe was stretched to the limit by the demands placed upon it elsewhere and lacked the forces to strike in any strength at undefended cities or, for that matter, military objectives.

On 24th-27th April, 1942, Bomber Command devastated the Baltic port of Rostock with 442 tons of high explosives and 305 tons of incendiaries dropped by 468 aircraft. This attack was a mixture of area and precision bombing; the Heinkel and Arado aircraft factories were seriously damaged, but the three main churches of the town and 1,760 houses were destroyed and sixty per cent of the inner town burnt to ashes. Four raids, on successive nights, completed the destruction of Rostock.

In reprisal for the Rostock attacks, the Luftwaffe hit at Bath, and later Norwich, with some success. A few weeks later, Winston Churchill considered and agreed to a plan for a saturation raid by a thousand bombers on a large German city, although the Prime Minister anticipated the loss of a hundred aircraft. Thus total war came to the citizens of Cologne on the night of 30th-31st May; and Harris was able to inform Churchill that 600 acres of the city had been devastated for a loss of only thirty-nine Bomber Command aircraft. "The dominating offensive weapon of the war was at last being used," wrote Air Marshal Harris in his memoirs.

In December, 1942, President Roosevelt informed Congress that 5,500 aircraft were being produced each month in the United States, an impressive figure dismissed with contempt by the leaders of the Third Reich. In one of his last public speeches, Goering had stated in October at a Harvest Thanksgiving: "Some astronomical figures are expected from the American war industry. Now I am the last to underrate this industry. Obviously the Americans do very well in some technical fields. We know they produce a colossal number of fast cars. And the development of radio is one of their special achievements, and so is razor blades. . . . But you must not forget there is one word in their language that is written with a capital B, and this word is Bluff." Unfortunately for the bulky Reichsmarschall, President Roosevelt was not bluffing; by the end of 1942 the United States had produced over 47,000 aircraft, including 2,600 four-engined Fortress and Liberator heavy bombers.

The Boeing B-17E Flying Fortress of 1942 was a far cry from the graceful XB-17 of 1936, no longer a thing of beauty but a powerful air weapon, heavily armed and heavily armoured. A bomb load of three tons; an operational height of 26,000 ft. and a maximum speed of 280 m.p.h.—this was the B-17E heavy daylight bomber. Earlier versions of the B-17, admittedly deficient in fire-power but otherwise an excellent aircraft, had been supplied to the R.A.F. under the Lease-Lend scheme in 1941 and failed disastrously in action. The British theory that daylight bombing brought little success for prohibitive losses was thus apparently confirmed; but the U.S.

Army Air Force remained faithful to the Fortress as an ideal air weapon. In fact, the R.A.F. Fortresses had failed only because they had been used at extremely high altitudes and in small, loose formations extremely vulnerable to fighter attack. The Americans assumed that large formations of B-17s, flying at their ideal operational height of 24,000 to 27,000 ft., would be able to precision-bomb a target and remain protected from fighter attacks by the concentrated fire-power of their massed defensive armament. From this British faith in night bombing and the American conception of the B-17 as a daylight heavy bomber originated the famous "round-the-clock bombing" technique that broke the back of the Third Reich and over-whelmed the Luftwaffe.

The Consolidated B-24 Liberator, though an ideal heavy bomber, never achieved the fame of the Flying Fortress. A rather ugly aircraft, with a deep, slab-sided fuselage, the B-24 could carry a bomb load of just over two tons and had a range of 1,600 miles. The defensive armament consisted of ten heavy machine-guns in nose, upper, ball and tail turrets and waist positions—more than enough to ensure a terrific concentration of fire against attacking fighters. Liberators were used in some numbers by R.A.F. Coastal Command, proving highly success-ful as anti-submarine aircraft, and B-24s of the U.S. 9th Air Force carried out the remarkable, if catastrophic, attacks on the Ploesti oilfields. As a daylight heavy bomber complementary to the B-17 Fortress, the Liberator remained unequalled; indeed, it was produced in greater quantities than any other American aircraft during the Second World War.

The special U.S. strategic bomber arm built up to undertake the daylight air offensive against Germany—the 8th American Air Force—was formed in February, 1942, under the com-mand of General Carl Spaatz, and two months later the first batch of some 1,800 U.S. airmen arrived in England, led by Brigadier-General Ira C. Eaker. On 23rd June, eighteen B-17s of the 8th A.A.F. took off from American bases to fly across the North Atlantic to Britain via Labrador, Greenland, Iceland and Northern Ireland, a distance of nearly 4,000 miles. This small formation of Fortresses proved to be the vanguard of an endless stream of thousands of heavy bombers destined to take the same route and find new bases in the airfields hurriedly constructed for them all over southern and eastern England.

In August, 1942, General Spaatz decided that the 8th A.A.F. was ready to take the offensive, and final plans were completed with the R.A.F. for a co-ordinated system of day and night bomber attacks on the Third Reich. On 17th August, less than six months after Spaatz had undertaken to shape an American air weapon, twelve B-17Es, including *Yankee Doodle* carrying General Eaker, took off on the first bombing mission of the 8th Air Force—an attack on the marshalling yards at Rouen-Sotteville in France. The bombers returned without loss from a fairly successful raid, and only two aircraft were shot down during the next ten missions, although these were admittedly carried out against short-range targets under strong fighter cover. This indication that the cautious General Eaker was allowing his inexperienced crews to feel their way before scheduling the more heavily defended German targets aroused further R.A.F. criticism; over and over again the question emerged: if the Americans had such faith in daylight bombing, why did they seem afraid to put it to the test?

Thus, with uncertainty and even a decided coolness between the Allies, evolved the round-the-clock bombing technique—the sword by day and the axe by night. It was basically a sound policy, but imperfect at birth, and during 1943 the Luftwaffe would have the opportunity to exploit its weaknesses. What then could the German fighter arm offer in defence of the Reich now that the fateful hour was at hand?

"If an enemy bomber reaches the Ruhr," Goering had told the German people, "my name is not Hermann Goering; you can call me Meier!" By 1942, the average German civilian was in no mood to call the Reichsmarschall Meier or anything else; he was wearying of the nightly air attacks that mocked Goering and his boastful speeches. The irritating, persistent raids by R.A.F. Bomber Command in 1940 and 1941 had steadily increased in numbers and intensity, culminating with the sledgehammer blows on Lubeck, Rostock and then Cologne. Those who survived in the tortured German cities remained steadfast, strengthened by Goebbels' surprisingly effective propaganda—"There is much suffering in the bombed areas, but even more determination"—and perhaps resigned to the cross they had to bear, but they could not help wondering what had happened to the Luftwaffe. "Where are our fighters?" was the inevitable question, to which there was no ready answer. Goering had virtually retired into the shadows, only occasionally appearing in public; and Hitler gave only vague promises that a terrible vengeance would be exacted on England, while refusing to visit any of the bombed cities.

Germany, at the outbreak of war, was supposed to possess a first-class air defence organisation. In fact, only a few fighters and a handful of ground defences had been provided, mainly for the protection of industrial and military installations in west and south-west Germany. As Adolf Galland has written, "All one heard was the slogan, 'The Luftwaffe must attack and not defend'." Night-fighting was regarded by Goering as an unnecessary luxury for an offensive air force, and Ernst Udet was one of the few high-ranking Luftwaffe officers interested in the air defence of Germany during the hours of darkness. He organised night-fighting exercises, using a single Gruppe of Bf 109s in co-operation with searchlight units, to the amusement of his associates, and persevered until he became disheartened by official opposition. When the R.A.F. began to raid Germany persistently by night during 1940, this system of fighters and searchlights—hitherto dismissed laughingly as "Udet's fun and games"—was used in action, but it proved so unsatisfactory in bad weather that Goering realised something would have to be pulled out of the hat as an improvement. He therefore ordered a complete reorganisation of Germany's air defences.

In July, 1940, General Felmay's former chief of staff, Josef Kammhuber, an outstanding officer and airman who had been dogged by misfortune, was recalled and given command of the first German night-fighter division. Nothing existed at that time for Kammhuber to command except a research Gruppe of modified Do 17s and Bf 110s, but he got to work and by the end of the year had formed the first two night-fighter groups, or Nachtjagdgeschwader. The Bf 110s of NJG 1 were intended primarily for operations over the Reich, while the long-range Do 17s of NJG 2 fulfilled the night intruder role, attacking the R.A.F. Bomber Command bases in East Anglia, Lincolnshire and Yorkshire.

During 1941 the highly capable Kammhuber built up his night-fighter force, using Goering's support to request production of more converted Do 17s and also adapting Ju 88s, equipped with the latest radar devices. The Ju 88C conversions were particularly successful, and in the hands of such outstanding pilots as Streib and Lent were responsible for many kills as the British bomber streams crossed the coast. Kammhuber hoped to form a chain of night-fighter zones from the Kiel across Hamburg, Bremen, Munster, Wesel, Arnhem, Venlo, Liège to Namur, a "Kammhuber Line" to protect the whole of Germany, and to this end he put forward an ambitious programme. He asked Goering for an interview with Hitler, and to his surprise found his plans approved by the Fuehrer and given priority. Above all, Kammhuber needed improved radar tracking devices for his aircraft and a specialised night-fighter; the development of German radar had been seriously neglected, and the Ju 88s were, after all, converted bombers. It was therefore agreed that the German electronics industry would provide more advanced radar devices, and the Ernst Heinkel A.G. was requested to develop the twin-engined He 219 as a night-fighter.

Backed by Hitler and Goering, Kammhuber was thus able to extend his defence zones, and in time these extended from Norway in the north to the Swiss frontier in the south, from Austria to East Prussia, and included the Ploesti oilfields in Rumania and areas of Italy and Tunis. By August, 1941, the original night-fighter division had become a night-fighter corps —Nachtjagdfliegerkorps XII. Nevertheless, the Luftwaffe was still desperately short of fighters for the defence of the Reich, and Ernst Heinkel was finding the Reichsluftfahrtministerium unwilling to authorise production of the He 219.

Then, in October, 1941, Hitler suddenly decided to stop Kammhuber's long-range intruder operations over England, on the grounds that the aircraft were urgently needed in Sicily and North Africa. This was, of course, true, but Hitler's decision was also affected by his own belief that R.A.F. bombers shot down over Britain were wasted losses because they did nothing to sustain the morale of the German people. Kammhuber asked Goering to intervene for him, but the Reichsmarschall did nothing, and the Do 17s and Ju 88s, together with their highly trained crews, were thrown into the furnace of the Mediterranean theatre of operations. The R.A.F. area bombing offensive was at hand—and the Luftwaffe night-fighter force was restricted to action over Germany without specialised aircraft for the purpose.

For day fighting, the Luftwaffe still possessed in any numbers only the Messerschmitt Bf 109 and the Focke-Wulf Fw 190. The Bf 109 had been subjected to an infinite succession of modifications since the outbreak of war; constant operational demands for increased engine power, heavier armament and additional equipment altering the original clean lines to such an extent that it had become known as "the bulge". By 1942 the basic Bf 109 design had passed the peak of its development, and the Bf 109G which appeared in the summer of that year was in many respects inferior to its predecessor, but the German aircraft industry had nothing better to offer as a replacement. Much the same situation existed with the Fw 190; it had been adapted as a close-support fighter, fighter-bomber, fighter-dive-bomber and night-fighter, and was in demand everywhere. These two types of single-seater fighter simply could not be produced in sufficient numbers, for they were needed to fulfil a dozen different roles, veritable jacks of all trades and masters of none.

Thus, on the eve of Germany's battle for survival the fighter arm of the Luftwaffe could only plead earnestly for better aircraft and soldier bravely on with improved versions of the Bf 109 and Fw 190. On 12th September, 1942, Goering commented frankly on the fighter problem—without doing anything to solve it. "By and large we have had a certain superiority . . . so far as fighters are concerned," he said, "the Bf 109 in its various developments and then the Fw 190. Both types have been caught up with and to some extent overtaken by the English and American fighters, particularly as regards climbing powers. To my annoyance they also seem to have a greater range . . . and this is very unpleasant. Above all, the Spitfire is ahead, a thing our fighter pilots don't like." As in Udet's lifetime, the promise of new, remarkable aircraft remained just around the corner; the Focke-Wulf Ta 152, a replacement for the Fw 190; the Me 209 and Me 309, projected replacements for the Bf 109; and the Dornier Do 335, a very fast tandem-engined fighter. Similarly, new types of bomber were under development, but progressing at a snail's pace, thanks to Erhard Milch's insistence on maximum production of the older types in a sincere attempt to achieve numerical if not technical superiority over the Allies.

On 27th January, 1943, fighters of the Luftwaffe took off to intercept the first attack on Germany by the United States 8th Air Force. This raid, directed against Wilhelmshaven, was indecisive for both sides, the Fw 190s being surprised by the heavy fire power of the American B-17s, and the twin-boomed P-38 Lightning fighters escorting the bombers proving no match for their more nimble opponents. Nevertheless, the Wilhelmshaven mission indicated that General Eaker had mustered sufficient B-17 squadrons to launch his daylight air offensive on Germany. In fact, he was prepared to sustain that offensive in the face of anticipated heavy losses.

A document signed by the Allied Chiefs of Staff at the Casablanca Conference the same month had sealed the fate of Germany before the sirens wailed over Wilhelmshaven. The Casablanca directive was the hinge that opened the door on the Allied air offensive; it gave Air Marshal Harris and General Eaker the green light to wage indiscriminate bombing war on the Third Reich, though each chose to interpret it in his own way. Expressed in the broadest possible terms, the Casablanca directive stated: "Your primary object will be the progressive destruction and dislocation of the German military, industrial and economic system, and the undermining of the morale of the German people to a point where their capacity for armed resistance is fatally weakened." To Eaker, this meant that the U.S. Air Force would merely extend its policy of daylight precision bombing attacks on selected targets in the German key industries, such as ball-bearing works and aircraft component factories, hitting at them again and again until they ceased production. Air Marshal Harris interpreted the Casablanca directive as an instruction to saturate any and every German town with bombs as he wished; in his book *Bomber Offensive* he writes: "I was now required to proceed with a joint Anglo-American bombing offensive for the general 'disorganisation' of German industry . . . which gave me a wide range of choice and allowed me to attack pretty well any German industrial city of 100,000 inhabitants and above. . . ."

On the night of 29th-30th May, 1943, the weight of Bomber Command fell upon the twin city of Wuppertal, at the eastern end of the embattled Ruhr. Over 700 bombers, using Wuppertal-Barmen as their aiming point, achieved such a high degree of concentration that the heart of the town was completely devastated and some 2,450 people killed. Wuppertal-Elberfeld escaped with slight damage, more by accident than intention, and Harris remedied this oversight a month later with a second raid that raised the death-roll for the twin city to 5,200. "This kind of aerial terrorism is the product of the sick minds of the plutocratic world-destroyers . . ." commented Dr. Goebbels at the mass funeral of Wuppertal victims on 18th June, 1943.

Yet Wuppertal was merely the beginning. Two months later Air Marshal Harris and his staff were ready to launch the great air attack code-named *Operation Gomorrah*—a triple blow calculated to achieve the maximum effect of air bombardment on a large German city. *Gomorrah* was intended to be a peak in the Bomber Command offensive, an outstanding example of the air weapon in its most fearful form; the Douhet theory put into practice, all the doubts and criticism of night bombing resolved for ever. At least two thousand bombers were scheduled to take part in three main raids, and Air Marshal Harris estimated that over 10,000 tons of bombs would have to be dropped "to complete the process of elimination". Large numbers of incendiaries were to be used.

The target for this gigantic, so aptly named operation was the city and port of Hamburg.

CHAPTER XIX

BOMBING ROUND THE CLOCK: 1943

ON the night of 27th-28th July, 1943, Hamburg became the first German city—and indeed the first city in history—to endure a firestorm. That is to say, so many tons of incendiaries fell on Hamburg during the R.A.F. attack, such an intense heat was generated, that individual fires fed upon each other, linked up and turned into a vast conflagration. This became a man-made tornado, a column of heated air more than two and a half miles high and one and a half miles in diameter. The Police President of Hamburg reported afterwards that the unique situation arising in a firestorm could be realised only by: "... analysing it soberly as a meteorological phenomenon: as a result of the sudden linking of a number of fires, the air above was heated to such an extent that a violent updraught occurred which, in turn, caused the surrounding fresh air to be sucked in from all sides to the centre of the fire area. This tremendous suction caused movements of air of far greater force than normal winds. In meteorology the differences of temperature involved are of the order of 20 deg. to 30 deg. C. In this firestorm they were of the order of 600 deg., 800 deg., or even 1,000 deg. C. This explained the colossal force of the firestorm winds." On that awful night when the anger of *Gomorrah* fell on Hamburg, the firestorm could not be analysed soberly, scientifically or any other way; it simply exploded into life as a monstrous, writhing thing of flame, utterly beyond control. Great trees were up-rooted and whisked away. People were sucked up into the inferno. Nothing, literally nothing, survived in the centre of the Hamburg firestorm; everything that would burn burned, and anything that would not burn melted.

To understand the importance of the fate that overtook Hamburg in July, 1943, it must be considered as a battle, for that is what the offensive became—the Battle of Hamburg. The first attack, on the night of 24th-25th July, was carried out by 740 aircraft of Bomber Command, and numerous large fires

231

were started. Nevertheless, Hamburg rightly prided itself on having the most efficient system of civil defence in Germany, and by the following morning some sort of order was being restored. Then, unexpectedly, came the Allied hammer blows calculated to finish the job once and for all. The same day the U.S. 8th Air Force appeared over the still burning city and stoked up the fires; on 26th July, Bomber Command mounted a second raid which resulted in the firestorm, and completed the triple blow the following night with another force of over 700 bombers. A fourth R.A.F. attack on the night of 2nd-3rd August failed to achieve any measure of success, owing to adverse weather conditions. In the three main Bomber Command raids, over 2,350 aircraft dropped 7,200 tons of high explosive and incendiaries on Hamburg, and during the w' le nine-day battle about 9,000 tons hit the target, just a little below Air Marshal Harris's estimate of the tonnage needed to ensure complete destruction.

Harris was well satisfied with the results of Operation *Gomorrah*, as he had every right to be. When at last the huge pall of smoke hanging over Hamburg had cleared away sufficiently for aerial photographs to be taken it was seen that eight square miles of the city had been completely destroyed, the transport system paralysed and the port turned into a shambles of wrecked and burning shipping. 277,500 houses and 183 factories had been destroyed, all the dock installations seriously damaged, and 180,000 tons of shipping sunk in the harbour. In Air Marshal Harris's own words, Hamburg after the battle presented "a scene of unimaginable devastation"—and all achieved for a loss to Bomber Command of only fifty-seven aircraft.

Unfortunately, the many aerial photographs taken during and after the raids could not be expected to reveal the human agony of Hamburg. Bodies were still being recovered from the masses of debris two months later, and not until 1957 did the city authorities arrive at a final total of 50,000 dead, including 7,000 children and young people. Conditions in the firestorm centre were so appalling that the access streets had to be sealed off with barbed wire until clearance could be affected, a horrifying task that took a long time. In this densely populated area, the tornado had exacted a terrible toll in human life; huge shelters and bunkers built to protect hundreds of people had been turned into ovens by the intense heat and were found to contain nothing but ashes. Pans and other cooking utensils carried into the shelters had melted; whole blocks of houses had been consumed by heat estimated to have reached temperatures of 1,000-1,500 deg. F.; and the streets and squares were choked with pitiful, charred remnants that had once been human beings. Twenty years later, the catastrophe of Hamburg has not been erased from the minds of those who survived the fearful days and nights of July, 1943, and a monument has been erected to the memory of the 55,000 people of the city who died as a result of aerial bombardment during the Second World War. With awful simplicity, the inscription reads: "May those generations who come after us be spared this. May this mass grave be a warning and exhortation to all who exercise charity towards their fellow men."

Adolf Galland has called the destruction of Hamburg "the fateful hour of the Luftwaffe" and it is true that after Hamburg German air power rapidly fell to pieces. The summer of 1943 saw Goering lose his last opportunity to improve the air defence of the Third Reich and step up the production of fighters under the Milch programme, already falling behind schedule because of Hitler's insistence on a large bomber force. The Reichsmarschall did, in fact, attempt to stop the rot by calling a conference of his generals at Hitler's headquarters in East Prussia and informing them that, in his opinion, the Luftwaffe had served its purpose as an offensive air force and must now become a defensive arm, concentrated on the protection of the homeland. This proposal, so long overdue, was welcomed by all who heard it; even Peltz, the General of the Bombers, was prepared to agree that only a strong fighter arm could save the Reich. For the first time in many months, Goering and his commanders were of one mind. "It would be a tough job to reorganise the Luftwaffe in so short a time from an apparently strategic offensive arm into an effective defensive one," considered Galland, "but none of us doubted that we could do it."

Unfortunately, Adolf Hitler had the last word—and to the Fuehrer, any discussion on defence could be anticipation of defeat. Also, of course, Goering was already out of favour; Hitler was certain to be prejudiced against him. Nevertheless, the worried Reichsmarschall made up his mind to tell Hitler what had been decided and retired to the Fuehrer's bunker, leaving his commanders still seated round the conference table. Later, when Goering emerged, it was obvious that something was seriously wrong; without a word he walked slowly past his leaders into an adjoining room. Then he called for Galland and Peltz, and they joined him. "We were met with a shattering picture," writes Galland in his memoirs. "Goering had completely broken down. With his head buried in his arms on the table, he moaned some indistinguishable words. We stood there for some time in embarrassment until at last he pulled himself together and said we were witnessing his deepest moments of despair. The Fuehrer had lost faith in him. All the suggestions from which he had expected a radical change in the situation of the war in the air had been rejected; the Fuehrer had announced that the Luftwaffe had disappointed him too often, and a changeover from offensive to defensive in the air against the West was out of the question."

Goering went on to explain that Hitler was giving the Luftwaffe a last chance to prove its mettle by resuming the air offensive against England on a large scale. The Allied terror raids would be countered by German terror raids; and the need for defence thus eliminated. It was all very simple, the way Hitler explained it. Goering talked on with growing confidence and Galland listened, aware that all his hopes were being dashed to pieces. The bombers would retain production priority; the night-fighter system—the famous "Kammhuber Line"—would deteriorate; and the day-fighter squadrons would be wasted away. And all to no purpose, all because one man refused to heed sound advice. Then Goering rose to his feet. "Oberst Peltz," he said, "I appoint you assault leader against England!"

Peltz was a young, efficient and energetic commander, and he made a great effort to assemble a bombing force to strike at Britain. Eventually he managed to gather together from all fronts about 550 aircraft, including a few of the troublesome, unwanted Heinkel He 177s and a number of Junkers Ju 188s—improved versions of the ubiquitous Ju 88 bomber. Some fighter-bombers, mainly Me 410s and Fw 190s, were also pressed into service. This collection of assorted types of aeroplane, a far cry from the great air armada Goering had launched against

Britain in 1940, was all that could be spared for Peltz, designated Angriffsfuehrer England for what turned out to be the
last German bomber offensive of the Second World War. Also,
Luftwaffe resources were at such a low ebb that preparations
for the attack took a long time, and not until January, 1944, did
the first raids, directed against London, take place.

Meanwhile, the Allied air offensive continued to hammer the
Third Reich and its satellite countries with increasing vigour.
In August, 1943, a force of 177 Liberators of the U.S. 9th Air
Force successfully bombed the vast Rumanian oilfields at
Ploesti—and at low level, in daylight, in the face of murderous
flak and fighter opposition. Over fifty bombers were lost on this
raid, considered by one writer to be "the worst catastrophe in
the history of the U.S. Army Air Forces". Two weeks later, a
large formation of unescorted B-17s of the American 8th Air
Force struck at Regensburg, home of the Messerschmitt
industry, and a second force of B-17s bombed the vital ball-
bearing factories at Schweinfurt. Again success was achieved,
but only at the cost of frightful losses. Later in the year the 8th
A.A.F. returned to Schweinfurt, this time with 290 Fortresses,
and dealt the ball-bearing works another crippling blow; the
Luftwaffe rose in force and sixty B-17s failed to return. The
German fighter arm—some two hundred Fw 190s and one
hundred Bf 109Gs of Luftflotte 3 and the Fw 190s of Luftflotte
Reich deployed for the defence of the homeland—was flying and
fighting as never before, and the American daylight air offensive
was drifting into a war of attrition. General Arnold wrote afterwards : "No such savage air battles had been seen since the war
began. Our losses were rising to an all-time high, but so were
those of the Luftwaffe, and our bombers were not being turned
back from their targets. Could we keep it up? The London
papers asked the question editorially. . . ."

Whether or not the Americans could stand the pace undoubtedly posed a leading air question in the summer of 1943, and
one that would have to be answered in Washington before the
end of the year. President Roosevelt had no desire to see the
Luftwaffe vanquished by a Pyrrhic victory that left American
air power so crippled that it was in no shape to tackle Japan—
and the Mitsubishi Zero-Sen was already proving to be easily
as good a fighter as the Bf 109 and Fw 190. It could be argued

that, thanks to the remarkable Norden bomb sight, almost every daylight attack had been successful, thus vindicating the American theory of precision bombing; but behind locked doors it was admitted that the heavy losses in aircraft and trained crews could not be sustained. The concentrated fire-power of a B-17 or B-24 formation, though devastating, was simply not enough protection against determined fighter opposition.

As an intermediate solution to the American daylight bombing problem, a number of B-17s were converted as bomber escorts—literally flying fortresses—under the designation YB-40. These massive aircraft, carrying no bombs, but fitted with greatly increased armour and armed with twenty machine-guns and cannon of various calibres, were mixed into 8th Air Force formations on an experimental basis during the summer of 1943. By the end of the year, all YB-40s had been withdrawn from service for reconversion as bombers; they could not be shot down, but their great weight made them too slow to keep pace with the normal B-17s they were supposed to defend. Shortly after this failure, the B-17G, a version of the Fortress with additional defensive armament, was hurried into production, and the majestic formations of four-engined bombers continued to thunder over Germany with swarms of enemy fighters twisting and turning around them. The air battles that took place every day, even more savage than the great struggles over Britain in 1940, sometimes destroyed but never turned back the bomber squadrons; the courage of the B-17 and B-24 crews has been equalled but seldom surpassed. Four miles above the Third Reich, these men saw unforgettable sights; fighters plunging to earth in flames; huge bombers breaking into pieces; bodies tumbling through the air; and, always, the Fw 190s hurtling to meet the B-17s in suicidal head-on attacks, followed by the appalling impact of rockets and cannon shells crashing home. Then the long journeys back to base in limping aircraft, the targets successfully bombed, the bullet-riddled fuselages strewn with dead and wounded; and so many, many men who never returned at all.

Inevitably, the American air staff concluded that every bomber formation would have to be escorted all the way to the target and back by relays of long-range fighters—or the U.S. 8th Air Force would be annihilated. Unfortunately, the first

American fighter type to enter operational service with the 8th Air Force was the Republic P-47 Thunderbolt, a huge machine weighing some seven tons that not only lacked the range to penetrate deeply into Germany but also failed to match the performance of contemporary Luftwaffe fighters. Nevertheless, the P-47 was sturdy—it was actually the largest and heaviest single-seater fighter built during the war—and could be modified as a long range fighter by fitting a 200-gallon ventral drop tank, thus increasing its radius of action to over 300 miles. This was done, and once Thunderbolts so converted began to appear over Germany in strength bomber losses began to decline. This American introduction of long-range escort fighters led to an argument between Adolf Galland and Goering, who insisted that the Luftwaffe fighter arm should still concentrate on attacking the enemy bomber formations, avoiding battle with the escorting Thunderbolts. Galland, on the other hand, wanted the American fighters beaten and then the bombers destroyed, in that order. If the Americans could be persuaded to believe that their long-range fighters were no more successful than the abortive YB-40 flying battleships, they might revert to unescorted daylight raids—so reasoned Galland, with some justification. However, once again Goering had his way, with disastrous results for the Luftwaffe, which soon began to lose alarming numbers of day fighters.

The North American P-51 Mustang, which replaced the Thunderbolt as the principal American escort fighter, solved the daylight bombing problem once and for all. A very fast and highly manoeuvrable single-seater fighter, powered by a Packard-built version of the superb Rolls-Royce Merlin engine, the Mustang arrived in the United Kingdom in November, 1943, and began to re-equip Thunderbolt groups of the U.S. 8th Air Force a month later. When fitted with detachable extra fuel tanks under each wing the P-51 was without equal as a strategic fighter; it had the range of a heavy bomber and the performance of contemporary Luftwaffe fighters above 20,000 ft. As a typical example, in March, 1944, Merlin-powered Mustangs escorted B-17 and B-24 bombers all the way to Berlin and back, a distance of 1,100 miles. Introduced just when it was most needed, the P-51 to a great extent guaranteed the ultimate success of the American daylight air offensive, although there would be many savage battles over Germany before the Luft-waffe admitted defeat.

Air Marshal Harris, with none of the problems that beset General Spaatz and Eaker to disturb his policy, hit hard at the Third Reich during the summer and autumn of 1943. On the night of 17th-18th August came the famous Peenemunde raid, of which more later. On the night of 22nd-23rd October the tar-get for Bomber Command was Kassel, fated to become victim of the second German firestorm. Some 1,800 tons of bombs were dropped on Kassel in this single heavy attack, killing at least 5,000 people, leaving another 120,000 civilians homeless and crippling all the city's industrial and commercial resources. During the November, Harris decided to concentrate large bomber forces against Berlin, and by the end of the year the German capital, although heavily defended by night fighters and flak batteries, was fighting for its existence. The R.A.F. raids continued all that winter, and were, on the whole, success-ful; but Berlin was a very large city, and the weather was against the Bomber Command crews. In his memoirs Harris has com-mented : "In all, my Command made sixteen major attacks on the German capital. The whole battle was fought in appalling weather and in conditions resembling those of no other cam-paign in the history of warfare. Thousands upon thousands of tons of bombs were aimed at the Pathfinders' pyrotechnic sky markers and fell through unbroken cloud which concealed every-thing below it except the confused glare of fires. . . ."

The Battle of Berlin, often amounting to nothing more than blind saturation of the target area, typified aerial bombardment in its most primitive form, pitted against an efficient, if neglec-ted, night-fighter and anti-aircraft defence organisation. It was a weary and often unrewarding struggle, but Air Marshal Harris, believing that Berlin was the key to the whole strategic air offensive, willingly accepted the difficulties. "We can wreck Berlin from end to end if the U.S.A.A.F. will come in on it," he informed the Prime Minister. "It will cost us between 400-500 aircraft. It will cost Germany the war." But the Americans, who lacked the equipment and experienced crews to undertake long-range night operations and had not yet fully solved the problems of deep penetration in daylight, were reluctant to "come in on it". The squadrons of R.A.F. Bomber Command consequently had to bear the brunt of the Battle of Berlin, the U.S. 8th Air Force not taking any part until March, 1944, when the offensive against the capital was almost at an end.

Germany remained desperately short of night fighters. According to Galland, the total number of twin-engined night fighters available for the defence of the Reich during 1943 never amounted to more than 350, and before the end of the year Kammhuber was powerless to prevent his small force from being steadily whittled away. For some time, the remarkable adaptability of Germany's standard night fighter, the Ju 88, had caused Erhard Milch to be always calling upon the type for a host of other duties, and finally Kammhuber was left holding sections of his weakened defence line together with modified Me 110s, long obsolete and useless in almost any role. As for the specialised night fighter Kammhuber had urgently requested, this aircraft—the Heinkel He 219—continued to be dogged by opposition in high Luftwaffe circles. Goering had no interest in the He 219 because he failed to realise that night fighting was specialist work and thought that any aircraft would serve the purpose; and Milch favoured an improved version of the Ju 88, designated the Ju 188, which would be easier and more economical to build in large numbers. Several He 219s were transferred to Venloe in Holland for flight testing under operational conditions, and on the night of 11th-12th June, 1943, Major Streib, a leading German night-fighter pilot, destroyed five R.A.F. bombers. This successful debut of the He 219 was quickly followed by a number of other victories, including the destruction of six of the new and very fast De Havilland Mosquito light bombers, and Kammhuber requested mass production of some 1,200 machines. Milch agreed to authorise production of the He 219, but in fact he had already decided to introduce the slower Ju 188 (later Ju 388) into Luftwaffe service, to the detriment of the Heinkel type.

On 15th September, 1943, Kammhuber was ordered to disband his centralised command—Nachtjagdfliegerkorps XII—and place his night-fighter squadrons at the disposal of the area Luftflotten responsible for the overall defence of the Reich. Demoralised and embittered by this final blow to all his hopes, Kammhuber resigned his post in the November; like others before him he had been defeated in the end by the stubborn ignorance of Goering and the ruthless ambition of Erhard Milch. When Kammhuber left office, the German night-fighter command fell into a state bordering on disintegration, and the last chance of a specialised night fighter becoming available in large numbers went with him. "The story of the He 219 is the most unfortunate I have ever heard," he told Ernst Heinkel, "but let those who were responsible for it take the blame."

Without Kammhuber's guiding hand, the Luftwaffe night-fighter system was open ground for anyone with the wildest ideas on dealing with enemy bombers to go ahead and try them out. A certain Major Hermann, an ex-bomber pilot, considered that the highly organised system of night fighting by radar direction as developed by Kammhuber was unnecessary, because the huge conflagrations invariably brought about by heavy bombing attacks often lit up the sky over the target area for many hours. Hermann reasoned that a fighter pilot could make use of this phenomenon to locate and shoot down an enemy bomber without the aid of radar direction or any other special equipment. His method of "daylight" night fighting, familiarly known as the "wild boar" plan, could be improved by using large numbers of searchlights; the fighters could then engage bombers coned in the searchlight beams. The idea—a development of Udet's fighters-and-searchlights system—was a daring if somewhat unorthodox one to adopt at the height of the R.A.F. Bomber Command offensive, but its simplicity and ease of implementation impressed Goering. Also, of course, Hermann's "wild boar" tactics utilised only single-engined fighters, which meant that fewer of the Reichsmarschall's precious Ju 88 medium bombers would have to be modified as night fighters.

In due course, Jagdgeschwader (Wilde Sau) 300 was formed, commanded by Major Hermann and equipped with Focke-Wulf Fw 190s fitted with anti-dazzle screens and flame shrouds over the exhausts; later, this was expanded to three Geschwader, all using the same free-lance methods. Hermann's tactics resulted in a considerable number of R.A.F. night bombers being shot down, but large numbers of German night-fighters were destroyed by their own anti-aircraft fire or crashed because they were hopelessly lost. While the "wild boar" pilots fought as they wished, and incidentally became considered as national heroes, the night-fighter organisation was thrown into chaos, without any real knowledge of what was happening and therefore unable to exert any control over the air defences. The onset of winter increased the heavy fighter losses, until only the courageous, if swashbuckling Hermann remained convinced that his methods could still bring success. Finally, when even he was frequently landing by parachute and German pilots were occasionally fighting each other instead of the enemy, the night-fighter losses rose until they were out of all proportion. With some reluctance, Goering brought the ridiculous situation to an end, and Hermann's Wilde Sau Geschwader were dissolved.

After the failure of the "wild boar" scheme, the Luftwaffe reverted to radar directed night-fighting, using modified Ju 88s and Me 110s. "It is not right that I should always have to be drawing on the bombers," grumbled Goering. "Both day fighters and bombers are not one hundred per cent suitable as night-fighters." This, of course, was only too true; but Goering bore equal responsibility with Milch for delaying production of Germany's only specialised night-fighter, the He 219.

Peenemunde was a lonely little island in the Baltic, very close to the German mainland. In 1943 it was also the scientific experimental base for Hitler's "miracle weapons"—the mysterious weapons which, Dr. Goebbels assured the world, would change the course of the war and exact a terrible retribution on Britain. The first of these secret 'V' weapons—V for "Vergeltung" or vengeance—was a flying bomb, powered by a single Argus pulse-jet engine and armed with a warhead containing 1,870 lb. of high explosive. The V.1 flying bomb, intended as a long-range guided weapon against London, had been designed by the aircraft firm of Fieseler, and successfully launched for the first time at Peenemunde in December, 1942. Since that date, some seventy trial firings had been made, but it was still under development and remained temperamental. The second V weapon, the V.2 rocket—officially designated the A.4—was a true guided missile, perhaps the ancestor of all modern guided missiles. The result of a decade of German rocket development, the V.2 was a giant liquid-propelled missile, weighing over twelve tons and having a range of about 200 miles. Hurled straight up into the air with tremendous velocity, it could reach a height of sixty miles before falling out of the stratosphere faster than the speed of sound; the most efficient air defence was powerless against it. Surprisingly enough, the development of both these remarkable weapons had proceeded at first with only mild encouragement from Hitler, but after the destruction of Hamburg and other German cities the Fuehrer had approved of the work and ordered mass production at the earliest possible date. Simultaneously, the Goebbels' propaganda machine went into action, arousing the weary German people to fresh vigour with promises that the V weapons would wipe out Britain and bring victory at the eleventh hour.

Rumours reaching Britain from neutral sources had indicated as early as 1940 that Germany was experimenting with secret weapons, including rockets and pilotless aircraft; but not until 1942 did reports from Allied secret agents working in Denmark establish beyond doubt that Hitler's "miracle weapons" actually existed. The Photographic Reconnaissance Unit of the R.A.F. was therefore given the priority task of locating the home of the V weapons.

Evidence pointed more definitely to Peenemunde when a member of the Polish Underground movement, an engineer, named Kocjan, learned that some new weapons were being developed there. London urgently requested more detailed information and a number of Polish slave-workers employed in Germany managed to obtain transfers to Peenemunde. Their reports of "small, torpedo-shaped missiles fitted with wings" were soon verified by a wealth of aerial photographs, which also revealed the presence of A.4 rockets on the site. It was thus confirmed that Peenemunde was the experimental station for the German secret weapons. Mr. Churchill therefore instructed Air Marshal Harris to mount a heavy Bomber Command attack on the island, and on the night of 17th-18th August, 1943, in clear weather and bright moonlight, a force of 600 bombers arrived over the target. Too late, the defensive smoke screen billowed over Peenemunde; the surprised barking of anti-aircraft batteries mingled with the high-pitched scream of falling bombs. Extremely accurate marking of the three aiming points by the R.A.F. pathfinder force, the calm direction of an experienced Master Bomber and perfect visibility all combined to make the Peenemunde raid a great success. Within an hour, huge fires were sweeping the whole target area. The drawing offices, the assembly works and main administrative block were badly damaged, and the housing settlement for the Peenemunde engineers almost completely destroyed, while many other buildings were gutted before the flames could be subdued. Casualties were very heavy, 735 people being killed, including two prominent rocket scientists, Dr. Walter Thiel and Chief Engineer Walther. Forty-one Bomber Command aircraft were shot down, mainly by the German night-fighter force, which took advantage of the full moon to press home numerous attacks during and immediately after the raid.

Generalmajor Walter Dornberger, who was responsible for the V.2 programme, has stated that the attack on Peenemunde did not greatly delay development of the V weapons, but the loss of vital equipment and irreplaceable engineers, followed soon afterwards by the Anglo-American air operations code-named *Crossbow*—the systematic destruction of the V weapon launching sites—undoubtedly had some effect. Indeed, the V.1 flying bomb was not ready for use until the following May, and the first V.2 operations did not take place until September, 1944. If the V weapons could have been used at an earlier date, they would have brought more havoc than they did to London, and thereby fully satisfied Hitler's craving for vengeance; but the Peenemunde raid and *Crossbow* operations denied the Fuehrer even that doubtful pleasure. As decisive weapons, the V.1 and V.2 were, of course, valueless. "In sum, what was the V.2?" says General Dornberger, in his book *V.2*. "It was by no means a 'wonder weapon'. The term was in itself an exaggeration which did not correspond with the facts. By the middle of 1943 the military situation had long ceased to be such that by launching 900 V.2s in a month, each loaded with a ton of high explosives, over ranges of 160 miles, one could end the Second World War."

Nevertheless, Goebbels had persuaded thousands of Germans that the V weapons would bring victory for the Third Reich, and not least of those who awakened to reality after the Peenemunde attack was the Luftwaffe Chief of Staff, Generaloberst Hans Jeschonnek. The road to victory for Jeschonnek, that faithful servant of the Fuehrer, had always been a straight and narrow one, overcoming all obstacles to reach the goal; but by

1943 the road had become stony and pitted with disasters. For nearly three years, to Hans Jeschonnek—"the youngster"—Hitler and Goering had been the wise men who could neither speak nor hear any evil, and he had said "yes" to everything. Before the Battle of Britain, Jeschonnek had sincerely believed that Germany needed only large numbers of dive-bombers and twin-engined medium bombers; but even after the defeat of the Luftwaffe over England proved him mistaken he raised no objections to their continued production. He had stood by while the Luftwaffe was decimated over Malta, allowed Goering to transfer the fighters he knew would soon be urgently needed for the defence of Germany, first to Russia and then to the Mediterranean, and seen them wasted away there. Now, Mussolini had tumbled ignominiously from his throne; Sicily could not be held; and an Allied landing in southern Italy was only a matter of time.

The disastrous Stalingrad air lift marked the beginning of Jeschonnek's downfall. Admittedly, he had dared to point out the difficulties of such a vast operation, but Goering had simply over-ruled him and Hitler had refused to listen to his objections. Afterwards, Goering had been only too anxious to find a scape-goat, and Jeschonnek found himself becoming a second Udet, blamed for every failure of the Luftwaffe. The situation was going from bad to worse. Hitler's 1943 summer offensive on the eastern front had been defeated, with staggering losses; the Russians were advancing for the first time; and Goering was switching fighters and bombers from one sector to another at random.

After the 1,000-bomber attack on Cologne, Jeschonnek had been forced to face the wrath of Hitler alone, without a vestige of support from Goering. He had said "yes" once too often, abided by too many wrong decisions, and now he had to take the full responsibility for them. To whom could he turn for help? He had always treated Milch with contempt, and that feeling had been reciprocated. As for Goering, his curious way of life disgusted Jeschonnek; but he was the architect of German air power, and his word was law. Desperately, Jeschonnek begged for instructions that would bring some sort of order out of the chaos all around him. Finally, Goering refused to see his Chief of Staff at all for long periods, and Jeschonnek, the man who had always tried to obey orders without question, was left alone to do what he liked. Or to be more exact, to do nothing. On one occasion, when he transferred some Luftwaffe units on his own initiative, Jeschonnek had to listen to a shocking torrent of abuse from Goering; right or wrong, faithful or disobedient, he was the whipping boy, the successor to Udet.

The destruction of Hamburg was the last straw. In despair, Jeschonnek appealed to Hitler, begging him to take over command of the Luftwaffe, telling him that Goering was never available to make decisions. This strange request must have given Hitler considerable food for thought—he too despised Goering by then—but apparently he kept his peace and took no immediate action. Not so the Luftwaffe commander; when he heard that his scapegoat was turning against him he flew at once to headquarters. With icy calm, he informed his Chief of Staff that he could have him indicted for insubordination— unless, of course, Jeschonnek himself was prepared to find another way out of the situation he had created. The implication was there, and could not be ignored. Jeschonnek, the beast of burden, had rebelled against the yoke; he would not be given a second chance.

Jeschonnek, deserted by the gods he had served so well, clung to one last hope for the salvation of his beloved Third Reich. The V weapons were no myth conjured out of thin air by Dr. Goebbels; they existed, they were under development and, given time, they could win the war for Germany. So believed Hans Jeschonnek, as the reins of Luftwaffe organisation slipped from his hands, and so believed many others as they hurried to the shelters with the wail of sirens rising and falling around them. Then the bombs fell on Peenemunde. After that, who could say when, if ever, the amazing Vergeltungswaffen would be ready for use against England?

Two days after the Peenemunde raid, Hans Jeschonnek ended the last chapter of his life. On 19th August, 1943, at his headquarters in East Prussia, he remained behind when his staff strolled out into the sunshine to report for the customary morning conference. Then, alone in the little bunker he used as an office, Jeschonnek took out his service pistol and shot himself. "His death means a particularly cruel and painful loss to all the services," commented the *Volkische Beobachter* next day. "The Luftwaffe loses an outstanding soldierly personality who prepared the way for great military victories in many campaigns. As the closest and most loyal colleague of the Reichsmarschall, Generaloberst Jeschonnek, occupying a post of the highest responsibility, gave his life for Fuehrer and Fatherland. . . . Even an insidious malignant disease was totally unable to paralyse his inexhaustible energy up to the very last moment. . . . The name of our tried and trusted Luftwaffe Chief of Staff will never be forgotten."

With this highly coloured, typically German, and largely untruthful tribute, Goering rid himself at last of his "closest and most loyal colleague." Jeschonnek's simple policy had been to satisfy his superiors to the exclusion of all else, to say "yes" and "no" as required, and this one fault had destroyed him. During the last few months of his life he had tried to make amends, but like Udet he had drifted too far along the road to disaster. Even the abruptness of his end was not allowed to shock the Nazi rank and file; the eloquent pen of Dr. Goebbels was, as always, at hand to provide the sugar coating for yet another bitter pill in the Luftwaffe box.

CHAPTER XX

DISINTEGRATION: 1944

GENERAL PELTZ, the young Angriffsfuehrer England, watched the last German offensive against England by piloted aircraft go into action from Chateaudun on the evening of 21st January, 1944. He saw a force of 447 bombers take off in two waves in this first attack of the so-called "Baby Blitz"—Hitler's last desperate attempt to relieve the unceasing pressure of the Anglo-American air offensive. Far away in Germany, the nightly Battle of Berlin was at its height, and the Luftwaffe fighter arm was battling with the U.S. 8th Air Force for command of the air. The losses were staggering; over a thousand German fighters destroyed in a single month. Somehow, a blow had to be struck in return, and Peltz was unfortunate enough to be saddled with the thankless, almost impossible task.

If Hitler's latest assault leader hoped that his bomber crews would return flushed with the excitement of success, he was doomed to disappointment from the first night. The seasoned veterans of the Battle of Britain days knew from bitter experience what to expect over London, but they were unpleasantly surprised at the great improvements that had been made in the British air defence organisation since 1940. Nevertheless, the German bomber waves managed to reach London. Using similar tactics to the R.A.F., they attempted to bomb on the target markers released by pathfinder aircraft, dropping mixed high explosive and incendiaries. Here the similarity ended, for the results, compared to the widespread devastation wrought by Air Marshal Harris in Germany, were so ineffective as to appear futile. The heavy defensive fire caused wildly inaccurate bombing over a wide area, and twenty-five Luftwaffe aircraft were shot down. As Peltz had feared, the offensive was off to a bad start, but he lacked the resources to bring about an improvement.

On 29th January, Peltz mounted a second attack on London, this time with a force of 285 twin-engined bombers, mostly Ju

188s and the older Ju 88s. Again, the raid caused only scattered residential damage in the London area, for the loss of eighteen aircraft. During February, Peltz tried again and again to prove that the Luftwaffe still possessed a bomber force worth the name, sending over 1,300 sorties against London, without success. The R.A.F. Fighter Command reigned supreme over England; so much so that it became impossible for German reconnaissance aircraft to venture into the lion's mouth for photographic evidence of the bombing results. In the dark as to the effect of his attacks, Peltz could only hope for the best and continue with his shoe-string air offensive to the bitter end. Before another month had passed, he was left with only 300 aircraft.

By the end of April, 1944, when the German bomber losses became prohibitive, Peltz had launched twelve attacks on London and the southern counties, and about 2,000 tons of bombs had been dropped during the whole offensive—a fraction of the tonnage dropped by the R.A.F. on Hamburg in a single week. Some damage and casualties had been caused and a few large fires started, but nothing of any significance achieved; whereas the defences had destroyed nearly two hundred bombers, a third of Peltz's force. This small defeat—the complete failure of Hitler's "Baby Blitz"—was important in only one respect. It marked the end of the Luftwaffe bomber arm as an air weapon, dispelled the Fuehrer's pipe dream that he still possessed an offensive air force, and awakened him to the fact that Germany needed more fighters.

Between 20th and 26th February, 1944, the Allied air offensive devastated seventy-five per cent of the German aircraft industry, and from that time the first tentative steps were taken to change the Luftwaffe into a defensive air force. As a beginning, the ponderous, hidebound Reichsluftfahrtministerium way of life was abruptly interrupted by the influence of a civilian—the brilliant young Minister for Armaments, Albert Speer. A technical genius who allowed neither red tape nor personal ambition to interfere with his work, Speer was an excellent driving force for his chosen fighter production leader, Saur, who was an ardent party man, lacking in personality but not in common sense. Speer was the dynamo and Saur the bulldozer; between them they hoped to breathe fresh life into the dying Luftwaffe.

Thrusting Erhard Milch unceremoniously into the background, Speer swept through the German aircraft industry like a whirlwind. In a short time, he drew up a new and realistic production programme, calling for the increased production of fighters and a drastic reduction in the numbers of new bombers. Existing fighter types such as the Bf 109 and Fw 190 were to be still produced in quantity, as under Milch, but new types were to be developed more quickly and given priority for materials if they proved to be worth it. Development of certain over-worked bomber types such as the Ju 88 was to be curtailed, and development of the troublesome, already outdated tandem-engined He 177 abandoned unless it could be quickly modified as a normal four-engined heavy bomber.

Speer's emergency aircraft construction programme was placed before Goering at a conference on the Obersalzburg in April, 1944. The Reichsmarschall immediately objected to any curtailment in bomber production, and stated that he wanted a minimum output of 400 He 177s and 500 Ju 88s per month. "The heavy bomber remains the kernel of the armament in the air," he insisted, disregarding every argument that Speer and Adolf Galland put forward. Goering was, of course, merely voicing Hitler's orders. The Fuehrer wanted to have his cake and eat it; more fighters and also more bombers. And this with an aircraft industry virtually crippled! Finally, Speer allowed his production programme to be altered as Goering had directed; but he confided to Galland afterwards that he would not accept the Reichsmarschall's decision as final.

Albert Speer kept his word. Within three months, the Ju 188, Ju 288, Ju 352, Me 110 and even the four-engined version of the He 177 had all been quietly removed from the production lines. On the other hand, development of the unconventional tandem-engined Do 335 fighter was proceeding with renewed vigour, and production of the He 219 night fighter, terminated by Milch, had been reinstated, though only in small numbers. With Speer watching over the special Jagerstab, or Fighter Staff, he had created with Otto Saur at the helm, fighters had top priority in Germany for the first time. By June, 1944, the Luftwaffe had a day fighter reserve of some 600 machines. It remained to be seen if production could keep pace with the increasing losses; and the Allied invasion of Europe was at hand.

From the night of 5th June, 1944, when 5,000 tons of bombs fell on Hitler's vaunted Atlantic Wall and the first British and American paratroops began to land in Normandy, the Luftwaffe was overwhelmed. As the largest invasion fleet in history moved across the blustery Channel, it was preceded and escorted by nearly 13,000 aircraft of all types, including 5,400 fighters, thundering in over the French coast, hurtling across German airfields with guns blazing, attacking German vehicles, shooting at everything that moved. Emplacements, bunkers and huge concrete blockhouses, erupted in smoke and flame, and the Normandy beaches became a great, seething volcano, vomiting fire, debris and fragments of men. "The Luftwaffe! Where is the Luftwaffe!" screamed the shocked infantrymen cowering in their slit trenches, but over their heads flashed only the fast Spitfires and Mustangs and the big Thunderbolts and Typhoons, followed in slow majesty by the massive formations of Fortresses and Liberators. Far out at sea, vague in the early morning mist, appeared the ships of the invasion fleet, outlined by the gouting flame from thousands of guns.

On this fateful day for Germany, von Sperrle, the commander of Luftflotte 3 in France, possessed only 300 operational aircraft, of which less than a hundred were fighters. In the event of invasion this small force—useless against anything more formidable than fighter-bomber attacks or similar sharp raids—was to be reinforced by the transfer of a further 600 aircraft from the Reich to prepared forward bases. Unfortunately, the order to move could only be given by Oberkommando der Luftwaffe headquarters; and the order came far too late. "According to statements by its commanding general, Fliegerkorps II learned of the start of the invasion only on 6th June at about eight o'clock in the morning," writes Adolf Galland. "Communications had been greatly disrupted and disorganised by the preceding air raids."

In the grey dawn the ramps of the assault craft began to crash down on the five invasion beaches: three British, code-named *Gold, Juno* and *Sword*, and two American, *Utah* and

Omaha. Ahead of the men who stumbled out into the shallows on the British beaches, smoke drifted over the shattered defences and the sand was littered with wreckage and broken obstacles. Miraculously, a few gun emplacements had survived the terrible preliminary bombardment, and here and there British troops began to fall as machine-gun fire cut them down. As the shocked defenders came to their senses, accurate shell and mortar fire blew great gaps in the masses of men streaming ashore, but still they came, wave after wave, until the beaches were choked with landing craft. By the afternoon of 6th June—D-Day—the German forward defences had been overcome and the invaders were fighting their way inland.

On *Utah* Beach the Americans, tanks and infantry together, were landing against wildly scattered fire that failed to stop them pouring across the cratered wilderness of tangled wire, overturned pillboxes and dead and wounded men. Soon, German 88 mm. guns—the deadly, superb dual-purpose 88s—were wreaking havoc and the intermittent flame of Spandaus was stabbing death through the smoke, but the American infantry continued to swarm through the inferno and press inland. More and more of the packed landing craft struck the beaches, sending wave after wave of men into the reeking shambles of the Normandy battlefield. The noise was indescribable; the shouts of command mingled with the screams of the wounded and the appalling racket of the guns. In an endless flood, tanks, trucks and men surged into France. It was a great and amazingly successful invasion—except on *Omaha* Beach.

Omaha Beach was a disaster. Over three hundred bombers had been sent to pound the defences there into rubble, but thick cloud obscured the *Omaha* area that morning and 13,000 bombs were dropped blindly up to three miles inland. Shaken by the naval bombardment but otherwise unscathed, the German guns remained silent until the first assault craft were almost ashore, then opened up with a murderous, raking fire. The ramps fell, and the heavily laden American troops plunged forward to be mown down like corn before the scythe. "They came ashore on *Omaha* Beach, the slogging, unglamorous men that no one envied," writes one D-Day historian. "No battle ensigns flew for them, no horns or bugles sounded. But they had history on their side. . . ." They fell in dozens and then in hundreds, until the first wave was decimated and *Omaha* Beach a scene of frightful carnage, with landing craft burning all along the water's edge and the shallows a jumble of bodies and wreckage. The second wave landed, trickled a few yards up the beach, and remained there in death; the third and fourth waves arrived and were at once pinned down by the devastating German fire. Time passed without any respite in the hail of steel from hundreds of guns, until *Omaha* Beach was strewn with American dead and the smoking, gutted hulks of destroyed landing craft were surrounded by drifting bodies.

Not until afternoon did the men thrown into the bloody desolation of *Omaha* Beach begin to fight their way inland, harried relentlessly by those among them who emerged as leaders. "Two kinds of people are staying on this beach," shouted Colonel George A. Taylor, as he strode up and down with bullets flying around him, "the dead and those who are going to die. Now let's get the hell out of here!" Slowly, the men of *Omaha* turned defeat into victory and finally reached the heights beyond the beaches, leaving behind them 2,500 dead, wounded and missing. Below, the sea was dotted with countless landing craft, still moving in under cover of the protecting warships; overhead, the sky trembled to the thunder of many aircraft engines. It was a splended, unforgettable and yet strangely awful sight, a great achievement made possible by untold wealth in material and the sacrifice of those who had almost, but not quite, lived to fight in Normandy.

Two Luftwaffe fighter pilots, Joseph Priller and Heinz Wodarcsyk, were probably the only German airmen to see action during the morning and afternoon of D-Day. While confused messages hummed along the wires from the forward areas and confusion reigned at Luftwaffe headquarters, Priller and Wodarczyk raced their Fw 190s into the air and set out to discover the truth about the invasion. Flying very fast and skilfully taking cover in the clouds, they arrived over Le Havre, turned along the coast—and abruptly found the vast Allied invasion fleet spread out below them. Priller was astounded, but he reacted with the speed of the trained fighter-pilot. At his signal the two Fw 190s fell away towards the mass of ships and levelled out over the British beaches, hurtling across *Sword* at less than fifty feet with cannon and machine-guns stabbing flame. Under the knife-edged wings, men hurled themselves to the sand or blazed away with automatic weapons. Then, as swiftly as they had arrived, Priller and Wodarczyk were gone, climbing furiously for the clouds with every ship in the Allied fleet hurling anti-aircraft fire after them.

After the daring hit-and-run raid by Priller and his companion, the Luftwaffe took no further part in the fight for the beaches until the night of 6th-7th June, when a few Ju 88s dropped a number of scattered bombs. The invasion had been expected for weeks—particularly during the perfect May weather—yet the Luftwaffe had been taken by surprise. Indeed, on the German side there was little else but disbelief and confusion for many hours. At Berchtesgaden, Hitler slept peacefully until the middle of the morning, blissfully unaware that his Atlantic Wall was crumbling, and even when awakened he decided to sit tight and await developments. According to the omniscient Fuehrer, the Normandy landings were a feint, and the main invasion was still to come. He, and he alone, could release the two key armoured divisions scheduled to go into action immediately Allied forces attempted to invade France, but despite urgent requests from von Runstedt's headquarters he refused to do so.

Even Erwin Rommel, the Desert Fox, commander of Army Group B in the west and more directly responsible than his superior, von Runstedt, for repulsing an Allied assault, had been tricked by the foul weather on 4th June into snatching at the chance of a few days leave in Germany. When D-Day came— also his wife's birthday—Rommel was many miles away at his Herrlingen home, his thoughts often returning to the coast he had worked so hard to fortify against invasion. Unlike von Runstedt, he believed that it was essential to hurl the Allies back into the sea before they could gain the slightest foothold. "Believe me, Lang, the first twenty-four hours of the invasion will be decisive . . ." he had confided to his aide on one occasion, and added, ". . . for the Allies, as well as Germany, it will be the longest day. . . ." On the fateful 6th June, it was 10.15 a.m. before he was informed of the landings, and he would spend the afternoon and most of the night driving back at top speed to his headquarters at La Roche-Guyon.

Too late, always too late. Within five days the German defences had been broken, sixteen Allied divisions were ashore and the armoured spearheads were thrusting inland. On 12th June, Rommel reported: "The strength of the enemy on land is increasing more quickly than our reserves can reach the front.... Our operations in Normandy will be rendered exceptionally difficult and even partially impossible by the extraordinarily strong and in some respects overwhelming superiority of the Allied Air Force and by the effect of heavy naval artillery... the enemy has complete control over the battle area and up to sixty miles behind the front. Almost all transport on roads and in open country is prevented by day by strong fighter-bomber and bomber formations.... Artillery taking up positions, ranks deploying, etc., are immediately bombarded with annihilating effect.... Neither our flak nor the Luftwaffe seems to be in a position to check this crippling and destructive operation of the enemy Air Force.... The material equipment of the Anglo-Americans, with numerous new weapons and war material, is far superior to the equipment of our divisions...." The acute situation brought Hitler from his lofty eyrie on the Obersalzburg five days later to attend a conference at Margival, near Soissons. Rommel, supported by von Runstedt, stated frankly that the Allies were on the verge of breaking out across France, and requested a strategic withdrawal to form a defensive line behind the Orne. Hitler refused; except for biting sarcasm and his automatic "no retreat" he had nothing to offer his commanders.

"Where is the Luftwaffe?" became the despairing cry of every German soldier in the west, from Rommel down to the merest private. Until 8th June, Luftflotte 3 possessed only eighty serviceable fighters; and on that date, when the transfer of some 600 aircraft from Germany commenced, many pilots arrived in Normandy to find their advanced airfields under attack by Allied bombers. So many landing grounds were unusable that large numbers of aircraft had to be diverted at the last minute, often by individual commanders acting on their own initiative. The few intact airfields quickly became overcrowded, and the confusion of mixed squadrons resulted in chaos. Allied fighters thronged the skies, and most of the transferred German aircraft were involved in dog-fights before they could make a landing. Even on this first day losses were very heavy, due to enemy action, crashes and the general disorganisation.

The Allied air superiority was overwhelming. "They bomb and shoot at anything which moves, even single vehicles and persons," reported one German armoured corps commander. "Our territory is under constant observation. . . ." And also under constant air bombardment; as a prelude to the crossing of the Orne, 2,200 aircraft dropped 8,000 tons of bombs. Against such mighty demonstrations of Anglo-American air power, the achievements of the Luftwaffe forces in the west were like drops in the ocean. Lacking heavy bombers, and with only a sprinkling of twin-engined medium bombers, the Luftwaffe could only throw "penny packets" of fighters and fighter-bombers into the inferno of the invasion bridgehead again and again. By the end of June 1,000 German aircraft had been lost, but thanks to Albert Speer and his emergency fighter programme a reserve of 998 machines had been rushed to the front a week later— more fuel for the hungry furnace. Adolf Galland sent Oberst Trautloft, a famous fighter ace, to the invasion area as Inspector of the Fighter Arm, but he could do little except bolster up the declining morale of the decimated squadrons. Galland himself, also in France at the time, was shattered by the wholesale disintegration of his forces.

On 17th July Rommel fell victim to Allied air power. After visiting the forward headquarters of the 2nd S.S. Armoured Corps, he was motoring back to La Roche-Guyon when his big open staff car was spotted by a roving squadron of Spitfires. Two of the fighters dived to within a few feet of the road, then flew along it, opening fire on the car from behind. A burst of 20 mm. cannon shells exploded into the left side of the vehicle. The driver collapsed and the car swerved to the right, struck the stump of a tree, skidded and overturned. Of the five occupants, three were seriously wounded, including Rommel, who had been thrown out of the car. The brilliant Desert Fox, the hero of the Afrika Korps, would never have the opportunity to win a German victory in Normandy; he had sustained a fractured skull, severe facial injuries and concussion.

Generalfeldmarschall Hans von Kluge—the so-called "clever Hans"—personally assumed command of Army Group B in the west. But Kluge, too, was not fated to save the situation in

Normandy. A month later, he had been relieved of his command and ordered back to Germany, another victim of Hitler's terrible retribution on the conspirators who came to be known as "the men of 20th July"—the only active resistance group to strike a blow into the heart of the Third Reich and attempt to end the war. On the aircraft taking him to Berlin, Kluge thwarted his executioners by swallowing cyanide.

At last, the German officer corps had turned on the megalomaniac who straddled the military machine like a colossus, and with the bending of the stiff-necked Prussian Junker class the many and varied opponents of Hitler were drawn together for the first time. Since 1938 there had been at least five attempts on the Fuehrer's life, all hurriedly organised by men who were not lacking in courage but found it almost impossible to penetrate the hard shell of Hitler's immediate circle. Not until 1944, when such opponents of the Nazi Party as the retired Field Marshal von Witzleben, Generals Fromme and Beck, Admiral Canaris of the Abwehr and General von Stulpnagel, the Military Governor of France, became active members of the resistance movement, did the simmering antagonism against Hitler flame into a determined conspiracy to kill him. Apart from the actual assassination of the Fuehrer—beyond which all earlier plots had never ventured—the 20th July conspirators hoped to seize all military and government offices in Berlin and Paris, and an excellent staff plan, code-named *Valkyrie*, had been prepared for this purpose. Unfortunately in the light of later events, the release of the *Valkyrie* operational forces was made dependent on the assassination of Hitler; while he lived, the officer clique feared his twisted hatred.

And Hitler, the "Bohemian corporal" of the old aristocrat von Runstedt, had an astonishing capacity for surviving his enemies.

July 20th, 1944. . . .

Near the long wooden hutment, or Gastbaracke, temporarily in use as a conference room at Hitler's headquarters in East Prussia stood the bulky figure of Field Marshal Keitel, watching the high-ranking Wehrmacht and Luftwaffe officers strolling past him towards the building. From time to time Keitel glanced with a frown at his wristwatch, his gaze always returning for a moment to the closed door of the ante-room some little distance away.

Alone in the tiny ante-room, a certain Oberst Count Claus von Stauffenberg worked quickly but efficiently on the package which nestled amid the papers inside his open brief-case. Using small pliers—for a British mine in the desert had cost him his right arm, two fingers of his left hand and his left eye—Stauffenberg deftly gripped a tiny capsule inside the package and broke it. Then he carefully closed the brief-case, and as carefully slid it beneath his good arm. A moment later, he heard Keitel's brusque voice shouting: "Hurry, Stauffenberg!" The voice was irritable; Keitel, the Fuehrer's willing lackey, liked to throw his weight about when dealing with subordinates.

Stauffenberg unlocked the door of the ante-room, saw Keitel awaiting him, and walked out into the sunlight. Inside the brief-case, unseen acid ate away at the wire holding a detonator tightly in place; within ten minutes the firing pin would be released. Outwardly composed as he talked casually with Keitel, Stauffenberg's nerves must have been tuned to shrieking pitch, his brain almost bursting with the awful secret he carried with him. As they entered the conference room, he knew without glancing at his watch that three minutes had already passed, and no man can have been more aware of the vital seconds ticking inevitably away.

Around the heavy wooden table in the long room, uniformed men raised their heads as Stauffenberg and Keitel came through the entrance hall. Almost at once, Stauffenberg saw Hitler; he was leaning over the table, a large magnifying glass in his hand. On the Fuehrer's right, General Heusinger, the Chief of Operations, was speaking, his forefinger moving across the large map spread over the table. Keitel interrupted the gloomy report on the deteriorating situation in Russia to announce: "Oberst von Stauffenberg, my Fuehrer. He will report on the new Volksgrenadier divisions." Momentarily, Stauffenberg looked into the brilliant eyes of the foremost man in Germany. Then Hitler said, "Good. But first I will hear the rest of Heusinger's report." He nodded curtly and sprawled forward across the table again.

Stauffenberg took his place at the table. As Heusinger's voice droned on in the sultry air, Stauffenberg casually placed the brief-case under the table, leaning it against the inside of the oaken support, near Hitler's chair. Then he glanced quickly around him. The official stenographer, Berger, was intent on his notes; otherwise all eyes were on Heusinger. The Fuehrer was intently examining the map, Keitel on his left, Heusinger reaching over the table towards him. Unhurriedly, Stauffenberg faded into the background. He retreated to the door, reached it, and passed through the entrance hall into the open air. Behind him, the acid ate steadily through the wire.

As Heusinger's report drew to an end, Keitel glanced down the table, seeking to catch the eye of the next speaker, Stauffenberg. A moment later, frowning with annoyance, he was in the entrance hall. The soldier on duty there told him that Stauffenberg had left the building. "The Russian," Heusinger was saying in the background, "is driving with strong forces west of the Duna towards the north..." Perplexed, Keitel hesitated then turned back to the conference room.

At that moment—12.42 p.m.—the bomb in Stauffenberg's brief-case exploded. A great sheet of flame erupted from the floor of the Gastebaracke, bodies hurtled out of the windows, glass shattered, men screamed in agony and jagged splinters of wood flew in all directions. Stauffenberg, who was standing a couple of hundred yards away, said afterwards that the explosion was "like a direct hit from a 155 mm. shell". He was certain that all in the room must have been blown to pieces. Jumping into his car, he used his rank to pass through the check points and left Hitler's headquarters; within minutes he was racing to Rastenburg airfield, where a Heinkel He 111 bomber awaited him for the flight to Berlin.

Meanwhile, out of the wrecked and burning conference room staggered the coughing, blackened figure of a man, leaning heavily on Keitel's arm. His trousers in shreds, his hair awry, the Man of Destiny, the Fuehrer of the Third Reich reeled out into the dust-filled, choking air. Temporarily paralysed, injured by falling beams, deafened and scorched, by some strange trick of fate he had nevertheless survived. In this respect he was more fortunate than most of the others who had been standing in the immediate vicinity of the explosion. The stenographer, Berger, was dead; Colonel Brandt, Heusinger's chief of staff, and General Schmundt, Hitler's adjutant, were dying; and General

Korten, Jeschonnek's successor as Luftwaffe chief of staff, later died of his wounds. Generals Jodl and Heusinger and Karl Bodenschatz, Goering's adjutant, were seriously injured, and no single person in the room escaped unharmed.

Because Adolf Hitler still lived, the Berlin rebellion ended in failure. Three precious hours were wasted while the conspirators hesitated to set *Valkyrie* in action, and by the time Stauffenberg arrived on the scene it was too late. Goebbels spoke to Hitler on the direct line to Rastenburg, and once alerted soon had an S.S. cordon thrown around the offices where the conspirators were dithering and talking without doing anything. Before midnight the plot was shattered and some of the ring-leaders, including Stauffenberg, shot without trial by a firing squad. Old General Beck, after trying twice to shoot himself, was finally despatched by an S.S. bullet in the throat.

In France, there had been the same fatal hesitation. A worried von Kluge refused to throw in his hand with the conspirators at La Roche-Guyon—Generals Blumentritt, Speidel and Stulpnagel—until confirmation of Hitler's death was received, and the delay ruined all hope of success. When Kluge learned that Hitler was still alive, he refused to support the conspirators and the plot collapsed within a few hours. Stulpnagel, summoned at once to Berlin, attempted to shoot himself near Verdun. Despite blindness and a serious head wound, in due course he was dragged before the notorious People's Court in Berlin and sentenced to death.

Upon regaining consciousness in hospital, Stulpnagel had mentioned the name of Rommel, and the Field Marshal, by that time convalescent at his home near Ulm, was drawn into the net of Hitler's vengeance. Rommel, still a very sick man, was given the chance to die "honourably" by taking poison. For the sake of his family he agreed, and on 14th October, 1944, ended a glorious career huddled in the back seat of his car, a mile or so away from his Herrlingen home. Hitler ordered a state funeral for the hero of North Africa who had "unexpectedly died of his wounds" and von Runstedt delivered the oration in the city hall at Ulm. "His heart," said Runstedt, who now looked a broken and bewildered old man, "belonged to the Fuehrer."

For many months the slaughter of the 20th July conspirators continued. "It is my wish that they be hanged like cattle," stated

Hitler. The actual death roll will probably never be known, but at least 4,000 people were executed and many more sent to the concentration camps. The Luftwaffe would appear to have largely escaped Hitler's lust for blood, and perhaps this was just as well; the Fuehrer had long ago wearied of his air arm and its many failures. Like Goering, he continued to accuse the German pilots of cowardice—at a time when the Luftwaffe was losing 500 aircraft every week over France. On at least one occasion Hitler threatened to dissolve the fighter arm and strengthen the anti-aircraft units, but was restrained from doing so by Speer. After General Korten had been killed by the 20th July bomb at Rastenburg, General-Leutnant Werner Kreipe was appointed Luftwaffe Chief of Staff, but he could do nothing to relieve the desperate situation. By the end of the year Goering was looking around for a successor to Kreipe; the disorganisation and confusion was mounting to a climax of disaster.

Without the Luftwaffe, Hitler still tried to gasp defiance against Britain; the V weapons were his last chance to strike back. The first V.1 flying bombs had been launched against London on 13th June, 1944—D-Day plus 7—and during the next three months over 9,000 of the little jet-propelled missiles catapulted into the air. At least 2,000 proved to be faulty and crashed soon after launching or strayed off course and fell into the sea; forty per cent of those which crossed the English coast were shot down by the defences; and the remaining V.1s exploded somewhere in the London area. By the autumn of 1944 many of the launching sites in Northern France and Holland had been abandoned, and subsequent V.1s were launched from Heinkel He 111 bombers over the North Sea. About 1,200 flying bombs were launched from aircraft, but of these only 205 reached the target. The effect on London was that of another unwelcome but endurable "baby blitz"; the "buzz bombs" or "doodlebugs", as they were soon called, were treated with respect but normal life in the capital remained uninterrupted, though some 5,000 people were killed and 16,000 wounded in Britain by V.1 missiles.

So much for Vergeltungswaffen Ein, the weapon supposed to bring a German victory at the eleventh hour. The V.2 (A.4) rocket was a far more terrifying proposition; it could not be seen, heard or intercepted in flight. The first V.2s were launched against London on 8th September, 1944, and were used almost without interruption until 27th March, 1945. More than 1,000 V.2s were launched on London during this period, and a further 2,100 rockets fell on the supply port of Antwerp and the Allied bases of Liège and Brussels. In Great Britain, 2,700 people were killed and about 6,000 injured by V.2s, the cost in human life of a bombardment against which no defence existed. London was finally reprieved by Hitler's old spectre of too little and too late; with the Allied capture of most of the V.2 launching ramps the hail of rockets dwindled to a trickle until Germany collapsed.

What remained of the Luftwaffe? It is an astonishing fact—and an indication of the scope of Allied air power—that in September, 1944, German fighter production reached a total of 3,013 aircraft, the highest figure attained; yet there was a desperate shortage of fighters. Numerically, the Luftwaffe fighter arm should have been stronger than ever before, but the losses were so staggering that it was impossible to build up any reserves. Germany needed new types of aircraft, and again it is astonishing to find that at last the revolutionary fighters and bombers promised to Ernst Udet in 1940 were belatedly making an appearance. But only in pitifully small numbers; a Gruppe here, a Gruppe there, struggling to prop up the disintegrating structure. After having to soldier on for year after year with the same types of aircraft, often adapted to suit a dozen different roles, the Luftwaffe was presented with some truly remarkable machines when the war was already lost; the Messerschmitt Me 262 jet fighter and Me 163 rocket fighter; the Junkers Ju 488 and Ju 287 bombers; the Arado Ar 234 turbo-jet bomber and Ar 232 transport; and the Dornier Do 335 and 635 fighters.

Of all these aircraft types, the Messerschmitt Me 262 is perhaps the only one that could have saved the Luftwaffe from defeat in 1945. Delays in production, the disinterest of Goering and Milch and the intervention of Hitler contrived to kill the Me 262 programme. The history of the world's first operational jet fighter is therefore worth examining in some detail; for the tragedy of the Me 262 was the tragedy of the Luftwaffe.

CHAPTER XXI

FIGHTERS, BOMBERS OR FIGHTER-BOMBERS? 1944

IF you were serving with an American B-17 or B-24 squadron operating over Germany in the summer of 1944, the odds were against you being alive and well in 1945. Four miles above Wiener Neustadt, Regensburg, Schweinfurt or Berlin, it was very easy to die in the bright afternoon sunshine; too easy for men who were young and unwilling to trade life for a few hours of glory. To fly with those massed squadrons, the huge, staggered formations of majestic Fortresses or Liberators deploying hundred of defensive guns, was to venture into a man-made inferno created by packs of Fw 190s, Bf 109s and Ju 88s, attacking in waves through the smoking, criss-cross lines of tracer. "Fighters at twelve o'clock, high!"—and the guns from every bomber would be firing together, the knife-edged wings of the German fighters stabbing orange flame as they came in for head-on attacks, closing to point-blank range and then breaking gracefully away through the bomber formations, still firing. To stand behind the pilot and co-pilot of a B-17, with all guns pounding away and the pungent smell of burnt cordite filling the cockpit, was to stand poised on the brink of a nightmare; to glimpse awful scenes jumping into sight and then vanishing in a moment, like the flickering images on a cinema screen. Beyond that reeling glassed cabin, bombers would be dropping out of the formation in flames, coming apart at the seams like old battered toys or breaking quickly and neatly into two pieces, spilling men out into space like peas from a dry pod. American and German fighters would be hurtling past at nearly 600 miles an hour, cannon blazing; perhaps a stricken Fw 190 in a half roll, trailing great sheets of flame; a pair of yellow-nosed Bf 109s caught in the bomber cross-fire and exploding together; and below, more and more black-crossed fighters rising as though drawn hypnotically to the slaughter. And the B-17 or B-24 formations, all guns hammering, would fly relentlessly on to the target, to those few moments kaleidoscoped into an unholy climax of falling bombs, flak and fighters. Then back from the target, harried all the way, flying through the debris of the great daylight air battles of 1944; the emergency hatches, exit doors, tangled parachutes, bodies, fragments of fuselages and tail-planes, whole engines and wings; bits and pieces of men and machines, the drifting flotsam of war as it was fought in the air.

Into this bloody, embattled arena entered Willy Messerschmitt's greatest achievement, the Me 262 jet fighter. It streaked through the skies over Germany in the autumn of 1944 like a meteor—"as if angels were pushing" in the words of Adolf Galland—the classic bomber-destroyer, without equal anywhere in the world. After six Me 262s had shot down fifteen American four-engined heavy bombers in as many minutes, General Spaatz, commanding the U.S. Strategic Air Forces, was moved to report that he and General Eisenhower were aware that the deadly German jet fighters could make the losses of the Allied bomber forces "unbearable in the near future". Yet at the time—September, 1944—the Luftwaffe possessed only one operational Gruppe of Me 262s!

The history of German jet propulsion development can be traced back to the 1920s, when members of the Deutsche Rakete Geselschaft, or German Rocket Society, were carrying out research work on liquid-fuel rockets, and Fritz von Opel, the automobile magnate, was experimenting with solid-fuel rockets. The latter rockets were used with some success to power racing cars, and a special Opel rocket-powered sailplane was flown for the first time in September, 1929. When the National Socialists came to power three years later, the use of the rocket as a practical power unit was visualised, and a new department under the leadership of Dipl. Ing. Dornberger was created within the Reichsluftfahrtministerium to develop rocket propulsion. This department was later reorganised and installed in the new research establishment at Peenemunde, being divided into two sections, one dealing with test-bed work under Wehrmacht control, and the other section dealing with flight test work under Luftwaffe supervision. About the same time, Professor Helmuth Walther, a prominent German engineer, formed a company named Helmuth Walterwerke to develop and manufacture rocket-power units.

18—TL

In 1936 Walther's company was ordered to design and build a rocket-propulsion unit to power a high-speed aircraft envisaged by Dr. Alexander Lippisch, an exponent of the delta-wing and tailless aeroplane. A special single-seater monoplane, the Heinkel He 176, was used during 1937 to flight-test the Walther rocket motor, and the unit was also experimentally fitted into a standard Heinkel He 112 fighter. Meanwhile, the Ernst Heinkel concern was taking a practical interest in the principle of turbo-jet propulsion, and several units were completed as a private venture, continued experiments leading to the first successful German gas turbine, the He S 3. On 27th August, 1939, the world's first flight by a jet-propelled aircraft —the Heinkel He 178—took place. Later, the Heinkel test pilot Erich Warsitz demonstrated the He 178 to Milch and Udet, who were impressed but failed to arouse any enthusiasm in Goering or Hitler.

In January, 1939, Lippisch had accepted an invitation to join the Messerschmitt company in order to accelerate and enlarge upon his experimental and practical work, and a year later the Lippisch-designed tailless single-seater fighter, designated the DFS 194, made an appearance. Powered by a Walther liquid-fuel rocket unit, the DFS 194 attained a maximum speed of 350 m.p.h. with an initial climbing speed of 5,300 ft. per minute. As a result of this phenomenal performance, the Deutsche Luftfahrtministerium decided that the fighter should go into quantity production, and this was undertaken by the Messerschmitt works at Augsburg. The production development of the DFS 194 was redesignated the Messerschmitt Me 163, with the code name Schwalbe (Swallow) and the more apt nickname Komet, or Comet. Later, Professor Lippisch disagreed with Messerschmitt over the handling of the Me 163 project and returned to his native Vienna.

The Messerschmitt Me 262 was envisaged in 1938, when the Messerschmitt A.G. was asked to design a suitable aircraft to accommodate two new gas turbines—the BMW 003 and the Junkers Jumo 004—which were being developed and bench-tested at the time. The year 1941 saw the appearance of two prototype jet fighters: the Heinkel He 280, designed around the Heinkel He S 8 gas turbine, and the Messerschmitt Me 262, intended as an airframe for the Junkers Jumo 004. Both airframes were completed in advance of the power units, and for flight-testing purposes the He 280 was flown as a glider, with streamlined dummy engine nacelles, and the Me 262 with a Junkers Jumo 211 air-cooled inverted-Vee motor driving an airscrew in the nose. When the Heinkel He S 8 gas turbine unit became available, it was installed in both the He 280 and the Me 262, but proved to be unsatisfactory and later had to be dropped in favour of the BMW 003 and Junkers Jumo 004. The amazingly simple Argus impulse-duct jet motor was also flight tested for the first time in 1941 and later produced in large numbers to power V.1 flying bombs.

In 1943, the first turbine-powered flights of the twin-jet Me 262 Sturmvogel (Stormbird) took place, the power units being the production-version Junkers Jumo 004B, mounted in underslung nacelles beneath the sweptback wings; because of these underslung units a tall tricycle undercarriage had of necessity to be fitted. The flight tests were highly successful, and after various minor modifications the Me 262 was cautiously ordered into quantity production as the Me 262A. All further work on the He 280 was abandoned.

Goering and Milch continued to remain indifferent to the possibilities of the Me 262, although Professor Messerschmitt had long ago pleaded to be allowed to produce "at least a few hundred fighters with jet propulsion". He had also proposed the production of a fast bomber, but with a petrol engine. Milch at first professed an interest in jet bombers, but later changed his mind in favour of jet fighters. Hans Jesschonnek sat on the fence as usual, and said nothing; official apathy hung like a grey cloud over the Me 262 programme. Meanwhile, the Reichsluftfahrtministerium had decided that a production rate of twenty machines per month should be attained in 1944.

In an effort to arouse official interest, Professor Messerschmitt invited Adolf Galland to flight test an Me 262. "On landing I was more enthusiastic than I had ever been before," recalls Galland in his memoirs. "Feelings and impressions were, however, no criterion; it was the performance and characteristics that mattered. This was not a step forward. This was a leap!" He immediately sent a telegram to Milch: "The 262 is a very great hit. It will guarantee us an unbelievable advantage in operations while the enemy adheres to the piston engine. Its airworthiness makes the best impression. . . . This aircraft opens up completely new tactical possibilities."

The opinion of a fighter leader like Galland was still of some value in the hidebound Luftwaffe, and he was not content to let written reports speak for him. Having made up his mind about the Me 262, he went to see Goering, who was soon sharing the enthusiasm of his subordinate. While Galland was still with him, the Reichsmarschall telephoned Milch, and the subsequent conversation left Galland in no doubt that the Me 262 had at last been accepted. Goering said that he would ask Hitler the very next day for permission to mass produce the new fighter; but he had forgotten—or still failed to realise—how much the Fuehrer distrusted him.

Hitler received Goering coldly, and showed little interest in the Me 262. He was quick to remind the Reichsmarschall that he had been promised the He 177 heavy bomber in 1941 and it was still not ready for quantity production. As for the Me 262, Hitler felt that it would have to wait a while until he reached a decision about its value. In the meantime, he expressly forbade any preparations for mass production. Later, the Fuehrer held a conference of aircraft engineers and designers, supposedly to discuss the jet fighter programme, but actually to reiterate his orders without bothering to heed outside suggestions. Flight tesing of the Me 262 was to be continued with a few prototypes; mass production was still strictly forbidden.

Then Hitler began to wonder if the Me 262 could be used as a fast bomber. On 2nd November, 1943, Goering visited the Messerschmitt works and asked Professor Messerschmitt : "Would the Me 262 be able to carry one or two bombs so that it could be used as a surprise fighter-bomber?" He added that the Fuehrer was taking a personal interest in the matter. Messerschmitt replied that the aircraft could indeed be modified to carry two externally mounted 1,100 lb. bombs or one 2,200 lb. bomb; a factually correct answer which meant precisely nothing, for almost any fighter could be adapted as a fighter-bomber—provided the drastic loss of performance was acceptable. The carrying of a bomb load would reduce the maximum speed of the Me 262 by as much as 120 m.p.h. Nevertheless, Goering was apparently delighted, and hurried back to Hitler with the good news that Germany had a new type of fast bomber.

Yet, in August of the same year, the General of the Bombers, Werner Baumbach, had stated: "As home defence must be made strong first—I say that as a bomber officer, although any-one can appreciate that it must go against the grain—I propose that in the present situation we give up the He 177 (heavy bomber) and its capacity in favour of the jet fighter and jet propulsion."

On 26th November the Me 262 was demonstrated before Hitler at Insterburg in East Prussia. The Fuehrer asked at once, "Can this aircraft carry bombs?" Goering turned to Professor Messerschmitt, who replied carefully, "Yes, my Fuehrer. Theoretically, yes—there is enough spare power to carry 1,000 lb., perhaps even 2,000 lb."

Hitler nodded. "For years I have demanded from the Luft-waffe a fast bomber which can reach its target in spite of enemy fighter defence," he said. "In this aircraft you present to me as a fighter plane I see the Blitz Bomber, with which I will repel the invasion in its first and weakest phase. Regardless of the enemy air umbrella, it will strike the recently landed mass of material and troops, creating panic, death and destruction. At last this is Blitz Bomber! Of course, none of you thought of that!" And he looked triumphantly at the men who faced him.

Messerschmitt apparently deemed this to be an occasion when silence was golden, and Goering, who should have acted as spokesman for the fighter experts, also chose to say not a word. Nevertheless, for once a decision of Hitler's was ignored. The existing programme for production of the Me 262 as a fighter remained virtually unchanged, and the first Me 262A-O fighters for service evaluation were used in action during March, 1944. Meanwhile, Adolf Galland was openly pressing for production of a thousand jet fighters a month, and at the end of April he again drew attention to the Me 262 in a résumé of the air situation, commenting as follows:

"The problem which the Americans have set the fighter arm is—I am speaking solely of daytime—quite simply the problem of superiority in the air. As things are now, it is almost the same thing as command of the air. The ratio between the two sides in day fighting at the present time is between 1:6 and 1:8. The enemy's proficiency in action is extraordinarily high and the technical accomplishment of his aircraft so outstanding that all we can say is—something must be done! In the last four months we have lost well over a thousand men in the day-time. Of course, that figure included many of our best Gesch-wader, Gruppe and Staffel leaders. I have mentioned this last possibility in many a report and conference, and gone so far as to talk of the danger of collapse. Now we have reached the point, because the numerical superiority of the enemy has become so great that we must ask ourselves whether the fight is not becom-ing extraordinarily unprofitable to us.

"What can we do to alter this situation?

"First, we must change the ratio. This means that the industry shall produce aircraft in numbers which will enable us to build up the fighter arm. Secondly, as we are numerically inferior, and always will be—let there be no doubt about that—technical performance must be improved. . . . I am convinced that we can do wonders even with a small number of greatly superior air-craft like the Me 262 or Me 163. The battle between the fighters —which in daytime is a preliminary to attacking the bombers— is largely a matter of morale. We must break the enemy's morale. With the help of the two factors, numbers and performance, the fighting value of our formations and the level of their train-ing will inevitably be raised. I do not expect that we shall ever be on equal terms with our opponents, but I think that we shall achieve a reasonable ratio.

"In the last ten battles we have lost on an average more than fifty aircraft and forty men. That means five hundred aircraft and four hundred airmen in ten great raids, and at the present rate they cannot be replaced. . . . We need higher performance to give our own fighter force a feeling of superiority even if we are inferior in numbers. For example, to give some idea of values : at the moment I would rather have one Me 262 than five Bf 109s!"

So far, so good. Production of the Me 262 as a fighter con-tinued, although Messerschmitt was also developing a bomber prototype, the Me 262V10. Then, at a conference held on the Obersalzburg in the summer of 1944, Hitler again mentioned the Me 262. "How many have been produced so far?" he demanded.

"One hundred and twenty, my Fuehrer," replied Erhard Milch.

"And how many of these can carry bombs?"

"None, my Fuehrer," came the inevitable answer. "The Me 262 is being produced exclusively as a fighter aircraft."

The words Milch spoke exploded in Hitler's ears like a succession of firecrackers. Two minutes later the Fuehrer was on his feet, hammering with his fists on the table and roaring insults and wild accusations. "You have constantly lied to me and deceived me!" he screamed at Milch. "The Luftwaffe is disobedient, unreliable and disloyal. Look at all the promises! And yet what has it achieved? Nothing. My orders have been systematically disobeyed. I will not stand it any longer!"

Stunned by the tirade, Milch was unable to find his voice; and in the background the amazing Goering nodded agreement with everything Hitler said. Soon afterwards, Milch was dismissed all his appointments; hurled out into the darkness like so many who had briefly crossed swords with the Fuehrer. As for the Me 262, Hitler ordered the modification of all existing machines as bombers, and forbade any mention of the aircraft as a fighter or even as a fighter-bomber. There would be no further discussion or argument about the Me 262; it was a Blitz bomber. All training and testing work on the Me 262 was at the same time taken away from Adolf Galland and handed to the bomber leader, General Peltz. Both Galland and Messerschmitt tried desperately to make Goering fight against the decision, but the Reichsmarschall chose to retire into his shell. When Galland became too persistent, Goering brought the discussion to an end by stating firmly : "So that we may understand each other clearly, I must report that there is no longer any question of debating the fundamental point at issue."

Having cut the Me 262 fighter programme to pieces, Hitler later relented slightly and made it known that "the tests should be continued with some of the prototypes as fighters". Meanwhile, the various modifications and problems arising from the fighter-to-bomber conversions naturally delayed tactical employment of the Me 262, and not until after the Normandy landings had taken place did Hitler's "fast bomber" make an appearance. The conversion of the Schwalbe fighter finally resulted in the Me 262A-2a, code-named the Sturmvogel or Stormbird, which entered service with Kampfgeschwader 51 when the Allied forces were already surging across France. By the time Kampfgeschwader 6, 27 and 54 had been re-equipped with the type, the German army in the west was in full retreat. Behind the scenes, Peltz was floundering in the confusion of trying to train his bomber pilots to fly an aircraft designed and built as a fighter; and all for the sake of dropping one or two bombs that could do no real damage.

Adolf Galland, who had been left to amuse himself with a test commando unit of a few Me 262 fighters, at last received orders to form a jet fighter unit, the nucleus of Jagdgeschwader 7, later to take a heavy toll of Allied bombers. There were two reasons for this change of heart by Hitler; the Arado Ar 234B jet bomber was beginning to roll off the production lines; and Albert Speer, with the unexpected support of Himmler, was pressing for release of the Me 262 as a fighter. The first Me 262 fighter unit was commanded by Major Walter Nowotny, a brilliant young Luftwaffe fighter ace and holder of the diamonds, who had shot down over 200 enemy aircraft. He was killed in action on 9th October, 1944.

Towards the end of 1944, when the defeat of Germany remained only a matter of time, Hitler decided to give priority to the Me 262 in the fighter role. The Me 262 fiasco thus reached the point of absurdity with the Fuehrer's order that all the Me 262 fighters converted to bombers must now be reconverted to fighters! More time was lost while this work was undertaken, and the production figures for the Me 262 serve to highlight the ridiculous situation. A total of 1,433 Me 262s were built during the war years, of which 568 had been produced by 31st December, 1944, and 865 completed during the first four months of 1945. Of these, only about 100 aircraft were used in action, some having to be reconverted into fighters at the front under enemy fire.

The many delays with the Me 262 had inspired the Reichsluftfahrtministerium to issue a specification calling for a cheap jet fighter which could be mass produced and hurriedly rushed into service in large numbers. Galland immediately took up arms against this idea, as he correctly judged that the limitations imposed by the specification spelled failure to any jet fighter. Also, production of the Me 262 would be further delayed. And supposing the miracle did take place and a fighter appeared which could indeed be manufactured in large numbers, how was the desperate shortage of trained pilots to be overcome? Galland suggested that all new projects should be dropped in favour of the Me 262, which had proved its worth in action; the situation was too desperate for the time-wasting development of new types.

Galland's arguments fell on deaf ears, and Professor Ernst Heinkel's latest design, the He 162 jet fighter, was accepted by Goering as the aircraft that would break the Allied bombing offensive. The He 162 Salamander, more popularly known as the Volksjager, or People's Fighter, was of mixed wood and steel construction and powered by a single Jumo 004 turbo-jet engine mounted above the fuselage and behind the cockpit. Imperfectly developed and produced in very great haste, the He 162 progressed from drawing-board to initial flight tests in the amazingly short period of sixty-nine days, and was so light and simple in concept that it was almost as primitive as the V.1 flying bomb. It could hardly be classed as a high-performance fighter, but Otto Saur, the fighter production leader, widely acclaimed the aircraft and sincerely believed that thousands of He 162s would soon be filling the skies over Germany. It was hoped to solve the pilot problem by using a year's intake of Hitlerjugend (Hitler Youth) boys of sixteen and seventeen years of age, who were to be hurriedly trained in gliders, then transferred directly to the Volksjager and thrown into battle. That such an insane idea could be put forward—let alone gladly accepted—indicates the disastrous state of affairs existing in the Luftwaffe hierarchy by the end of 1944.

On 10th December, 1944, the Heinkel test pilot Flugkapitan Peter demonstrated the He 162 to a party of high Nazi and Luftwaffe officials. During a low-altitude, high-speed run across the airfield the starboard wing leading edge suddenly broke away, followed by the starboard aileron and wing-tip, then the fighter performed several rolls and disintegrated, killing the pilot. It was discovered that the new type of wood adhesive used in the construction of the He 162 had failed under stress, but the crash made Saur and the other Volksjager advocates doubt the capabilities of their "miracle fighter" for the first time. Nevertheless, the He 162 was ordered into quantity production.

Fortunately for the Hitlerjugend boys who were supposed to fly the He 162, only about 100 machines were delivered before the shortage of fuel, Allied bombing and the German capitulation brought production to an end. During the last weeks of the war, all the wooden parts of the aircraft were being made in carpenters' shops in Thuringia and Wurttemberg and then assembled in three main centres, and large numbers of semi-completed Volksjager were captured during the Allied advance. A few airworthy He 162s were later flown to Britain and tested at Farnborough, but they were found to be anything but "miracle fighters", being prone to many defects and extremely difficult to handle at speed.

Adolf Galland's outspoken comments on the Me 262 fiasco, followed by his lonely struggle against Saur and the other He 162 advocates, had made him a marked man. In January, 1945, Goering virtually relieved him of all his duties by sending him on indefinite leave without bothering to appoint a successor, a move that inadvertently blew the lid off the crisis seething in the German fighter arm. Obersts Lutzow and Trautloft, heading a delegation of veteran fighter pilots, drafted a memorandum for Goering, which, in effect, blamed the Reichsmarschall for the disastrous state of the Luftwaffe and demanded immediate action to save the situation. The "fighter pilot mutineers" hoped to be granted an audience by Hitler, but had to be satisfied with Goering, who met them in the Haus der Flieger in Berlin. He was accompanied, among others, by General der Flieger Karl Koller, the last Chief of Staff of the Luftwaffe, who had reluctantly accepted a post nobody wanted when Goering agreed to give him a free hand. (Koller criticised Goering to his face for taking no interest in Luftwaffe affairs, and the Reichsmarschall promised roguishly to "be a good boy in future"; in this mood, according to Koller, he was "irresistible".)

Silently, Goering read the memorandum placed before him. It pointed out that the fighter arm of the Luftwaffe had suffered fearful losses for a considerable time, yet the Reichsmarschall continued to charge his fighter pilots with cowardice, mentioned the increasing influence of the bomber arm in fighter matters and stated that the dismissal of Galland at such a time seemed to be a grave error. The equipping of bomber units with the Me 262 was also considered a terrible mistake. Finally, the memorandum demanded the removal from their posts of a number of high Luftwaffe officers—Goering's cronies—and concluded with the blunt words; "The fighter arm is of the opinion that the Reichsmarschall is being ill-advised by his staff and it is also of the opinion that all officers without long war experience should now be removed and replaced by experienced fighter commanders."

Before Goering could open his mouth, Lutzow, in defiance of all protocol, rose to his feet and spoke. "Herr Reichsmarschall," he said quietly, "in the name of my comrades I must ask you to give me fifty minutes uninterrupted time to speak, as otherwise our intention of making the situation clear to you will be frustrated."

Goering was crimson in the face with anger. "What impudence!" he shouted. "Are you suggesting that I didn't build up a strong Luftwaffe?"

Lutzow looked directly at him. "Yes, Herr Reichsmarschall, you did build up a strong Luftwaffe," he replied. "And it won you many victories in Poland and France. But afterwards you went to sleep."

The last remark brought the meeting to an abrupt end. Goering seemed momentarily paralysed with rage, then he yelled, "This is the limit! You're all mutineers!" and stalked out of the room. Once back at Karinhall and away from the accusing eyes of his subordinates, he became the old ruthless Goering, ready to swing the axe without pausing to consider the facts. Lutzow was relieved of all his duties and virtually banished from his native Germany, for he was placed in command of a fighter unit in the Italian theatre of operations. Trautloft was also dismissed. Adolf Galland, who Goering suspected had instigated the "mutiny" while remaining in the background, was ordered to leave Berlin at once and not return without permission, an indication that he was about to be publicly dragged through the mire as yet another scapegoat to save the Reichsmarschall's skin. What is history to make of this vain, grotesque man who buried his head in the sand to the bitter end, and used his authority only to silence the voices of reason?

Just how much of the so-called Galland affair had leaked out to the ears of Hitler is not known, but at this juncture he intervened. Goering unexpectedly called Galland to Karinhall and told him that in view of his past services to the fighter arm, no further disciplinary action would be taken. For obvious reasons Galland could not be reinstated, added Goering, but the Fuehrer was giving him the opportunity to prove the value of the jet fighter by forming a free-lance Jagdgeschwader of Me 262s, selecting his own pilots. Goering cunningly recommended the most rebellious of the fighter leaders for service with what he considered would prove to be a suicide unit, and for once Galland was in complete agreement; he knew that the "mutineers" were without equal in the Luftwaffe.

In due course, Jagdgeschwader 44, perhaps the most élite unit in the Luftwaffe, was formed at Brandenburg-Briest. The pilots included such outstanding aces as Barkhorn, Steinhoff and Lutzow, who had been recalled from Italy; all were veterans, and many wore the highest decorations for bravery, including the Knight's Cross. In March, 1945, Jagdgeschwader 44 became ready for active service from Munich-Reim, and the last and greatest of the Luftwaffe fighter pilots were able to fly the world's first operational jet fighters into the cauldron of the German skies. Among these unique airmen, Adolf Galland, their commander, held a unique position. "The circle was closing," he writes . "I went into the war as lieutenant and squadron leader, and should end it as lieutenant-general and squadron leader ! I was the fortunate man who was allowed to form and lead the most powerful squadron of fighters in the history of war."

CHAPTER XXII

DRESDEN AND BERLIN: 1945

"GOERING has reported that he has 3,000 planes available for the operation. You know Goering's reports. Discount one thousand, and that still leaves a thousand for you and a thousand for Sepp Dietrich." Thus spoke Adolf Hitler to one of his generals in the autumn of 1944, commenting on the Luftwaffe support he expected for what proved to be the last German offensive of the Second World War. This was to be the haggard Fuehrer's final throw of the dice, the breakthrough in the Ardennes supposed to bring a last-minute German victory. For the Ardennes offensive, code-named *Herbstnebel*, or Autumn Fog, Hitler demanded all available men and war material—more than twenty divisions—and almost every remaining aircraft the Luftwaffe possessed. It was to be the famous Blitzkrieg technique all over again, a powerful blow spearheaded by armoured divisions cutting a great gash through the Allied lines all the way to the Channel coast. "I am determined," Hitler said, "to carry out this operation despite all risks. . . ."

On 16th December, 1944, the Ardennes offensive broke in fire and steel over the heads of the surprised Allied commanders. In one day, von Runstedt's armour rolled forward a dozen miles, and within a week a wedge forty-five miles long had been driven into the Allied lines. In fog, sleet and snow the battle swayed through the Ardennes, with the American forces falling back in confusion, until at last the U.S. 10th Armoured Division met the German Panzers head-on outside Bastogne and in a series of bitter tank duels brought the offensive to a standstill. Von Runstedt hurled his élite S.S. troops into the battle, Lieutenant-General George S. Patton's huge force of armour and infantry thundered through Luxembourg to relieve Bastogne, and thus began the Battle of the Bulge, which would delay the Allied advance for less than a month at a cost of 120,000 German casualties. The ill-fated *Herbstnebel* offensive never amounted to more than a hopeless gamble, and is memorable less for Hitler's strategy than the outstanding courage of the American troops who fought and died to hold Bastogne, and the appalling weather conditions that winter, the unbearable, shocking cold of the Ardennes.

In the grey, cold dawn of 1st January, 1945, the last attack in any force by the Luftwaffe—Goering's so-called "Great Blow"—struck at the Allied air bases from Brussels to Eindhoven. The previous evening the men of ten élite Jagdgeschwader had been sworn to secrecy and informed that they were to undertake a massive attack on the Allied airfields in Belgium and Northern France, at low level, with machine-guns, cannon and light bombs. Some two thousand fighters were said to be involved in the operation, but in fact General von Sperrle could only muster about 650 Focke-Wulf Fw 190s, 450 Messerschmitt Bf 109s and a few jet aircraft. As church bells all over Germany rang in the New Year, the weary Luftwaffe pilots were awakened to prepare for their "Great Blow" while Goering hurried from unit to unit scattering a few words of encouragement. On every German airfield, whirling propellers threw up clouds of snow as engines burst irritably into life in the icy air. Then the Fw 190s and Bf 109s were thundering away into the early morning sky, with cine cameras on the ground recording what had become an unusual sight—a massed take-off by German aircraft.

Led by three navigating Junkers Ju 188s, the huge formations of fighters flew at ground level towards the Allied lines. About 300 machines streaked over the Zuyder Zee, heading for Brussels; a second force came through Arnhem, seeking Eindhoven; and the third massive formation, passing over Venlo, struck at the American forward bases. For once, fortune smiled briefly on the Luftwaffe, and the surprise was complete. At unsuspecting Brussels-Evere, hundreds of Allied aircraft were lined neatly along the airfield perimeter, and soon cannon fire was jumping along the ranks of bombers and fighters, men running for cover were being mown down and black smoke was rising from burning hangars. A few Spitfires succeeded in taking off, others ran into the raking German fire and overturned or crashed in flames. Then the anti-aircraft defences were hammering away, and the first black-crossed fighters falling; but within thirty minutes over a hundred Allied aircraft had been destroyed on the ground.

Death and destruction struck at Eindhoven only seconds after a little unarmed Taylorcraft Auster artillery-spotting mono-plane had frantically radioed : "Have just seen formation of at least 200 Messerschmitts flying low on course 320 deg." Again it was a violent awakening, with tracer flashing in all directions, cannon shells striking along the lines of parked aircraft, fires blazing and men falling. The few Spitfires and Tempests already airborne whirled into battle, and within minutes the terrific anti-aircraft fire was taking a heavy toll of the attacking force. Nevertheless, the damage at Eindhoven proved to be devastat-ing, with a Typhoon Wing and a Spitfire Wing virtually wiped out on the ground. On the twenty-seven Allied bases attacked, at least 300 aircraft had been destroyed, and for a week the sky over the Ardennes was strangely empty of British and American machines. But only for one week.

When the last German fighters had staggered back to their home bases, Hugo von Sperrle and his subordinate, Dietrich Peltz, were able to calculate their losses. More than a hundred Luftwaffe aircraft had been destroyed by Allied fighters and gunfire and many others damaged beyond repair; Galland later assessed the total as high as 300 machines. This was the price that had been paid for a week of grace at a time when new fighters were worth their weight in gold and experienced pilots were irreplaceable. In assembling the Fw 190s and Bf 109s needed to mount his "Great Blow" against the Allied airfields, von Sperrle had sacrificed all Luftwaffe fighter reserves—every-thing that remained, including night fighters—and the opening of 1945 saw Germany, now carpeted with bombs by day and night, with only the scattered remnants of an air force.

What, then, had the "Great Blow" achieved? In the west, the Allied armies were hurling the beaten Wehrmacht back and back, and within a month eighty-five divisions were closing in on the Rhine. General Eisenhower's armour and infantry had slogged a long, hard road since leaving the Normandy beaches, and along that path the military might of the Third Reich had been broken : by way of the Falaise pocket, that vast charnel-house of German troops and vehicles; Caen, reduced to rubble by hundreds of Allied bombers; and more recently the Ardennes, scene of reeling tank battles and slaughter in the snow. Now the end was in sight. With the Allied forces about to flood into the German homeland, Hitler had played his last card. He had no more "bold strokes" to shake an unsuspecting world, no "eleventh-hour victories" to announce with unswerving confidence. But—". . . I have never learned to know the word 'capitulation'" he had stated at a conference during the Ardennes offensive, and now that battle was lost he was ready to blame his leaders—and not himself—for the catastrophic situation. On 10th March he dismissed the ageing von Runstedt and replaced him with Kesselring, who had stubbornly defended the Italian front until the bitter end.

Meanwhile, in the east, the great masses of booty-laden soldiers, tanks, cars, lorries, horses and carts and captured vehicles that composed the Red Army were rolling inexorably forward into Poland and East Prussia in the greatest Russian offensive of the Second World War; 180 divisions carrying all before them, capturing Warsaw, crossing the Oder, rumbling through the vital Silesian industrial basin. Before the end of January, 1945, the Soviet armies were within a hundred miles of Berlin, and Albert Speer, coldly accepting each new disaster, was drafting a memorandum on the loss of the Silesian mines. "The war is lost," he reported calmly to Hitler, who surprisingly made no comment, but merely had the memorandum filed away. On 18th March, Speer personally handed Hitler a second memorandum, which stated: "In four to eight weeks the final collapse of the German economy must be expected with certainty. . . . After that collapse the war cannot be continued. . . ."

The Allied round-the-clock bombing offensive continued without respite, although the German war potential was virtually paralysed. In fact, by 1945 all industry in the Third Reich had been destroyed to such an extent that the Allied Chiefs of Staff decided at a conference held in Malta on 30th January to revise the bombing offensive, switching top priority to "Berlin, Leipzig, Dresden, and other German cities where heavy raids would cause great chaos amongst the civilian population swelled by refugees from Eastern Germany". The immediate result of this high-level decision was a thousand-bomber raid on shattered Berlin, laying waste to whole districts and killing at least

25,000 people. Other mass attacks on the German capital followed on 21st and 26th February, 6th, 13th, 18th, 20th and 24th March; a terrifying chronicle of merciless destruction from the air.

At the height of this wholesale slaughter now overwhelming every inhabited area in Germany, the lovely rococo city of Dresden became the target ever afterwards to be remembered by the Allies with a twinge of conscience and by the German people with agony and horror. Although it was a railway centre of some importance, in five years of total war Dresden had never been bombed, and slowly but surely the anti-aircraft defences of the city were whittled away for service on the eastern front. During 1944 many of the night fighters based in Saxony had also been withdrawn and hurled into the inferno of the daylight air battles, leaving Dresden unprotected. Helpless, and also unsuspecting in her nakedness, why should Dresden be bombed after five peaceful years, when Germany was on the verge of collapse?

Why indeed? Since the beginning of 1945, the roads and railways from the east had been packed with refugees fleeing in terror before the onslaught of the pillaging Red Army, pouring in wild disorder through Saxony and drawn at last in their thousands to the deceptive security of Dresden. By 13th February the normal population of the city—about 633,000— had swollen to a fantastic figure, perhaps a million people. The railway station was jammed with trains, all filled, yet still surrounded by masses of homeless men, women and children; carts and farm wagons piled high with household goods trundled through the crowded streets; and, with the approach of night, even the parks and river banks became strewn with exhausted wanderers seeking a place to rest. Dresden—"the German Florence"—was ripe for the slaughter, and the hour of execution was at hand.

On the night of 13th-14th February, 1945, a force of 250 multi-engined Lancasters of R.A.F. Bomber Command drummed steadily over Dresden, dropping a massive concentration of high explosive and incendiary bombs into the centre of the city. Fires began to sweep unchecked through the ancient buildings, and within an hour whole streets were burning. While the many conflagrations were still raging, a second wave of

529 R.A.F. Lancasters arrived over the target area, scattering heavy 4,000-pound block-buster bombs and thousands of incendiaries at random into the spreading fires. At dawn, as the last bombers throbbed homeward, the heat rising from the great sea of fire that consumed Dresden could be felt at 20,000 ft., and from that height every street could be seen etched vividly in flame. Dresden, beautiful doomed Dresden, was burning; and would continue to burn for seven days and eight nights.

The famous Allied triple blow, hall-mark of the Hamburg catastrophe, was repeated against Dresden. On 14th February— Ash Wednesday—a force of 300 Flying Fortresses of the U.S. 8th Air Force passed over the city, dropping over 700 tons of radar-directed bombs into the dense pall of black smoke rising many thousands of feet into the sky. During the three major raids at least 3,000 tons of high explosives and incendiaries had fallen on Dresden, but it seemed to the survivors that a juggernaut had been set in motion which could not be halted. To their horror, another huge formation of American B-17s returned to the city on 15th February, raining down a further 461 tons of bombs to effect complete saturation.

Afterwards, the scenes in the heart of Dresden defied description. At the height of the first attack, the thousands of fires had leaped together to create the last and most terrible firestorm to be endured by a German city; a great pillar of seething flame burning out everything within an area of eight square miles. This man-made tornado, reaching a temperature of 1,000 deg. at its centre, wrenched giant trees out of the ground and snapped them like twigs, seized hundreds of people and drew them into the inferno, tossed furniture high over the city and ripped the roofs off houses. As in Hamburg, nothing touched by the firestorm survived; jars, pots, pans, tiles and bricks were incinerated. The dead—numbering at least 135,000, and perhaps many more—choked the streets, the railway station, the parks, the river banks.

Consider this. So many people had been killed in Dresden that insufficient able-bodied survivors were left to bury the dead. During February, great mounds of mutilated bodies accumulated at the cemeteries, until the S.S. ordered that they be bulldozed into mass graves dug by excavators. The weeks passed, and the unidentified dead were still being tipped by the lorry-load into great pits; an awful stench of decay hung over Dresden, and doctors began to fear an outbreak of typhus, about 9,000 victims were cremated on five funeral pyres lit in the cordoned-off city centre, and the ashes reverently buried. Many bodies were still being recovered from the ruined streets two months later.

The destruction of Dresden carried Air Marshal Sir Arthur Harris's area bombing policy to its ultimate conclusion; even the atomic bombs dropped later on Hiroshima and Nagasaki could not equal such wide devastation or surpass the death-roll. In 1940, at the height of the Blitz on London, Harris had gazed at the great fires raging around St. Paul's and remarked calmly to the officer at his side, "Well, they are sowing the wind." Within three years, he had lit a mighty torch to Hamburg; in less than five years he had turned every major German city into a rubbled wilderness; and now Dresden had been taught the dreadful lesson.

Compare the bombing of London, Plymouth or Coventry with the deluge of fire and steel that consumed Berlin, Hamburg and Dresden. In truth, the German people had reaped the whirlwind.

Hands clasped behind his back, Hermann Goering wandered sadly through the great house-cum-mausoleum he had named Karinhall. Many of the rooms were empty now; for weeks a large staff had been carefully packing the hundreds of art treasures for transporting to Berchtesgaden and other places. Valuable paintings, statues, priceless glass and porcelain, all had departed by lorry and train to the south, to be followed very soon by the crockery, furniture and a mountain of personal baggage. Within a month, nothing would remain at Karinhall except empty showcases, leaving the last evidence of Goering's years of triumph a deserted shell to be destroyed by high explosive on his orders. He was living in a nightmare: evacuating Karinhall before the Russian tanks and infantry blasted a path through the beautiful estate; trying to salvage a few baubles out of the wreckage of his former glory. He was already a commander without any forces; soon he would be a prince without a palace.

Thus far had the mighty fallen; and Goering wept to think

that at a time when Soviet guns were massed against Berlin, at the moment Karinhall would crumble into ruins, the amazing new aircraft that could have saved the Third Reich—and the Luftwaffe—were entering operational service. The Me 262, haunted by Hitler's interference; the Ta 152, Kurt Tank's replacement for the Fw 190; the rocket-driven Me 163 interceptor; the tandem-engined Do 335; all exceptional fighters, yet available in such pathetically small numbers. And Germany had new bombers, too: the Me 264, intended for the bombing of New York; the Ju 287; the Ar 234, first turbo-jet bomber in the world. Dozens of other projects still lay on abandoned drawing-boards, soon to be studied by the Allies. Did Goering, as he walked aimlessly through the vastness of Karinhall, remember Ernst Udet, and the wonderful new aircraft he had been promised back in 1941? There had been too many delays, too many tactical errors, too many wrong decisions. Now, time was the strongest enemy; the trees with their ripening fruit were about to come crashing down.

There were other Wunderwaffen that had more than a hint of the suicidal about them. In 1941 the chief test pilot of the Junkers concern, Holzbauer, had experimented with a new device for automatic bombing, and the success of his trials had resulted the following year in the appearance of the Mistel (Mistletoe) pick-a-back aircraft. In this unusual combination, an Fw 190 (or Bf 109) fighter rested uneasily above a Ju 88A-4 bomber modified to incorporate a large hollow-charge warhead. The upper component of the Mistel combination controlled both aircraft, the fighter pilot releasing the Ju 88 on the approach flight and then directing it on to the target. The bomber leaders, Peltz and Baumbach, showed considerable interest in the Fw 190/Ju 88 "Father and Son" project, as it was commonly called, and permission was given for the construction of an initial batch of fifteen pick-a-back aircraft. During 1944, Mistel combinations were used operationally against the Allied invasion fleet, sinking the old French battleship *Courbet* and two or three merchant ships. Dazzled by these successes, the gullible Reichsluftfahrtministerium ordered the production of a further 100 pick-a-back machines.

Early in 1945, Werner Baumbach proposed that all remaining aircraft of the Luftwaffe bomber arm be thrown into a sink-orswim attack on the vital Soviet power installations beyond the Urals. Code-named *Eisenhammer*, this offensive—yet another "Great Blow"—was entrusted to Kampfgeschwader 200, which received an assortment of bombers, including the Mistel combinations; in all about 200 aircraft, operating from bases in East Prussia. However, before the attack could take place the Russian armies flooded into East Prussia and the *Eisenhammer* operation had to be hurriedly abandoned. Another astonishing scheme involving pick-a-back aircraft, the destruction of the British Fleet at Scapa Flow, also never reached fulfilment. The last Fw 190/Ju 88 combinations were destined to attack the bridges across the Rhine and Oder, in a vain attempt to halt the Allied advance.

Meanwhile, the German engineer and inventor Erich Bachem had developed a "wonder weapon" at the last moment to serve a very different purpose. This was a short-winged manned rocket aircraft named the Natter, or Adder, intended to break up enemy bomber formations by taking off vertically to fire a devastating salvo of rockets into the masses of Fortresses or Liberators throbbing endlessly over the Reich. The Natter was then supposed to disintegrate, ejecting the pilot, who descended by parachute; a second parachute automatically opened to bring the complicated and expensive rocket motor to the ground for further use. Bachem credited the aircraft with a startling performance; a height of 30,000 ft. in ten seconds, and a maximum speed of 900 m.p.h. When he approached Galland and Albert Speer, they approved of the Natter project, but Goering refused to authorise mass production. Bachem, a man of great determination, at once sought an interview with Goering's most powerful enemy in the party, Heinrich Himmler, who gave permission for the building of a number of Natter aircraft; but with the proviso that only convalescent soldiers and disabled men be used as labour.

Three months later, Erich Bachem found that he was being publicised as the inventor of a weapon capable of breaking the Allied bombing offensive. The Natter was given top priority, and within the space of a few weeks about thirty aircraft were ready for testing, using dummy pilots. It was found that the Natter unfailingly broke up as anticipated, the dummy pilot and the rocket motor returning to earth by parachute; but Bachem doubted if a human being could survive the terrific acceleration of the machine so unharmed. Despite his misgivings, Berlin insisted that a manned launching take place without delay, and in February, 1945 a young Luftwaffe pilot, Lothar Siebert, was strapped into the cockpit of a Natter and hurled into the air to the accompaniment of a loud explosion. The Natter reached five thousand feet, then flicked over on its back and, still inverted, fell into a steep dive. A moment later, the horrified spectators saw it crash in a sheet of flame. Siebert was instantly killed, his neck broken when the cockpit canopy became unfastened and wrenched his head back.

The Anglo-American forces had crossed the Rhine, the Soviet artillery thundered beyond Berlin, and necessity became the mother of Bachem's invention. Three further manned tests proved to be completely successful, and by April, 1945, the first ten operational machines were ready for launching at Kircheim. Bachem and his team waited for the American bombers to arrive, unaware that Air Marshal Harris had already stated that his strategic bomber fleet could no longer find a worthwhile target in battered Germany, and the Allied bombing commission, codenamed *Jockey*, had sent a final message: "Jockey has unsaddled". On 10th April, the U.S. 8th Air Force attacked Berlin for the last time; but before that date American tanks had reached Kircheim to find the Natters destroyed to prevent capture.

So many contributions to the deadly art of war; so little time left to use them. The R4M anti-aircraft rocket, the most powerful weapon to be used against Allied bomber formations, had been developed by a woman, Fraulein Doktor Schwartz, of the D.M.W. laboratories at Lubeck. Carried on rails under the wings of fighter aircraft, these 55mm. calibre rockets could be electrically fired in salvoes from a range of 900 yds. into an enemy bomber formation, exploding simultaneously with tremendous force. By April, 1945, a number of Me 262 jet fighters had each been equipped with twenty-four R4M rockets, in addition to the normal armament of one 30 mm. cannon, all directed by the remarkable new Ez 42 automatic sight. Six Me 262s, led by General der Flieger Gordon Gollob—Galland's successor—attacked a formation of B-17E bombers, blowing fifteen to pieces without loss to themselves, and a few days later a Geschwader of Fw 190s armed with R4M rockets destroyed forty American bombers. In all, some 20,000 R4M rockets were produced, large numbers falling into Soviet hands at the end of the war.

Suicidal or ingenious, the Wunderwaffen made no difference. The last Allied bombs crashed down; pulverising medieval Hildesheim; demolishing Nordhausen; ruining historical Potsdam. On 18th March, 1945, the last great air battle of the Second World War took place over Berlin, when 1,200 heavily escorted American bombers were engaged by Me 262 jet fighters of the Luftwaffe. Twenty-five B-17 bombers and five P-51 fighters were destroyed by the Me 262s, and at least sixteen more of the heavy bombers badly damaged by anti-aircraft fire. The following day, Germany's small force of Me 262s again took a heavy toll of American aircraft, but the jet fighter successes were drowned in the vast ocean of Luftwaffe losses; in just one week during April 1,700 machines were shot down or destroyed on the ground. Their airfields pitted with hundreds of craters, Galland, Lutzow, Steinhoff and the remaining pilots of the Luftwaffe fighter arm fought on, while the Third Reich burned to ashes.

From empty Karinhall the booty-laden lorries drove away to run the gauntlet of Allied fighter-bombers, and a dejected Goering prepared to leave for Berlin. In the suburbs of that tortured city, trenches were being dug by women and children at cross-roads and wire barricades had been hastily thrown up, manned by old men of the Volkssturm in French Army overcoats and fanatical schoolboys of the Hitlerjugend in uniforms too large for them. Fires were blazing everywhere; tank columns rumbled through the streets and wretched civilians scurried about among the helmeted and armed defenders, seeking a little coal or food. The smell of smoke and dust hung over Berlin; it had become a city of the damned.

In an air-conditioned steel and concrete bunker fifty feet below the Reich Chancellory garden, the architect of more destruction than the world had ever seen was receiving a stream of visitors, despatching absurd messages and making futile plans for the future. Adolf Hitler, aged and trembling, stooped and ashen of face, had retired to what proved to be his last headquarters after the failure of his Ardennes offensive, and there he continued to live an unreal, troglodyte existence, attended by a few faithful followers. Goebbels was there, with his wife and five children, the golden voice still telling the German people that a great future lay ahead. Eva Braun, Hitler's mistress, sat reading magazines and waiting complacently for the end; and always in the background lurked the sinister Martin Bormann, successor to Rudolf Hess. Yet in the Wagnerian atmosphere he had created in the bunker, the Fuehrer still reigned supreme, a megalomaniac determined that when he fell from his pedestal the world would tumble with him. He had already ordered Field Marshal Walter Model, who had replaced von Runstedt, to undertake a scorched-earth policy in the Ruhr, leaving only wreckage to be captured by the Allies. Albert Speer hurried to the bunker to protest against such useless waste, and Hitler told him: "If the war is to be lost, the nation also will perish. . . . The nation has proved itself weak, and the future belongs solely to the stronger Eastern nation. Besides, those who remain after the battle are of little value; for the good have fallen." Nevertheless, Speer persuaded Model to ignore the scorched-earth order, and it was never carried out.

During the period 1st-18th April, 1945, the twenty-one divisions of Model's Army Group B were encircled in the Ruhr and destroyed by the Allied forces, 325,000 prisoners being taken, including thirty generals. Field Marshal Model shot himself in a wood near Duisburg. The German front in the west was now ripped apart ,and the U.S. Ninth and First Armies were racing through the gap, over the Elbe and then beyond; the road to Berlin lay open, defended by only a few scattered divisions.

On 20th April, Hitler's fifty-sixth birthday, the Nazi hierarchy —Goering, Goebbels, Himmler, Bormann and von Ribbentrop —brought the Fuehrer their congratulations and pleaded with him to leave Berlin and withdraw to the Obersalzburg. Hitler said he could not make up his mind; he appointed Grand Admiral Doenitz supreme military commander in the north, but refused to delegate a southern commander. Meanwhile, he would await developments. After the conference, Himmler and Ribbentrop left the bunker, and the same evening Goering took his leave of Hitler, whom he would never see again. In the early hours of the following morning the unfortunate General Koller, trying to gather together the threads of the Luftwaffe, saw

Goering drive past his house at the head of a long convoy of cars and lorries without even a word of farewell to his last Chief of Staff. All the cars were travelling at high speed; the road to the south might be cut at any time.

In Berlin the evacuation of the ministries continued. Hitler, a pale ghost clutching sweat-stained maps with trembling hands, had ordered a final do-or-die attack by all the German forces in Berlin, led by an S.S. general, Obergruppenfuehrer Steiner. The telephones never stopped ringing in Koller's chaotic office; the familiar harsh voice screamed a strange mixture of instructions and insults into his ear without pause for a reply. "You will guarantee with your head that every man of the Luftwaffe is used! All Luftwaffe forces transferred immediately for ground fighting under Steiner! The whole Luftwaffe command should be executed for incompetence!" And so on and so on, while Koller wondered who Steiner was and rummaged through masses of paperwork.

During the night, contradictory reports of the Steiner attack poured into the bunker, culminating in a statement by Generals Jodl and Krebs at the morning conference that the Luftwaffe had never gone into action; the Steiner "offensive" had not been mounted after all. The very walls of the bunker resounded to the ensuing storm. "I have been deceived!" Hitler shrieked. "This is the end ... everyone has deserted me ... nothing but treason, lies, corruption, cowardice!" For the first time, he said, he despaired of his mission; nothing remained now but death. He had made his decision; he would stay in Berlin until the end.

Thus Hitler raged and ranted, the insane ruler of a kingdom bounded by steel doors and concrete walls, fifty feet under the ground. In the northern suburbs of Berlin, boys in oversized helmets hurled futile Panzerfausts at mammoth tanks and old men of the Volkssturm died under the clanking caterpillar treads as the Russian armoured spearheads thrust relentlessly forward to pierce the heart of the city. Finally, the human gramophone in the bunker began to run down; the needle was broken and almost worn out. "I will never leave Berlin—never!" Hitler repeated to Keitel and Bormann, then sat back highly pleased with himself. He did not know if he had convinced anyone else; but he had succeeded in convincing himself. The last "irrevocable decision" had been made.

CHAPTER XXIII

CRY HAVOC TO THE END: MAY, 1945

WITH the swelling music of *Deutschland über Alles* crackling from their radios, a tight formation of Messerschmitt Bf 109s hurtled out of the sun on an April morning in 1945. "Remember our dead wives and children, murdered by the American air pirates!" shrieked the voice of a woman announcer into the ears of the German pilots as they watched the massive array of Flying Fortresses below change from tiny dots into huge four-engined bombers with wide silver wings and perspex turrets sparkling in the sunshine. The martial music rose to a crescendo. and the sky became alive with tracer; the stammering guns from the Fortresses met the savage reply from flame-stabbing Mauser cannon firing from beneath wings and through airscrew spinners. First one Bf 109 and then another shook in the cross-fire from the bombers and abruptly exploded, but the remainder plunged on through the smoky, flame-slashed sky, until the Fortresses were dead ahead, sliding across the windscreens of the Bf 109s at an angle, the big oil-spattered tailplanes filling their reflector sights. The cannon of the leading German fighter thundered at point-blank range into the rear turret of a B-17, great pieces of metal flew away from the stricken bomber, then the two aircraft met in a vast ball of flame. An accidental collision? No—seconds later, another Bf 109 struck a Fortress and again came the shattering explosion. At once, blazing wreckage and drifting parachutes everywhere; a B-17 breaking in two, cascading men into space; crippled fighters streaming grey smoke through the whirling battle. A third explosion, and a tangle of twisted metal dropping to the ground 30,000 ft. below. In the background, the voice from the German radios still shouted "Remember our women, buried under the rubble of our cities! Remember! . . ." until drowned at last in the silence of oblivion.

This action, incredible even in the madhouse that was Germany in 1945, was undertaken by the Raubvoegel Gruppe of Sonderkommando Elbe, a so-called "suicide unit" of the Luftwaffe. Since the winter of 1943-1944, a few Sturmjaeger Gruppen, equipped with heavily-armed FW 190s piloted by brave and dedicated volunteers, had operated with some success against the Allied bomber formations by attacking at close range through the defensive fire and breaking away only at the last possible moment. In exploitation of this "death or glory" attitude, and in an attempt to imitate the more recent Japanese Kamikaze tactics, Oberst Hermann, the reckless exponent of "wild boar" night fighting, requested volunteers for certain "special and dangerous work" and in March, 1945, about 300 pilots arrived at Stendal for a short course in ramming Allied bombers. Suitably inspired by the political indoctrination which constituted most of the course, the fanatical Selbstopfer-manner—self-sacrifice men—later left Stendal for Prague, where Sonderkommando Elbe, which comprised four Gruppen, was formed. By the beginning of April the Raubvoegel Gruppe (Staffeln 9, 10 and 11) was based at Sachau, and ready for operations. On 7th April a number of Raubvoegel aircraft took off for action against Allied bomber formations, and assembled over Magdeburg to intercept the masses of B-17s heading for Berlin. At least five Fortresses were destroyed by ramming during this, the only attack by "suicide commandos" of the Luftwaffe, but seventy-eight German fighters were shot down and the Raubvoegel Gruppe decimated.

Hanna Reitsch, the famous German airwoman and test pilot, was largely responsible for the formation of a competitive suicide unit to Oberkommando Elbe during the autumn of 1943. Although Field Marshal Milch disliked the idea of self-sacrifice, he was persuaded by Reitsch that the V.1 flying bomb could be modified as a piloted missile, and also agreed that tests be carried out on the Messerschmitt Me 328, a new but unsuccessful type designed as a long-range fighter. The first V.1 conversion took only five days, and a number of single-seater (operational) and two-seater (training) piloted V.1s were tested at Rechlin and Larz. The Me 328 also proved adaptable as a "suicide bomb" and an aircraft factory in Thuringia received orders to undertake mass production. According to Hanna Reitsch, there was no lack of volunteers to fly the piloted V.1s and Me 328s. Out of the thousands who came forward, about seventy were accepted.

In the summer of 1944 the self-sacrifice men were taken on the establishment of an existing Luftwaffe squadron as a special unit, each man signing a declaration that he understood enrolment as the pilot of a glider bomb would entail certain death. The training of instructors commenced, but behind the scenes Milch was having second thoughts about the project, and the bomber general Werner Baumbach had condemned it as idiotic in the extreme. Himmler gave his blessing but objected to the wastage of experienced aircrew and suggested that criminals and neurotics should be used as suicide men. Later in the year, Goebbels gave the suicide pilots premature and unwanted publicity in a speech praising "their great sacrifice in an operation which might decide the war". Hitler, who always had the last word, finally squashed the project by rejecting all the proposed suicide operations. "The German soldier must always have a chance to survive," he said.

The only other self-sacrifice idea to emerge out of the twilight of the Third Reich came from Generalmajor Storp, the last Inspector of Bombers, who hoped to form a so-called Luftwaffe Suicide Division, the volunteers to be dressed in Wehrmacht uniform to confuse Allied intelligence! Needless to say, this unit, provisionally named the Hermann Goering Fighter Division, was never formed.

On 22nd April, General Koller learned that Hitler intended to remain in Berlin. The following morning, fifteen Ju 52 transport aircraft carrying Koller and his staff—the remnants of Oberkommando der Luftwaffe—took off from Gatow aerodrome and flew to Bavaria, where Goering waited anxiously for news. "Is the Fuehrer still alive?" asked the worried Reichsmarschall. "Has he appointed Bormann his successor?" Koller told him that Hitler was almost certainly still alive, but the Russians had reached the Alexanderplatz; Berlin could not hold out for longer than another seven or eight days. Koller then described the final conference in the bunker, the trembling ghost with staring eyes, the harsh voice screaming, "I will never leave Berlin—never!" as it had been reported to him by his liaison officer. Puffing nervously at his pipe, Goering listened intently, saying little, no longer in any doubt that Germany was in the hands of a raving madman.

"You must act at once!" implored Koller. The Reichs-marschall hesitated, deep in thought. At last, he decided to send Hitler a carefully worded telegram: "My Fuehrer, in view of your decision to remain at your post in the fortress of Berlin, do you agree that I take over, immediately, the total leadership of the Reich, with full freedom of action at home and abroad, as your deputy, in accordance with your decree of 29th June, 1941? If no reply is received by ten o'clock tonight, I shall take it for granted that you have lost your freedom of action, shall consider the conditions of your decree as fulfilled, and shall act for the best interests of our country and our people. You know what I feel for you in this gravest hour of my life. Words fail me. May God protect you, and speed you quickly here despite all. Your loyal Hermann Goering."

Goering had just finished dinner when Hitler's reply arrived at the Obersalzburg like a shell from a cannon. "Your action represents high treason against the Fuehrer and National Socialism. The penalty for treason is death. However, in view of your earlier services to the party, the Fuehrer will not inflict this supreme penalty if you voluntarily resign all your positions and offices." A second message stated: "Decree of 29th June, 1941, is rescinded by my special instruction. My freedom of action undisputed. I forbid any move by you in the indicated direction. Adolf Hitler." The same evening, a hundred S.S. men of the Liebstandarte surrounded Goering's house, and he was placed under close arrest, by order of Martin Bormann.

Generaloberst Ritter von Greim was appointed Commander-in-Chief of the Luftwaffe and ordered to report immediately to the Fuehrer in Berlin.

On 26th April, von Greim, accompanied by Hanna Reitsch, stepped from a Ju 188 bomber at Rechlin airport, 150 miles out of Berlin. The attractive woman test pilot, hastily summoned by the new Luftwaffe commander to fly with him into the burning German capital, hoped to achieve the journey by helicopter, but von Greim quickly ascertained that Rechlin's last example of the type had recently been destroyed in an Allied air raid. Von Greim, who apparently failed to see the absurdity of reporting to an underground shelter virtually surrounded by

Russian infantry, then determined to make the flight as far as Gatow in a Focke-Wulf Fw 190 single-seater fighter. A sergeant pilot and von Greim wedged themselves with difficulty into the tiny cockpit, while the more unfortunate Hanna Reitsch was pushed feet first into the tail, where she lay in total darkness, imprisoned by the fuselage framework. After dodging a number of roaming Soviet fighters, the Fw 190 arrived safely at Gatow, which was under heavy Russian artillery fire. With shells erupting all around them, von Greim and Reitsch hurried to the nearest air raid shelter.

Von Greim, realising that it would be almost impossible to reach the centre of Berlin, decided to telephone Hitler's bunker for instructions. He learned that all approach roads and most of the inner city were now in Russian hands, but was also told that he must report to the Fuehrer at all costs; exactly how he might attempt the hazardous journey was not revealed. Finally, von Greim agreed to Hanna Reitsch's suggestion that they use a Fieseler Storch liaison aircraft which was standing on the scarred airfield. Dashing through the shellfire, they climbed into the little machine.

As Hanna Reitsch had never flown an aircraft in action, von Greim took the controls while she crouched behind him, ready for any emergency. The Storch lifted at once into the air, and was soon flying low over the Wannsee, then skimming the trees of the Grunewald. Suddenly, the tiny aircraft shook in a gale of small arms fire; Russian tanks and infantry were shooting at it with hundreds of weapons. A blinding flash lit the windscreen, and simultaneously von Greim shouted, "I'm hit!" He collapsed in his seat, unconscious, and Hanna Reitsch reached over him, grasping the control column; the Storch lurched alarmingly before she regained control. With bullets and cannon shells hitting the wings and fuselage, the aircraft flew on, and in a darkness shot with flame Reitsch peered ahead, seeking her landing place—the East-West Axis.

The East-West Axis, that magnificent, wide highway connecting East and West Berlin, once the pride of the Third Reich, was a five-mile-long shambles of overturned vehicles and fallen trees, lined with rubble and the ruins of great buildings. The Kaiserdamm was a wilderness; the famous Unter den Linden a sea of wreckage; the Bismarckstrasse cratered like the face of the moon. Through the drifting smoke dropped the bullet-riddled Storch, bumping heavily along the street to stop at last facing the colossal Brandenburg Gate. Von Greim had recovered consciousness, and was helped out of the cockpit by Hanna Reitsch, who was aghast at the desolation all around her.

A battered Wehrmacht lorry, trundling slowly over the rubble and broken glass, moved towards the little monoplane standing so incongruously in the centre of Berlin. Supported by the driver and Hanna Reitsch, the wounded von Greim clambered into the vehicle on the last stage of his journey to the Fuehrer. In a few moments the lorry had travelled the short distance to the scarred Reich Chancellory buildings, and S.S. men were soon hustling von Greim down into the Bunker to receive the immediate care of Stumpfegger, Hitler's surgeon. Then, lying on a stretcher, with Hanna Reitsch still in her flying clothes at his side, von Greim found himself confronted by a stooping, glassy-eyed figure with trembling hands and dragging feet. The dying ruler of a dead city, looking and acting like a man in an alcoholic daze, Adolf Hitler waited for news from the outside world.

In great pain, von Greim nevertheless endeavoured to give a correct account of his journey. When he had ended his strange report, Hitler shook his hand, saying warmly to Hanna Reitsch, "Brave woman! So there is still some loyalty and courage left in the world!"

Producing the telegram from Hermann Goering, the Fuehrer turned back to von Greim. "I have dismissed Goering for treasonable conduct," he said angrily. "He has sullied the honour of the Luftwaffe; I have called you here to restore it." Growing visibly more agitated, Hitler waved the telegram with a fluttering hand as he read it aloud. With tears in his eyes, he shouted: "An ultimatum! A crass ultimatum! Nothing now remains, nothing is spared me, no loyalty is kept, no honour observed. There is no bitterness, no betrayal, that has not been heaped upon me. And now this! It is the end. No injury has been left undone!" When he had calmed down, he said, "And now, von Greim, I promote you to the rank of Generalfeld-marschall and appoint you commander-in-chief of the Luftwaffe in place of Hermann Goering."

Von Greim huddled motionless on his stretcher while Hitler's voice droned on. "You will play an important part in my plans for the relief of Berlin. . . . Wenck's army is at hand. . . . I need every available bomber. . . . the Soviet ring around the city must be broken. . . ." All hopeless dreams, the fantasies of an underground fairyland; von Greim knew only too well that the Luftwaffe no longer existed. He had flown through Russian bullets and artillery fire, risked his life, endured painful wounds to reach this place. For nothing; he might just as well have stayed in Munich.

That night, heavy Russian shells began to fall directly on the Reich Chancellory building.

The few German fighter units remaining in action continued to suffer appalling losses. In Adolf Galland's élite Jagdgeschwader 44, Steinhoff had been seriously burned on 18th April when his Me 262 crashed on take-off, and the brilliant Gunther Lutzow had been posted as missing, believed killed; like the World War One ace George Guynemer, he was destined to fly into the unknown, never to be seen again. Many others had died, so many and in such an obviously lost cause that Galland called his pilots together and spoke to them as bluntly as they would have wished. "Militarily speaking, the war is lost," he said. "Even our action here cannot change anything . . . I shall continued to fight, because operating with the Me 262 has got hold of me, and I am proud to belong to the last fighter pilots of the German Luftwaffe. Only those who feel the same are to go on flying with me. . . ."

On 26th April, Galland led six of his Me 262s into battle against a large formation of American Martin Marauders, apparently unescorted by fighters. As he attacked one of the sleek twin-engined bombers and saw it rock under the impact of his cannon fire, a burst of heavy-calibre bullets from an unseen P-51 Mustang fighter strewed the cabin of the Me 262 with flying glass and metal fragments as the instrument panel disintegrated. Immediately, Galland became aware of a sharp pain in his right knee. He fought to keep the Me 262 in the air, despite a second burst of enemy fire which damaged both jet engines, and finally managed to evade the P-51 by diving away through the low cloud.

Nursing the crippled jet fighter over the Munich autobahn,

Galland banked steeply to come in for an emergency landing at Riem airfield. At the last moment, he realised that Riem was under heavy low-level attack by Thunderbolts, but with a dead engine he had no alternative but to land; the Me 262 touched down at 150 m.p.h. and bounced along the runway. At last it screeched to a halt and Galland tumbled out of the cockpit into the nearest bomb crater. Soon afterwards, an armoured tractor came speeding across the airfield with scant disregard for the falling bombs and flying cannon shells, and Galland was swiftly rushed to a more secure shelter. He had fired his guns for the last time in the war; an X-ray of his wounded leg revealed splinters in the knee-cap and he had to go to Munich hospital for treatment. An outstanding pilot, who had seen action in Spain in 1937 and in almost every theatre of operations during the Second World War, Adolf Galland had become something of a rarity by 1945 : a great ace and holder of the coveted diamonds who had fought to the end—and survived.

The Russian bombardment of the Reich Chancellory was increasing to a terrible crescendo, fine cracks appearing in the ceiling of the Bunker as explosion after explosion reverberated through the concrete structure. The dismal reports continued to come pouring in, heaping one disaster upon another: Spandau and Potsdam had fallen to the Soviet forces; bitter hand-to-hand fighting was raging in the streets around Unter den Linden; and Zhukov's massive Stalin tanks were blasting a path of death to the Wilhemstrasse. In the seclusion of his study, Adolf Hitler lifted a haggard, waxen face to Hanna Reitsch and looked at her with dim eyes. "Hanna," he said, "you belong to those who will die with me. . . . I do not wish that one of us falls to the Russians alive, nor do I wish our bodies to be found by them. . . . Eva and I will have our bodies burned. . . ." He pressed into her hand two capsules of potassium cyanide, one for herself and the other for Ritter von Greim.

On 28th April came the heaviest blow of all, striking Hitler to the heart. A loyal assistant of Goebbels dodged through the bombardment and arrived breathlessly at the Bunker with an urgent radio message; it was handed to Hitler's valet, Linge, who took it at once to the Fuehrer. Instantly, a terrifying, in-human scream of despair came from the sanctum of the almighty, and Hitler emerged, waving yet another fateful piece of paper. The truth was out at last. Himmler—the faithful Heinrich supposedly holding the fort in the north—was secretly negotiating with Count Folke Bernadotte, head of the International Red Cross in Germany, and had offered to surrender the German armies in the west to General Eisenhower! "That he should do this to me!" shouted Hitler incredulously, gazing wildly around him. Then he limped jerkily across the corridor to von Greim's room. "Now Himmler has betrayed me. . . . You must leave the Bunker at once and see that he is arrested as a traitor. Also, I have news that the Russians may storm the Reich Chancellory tomorrow morning. You will prepare to mount an air attack at once!"

"With what, my Fuehrer?" asked the dazed von Greim.

A good question. "Every bomber must be summoned," continued Hitler, disregarding the details. "If the Russian troop concentrations in the streets leading to the Reich Chancellory can be destroyed by air attack, we can gain at least twenty-four hours. . . ." Finally, he said that a light aircraft had succeeded in landing on the embattled East-West Axis; it would take von Greim and Hanna Reitsch immediately to Rechlin. His last words to the airwoman were, "God protect you!" as he shook her hand.

Soon afterwards, von Greim, hobbling slowly on crutches, emerged from the Bunker into a tornado of shellfire and was helped into an armoured car by Hanna Reitsch. Through clouds of sulphurous smoke, under a blood-red sky, they were driven rapidly along the ravaged Tiergarten and on to the East-West Axis. With a skill and courage that defied description, the same Luftwaffe sergeant-pilot who had flown von Greim and Reitsch to Gatow in an Fw 190 had managed to land a little Arado Ar 96 training monoplane on the cratered boulevard, and this aircraft still remained, miraculously undamaged, in the meagre protection of a blast bay. Hanna Reitsch assisted von Greim into the rear cockpit and then dropped into the pilot's seat; within minutes the diminutive Argus engine had burst into life and the Ar 96 was trundling along the street.

The airwoman pulled gently back on the control column and the monoplane rose gracefully into the air, passing low over the Brandenburg Gate, which was lit by the glare of Russian searchlights. Tracer flickered lazily past as the Ar 96 climbed steadily, then the great heaving sea of flame that was Berlin lay far below, and Hanna Reitsch settled herself more comfortably in the darkened cockpit, setting course for Rechlin. Behind her sat a very tired, grey-faced man, in agony from an infected foot wound; the commander-in-chief of a Luftwaffe he had never had the opportunity to command. They were Hitler's last visitors from the forgotten world outside Berlin; the Ar 96 was the last aircraft to leave the beleaguered city.

On arrival at Rechlin, von Greim ordered Hanna Reitsch to fly him to the field headquarters of Grand Admiral Karl Doenitz, where a conference was held, and then to Keitel's headquarters, for another hasty conference. What was discussed was of no importance; nothing now was of any importance. Von Greim, flying and then motoring from place to place, hiding in ditches while Allied aircraft roamed overhead, was a dedicated and loyal soldier, and he was going through the motions of obeying Hitler's last insane orders, but he must have realised before he left Berlin that the curtain had fallen for the Third Reich. He was merely playing for time while he waited for the end.

On the afternoon of 30th April, 1945, in the depths of the Bunker, behind the closed doors of Hitler's suite, a single shot rang out. Immediately, the group of men assembled in the corridor, including Goebbels and Bormann, moved forward; the study door was thrown open and they crowded into the room. Adolf Hitler lay sprawled on the sofa, shot through the mouth, a Walther pistol near his dangling right hand. Beside him, also dead, was Eva Braun, who had swallowed a poison capsule; her Walther pistol, unfired, lay on the rug at her feet. For perhaps ten minutes, Joseph Goebbels, also soon to die by his own hand, remained in the room in silent contemplation, while the others tried to understand that the trembling madman who had ruled their lives would haunt the Bunker no more. Above their heads, the anger of the Russian guns pounded without respite. Nothing had changed; the imitation Siegfried was dead, but the mighty Wagnerian opera would have to reach a finale without him.

In Berlin, a Viking funeral pyre burned in the Reich Chancellory garden. In Lubeck, Ritter von Greim and Hanna Reitsch listened in silence to the voice of a radio announcer from

Hamburg: "Our Fuehrer, Adolf Hitler, fighting to the last breath against Bolshevism, fell for Germany this afternoon in his operational headquarters in the Reich Chancellory. On 30th April the Fuehrer appointed Grand Admiral Doenitz his successor. ..." At that moment, Russian tanks were clambering over the debris of Wilhemstrasse, and the four bronze Horses of Victory crowning the Brandenburg Gate quivering to a tattoo of bullets. In 1935, Hitler had told the German people, "Give me ten years and you will not recognise the face of Germany." He was a man who during his life dreamed many dreams and made many empty promises, but this undertaking at least he had fulfilled to the letter. On 1st May, 1945, Germany was unrecognisable.

On Salzburg aerodrome, the last base of Jagdgeschwader 44, the uncamouflaged Me 262s stood on their tricycle undercarriages, grounded and silent for lack of fuel. The roar of engines rose and fell overhead as the American fighters flew lazily around in wide circles, not bothering to open fire, content to await the arrival of the Allied armour about to enter Salzburg. As the rumble of heavy caterpillar treads was heard in the distance, one of the Luftwaffe jet fighters was abruptly shaken by a violent internal explosion, and a sheet of flame erupted from the cockpit. A second Me 262 lifted on its wheels with a deafening roar, greedy crimson fire surging towards the sky. Before the first American tanks had reached the airfield, all the German fighters were burning with an intense white heat. The war was over for the pilots of Jagdgeschwader 44, but their beloved Me 262s would never be appraised or flown by the airmen of other countries.

All over Germany, on airfields, along the wide autobahnen, in secret underground factories, hidden by camouflaged hangars and sheltered by great pine trees, could be found the last aircraft of Goering's Luftwaffe. The Bf 109s, Me 163s and Me 262s of Willy Messerschmitt; the He 111s and He 162s of Ernst Heinkel; the Fw 190s and Ta 152s of Kurt Tank; and a myriad other types, large and small, all grounded, with empty fuel tanks: a dead, scattered air force. High in the heavens, other wings glittered briefly in the sun, Allied aircraft twisted and turned gracefully in the joy of victory, while the German pilots gazed wistfully up at them, envying the British and American airmen their freedom of the sky.

On 8th May, 1945, the road to Radstadt was jammed with refugees, a hopeless tangle of horse-drawn carts, lorries, cars and laden barrows. Through the chaos moved a magnificent, super-charged Mercedes saloon, heading a column of staff cars and lorries piled with expensive baggage; the colourful procession of a rich eastern potentate. In the Mercedes reclined Hermann Goering, released by order of Albert Kesselring, and now on his way to meet the Americans, confident that he would be able to negotiate peace terms with General Eisenhower. He was dressed, very simply for him, in grey-blue Luftwaffe uniform, with only three medals—the Iron Cross, the *Pour le Mérite* and the Golden Air Medal—and carried his heavy, diamond-studded marshal's baton in his right hand. Apart from his vast amount of personal luggage, in monogrammed pigskin suitcases, Goering also had with him four gold watches, a number of gold cigar-ette and cigar cases, gold pens and pencils, a single huge emerald, and three massive ornamental rings. He was, perhaps, the wealthiest refugee adrift in Germany that May morning.

The column of vehicles came to a halt as the wail of sirens preceded the sudden arrival of several American jeeps, which blocked the road. First Lieutenant J. N. Shapiro, United States Army, stepped from the leading jeep; recognising Goering at once, he saluted. The Reichsmarschall limply raised a hand in response, and within minutes the cavalcade was on the move again, led by a jeep with screaming sirens. At peaceful Zell am See, the headquarters of the American 36th Division, Goering was met by Brigadier-General Robert J. Stack, and the two men shook hands. The next few hours were spent by Goering enjoy-ing the minor luxuries he had come to take for granted. He had a hot bath and changed his silk underwear; was provided with a good lunch and posed happily over and over again for the photographers. A glass of champagne in his hand, high-ranking American officers listening eagerly to his every word, the bulky Reichsmarschall became increasingly more cheerful and optimistic for the future. He had no doubt that he would soon be having the "man to man chat" he desired with General Eisenhower.

But after the sparkling champagne came the douche of cold

water. General Eisenhower was furious when he heard of Goering's friendly reception at Zell am See and the crestfallen Reichsmarschall found himself whisked away with scant ceremony to a dreary house in Augsburg for interrogation. His medals and his marshal's baton were taken from him, and his vast intake of drugs reduced to eighteen pills a day; he became moody, dispirited and careless of his personal appearance. Later, he was flown to Bad Mondorf, in Luxembourg, where he had to undergo questioning for the greater part of each long, weary day, and finally he arrived at Nuremberg to stand trial before the International Military Tribunal.

For month after month during the summer of 1946 Hermann Goering sat in the dock beside Hess, von Ribbentrop, Keitel and the other defendants, eyes sunken in his head, the grey-blue Luftwaffe uniform hanging in folds on his shrunken frame. Despite his haggard appearance, he was mentally alert and followed the trial closely; during his cross-examination he crossed swords so deftly with the prosecution that the United States Prosecutor, Justice Robert H. Jackson, lost his temper. In his final statement, the former Reichsmarschall said : "I did not want a war, and I did not bring it about. I did everything to prevent it by negotiation. After it had broken out, I did everything to assure victory. . . ." It was his last public speech, and there was no applause.

On 1st October, 1946, Goering rose to hear the verdict of the Tribunal. "There is nothing to be said in mitigation," came the measured tones of the President of the Court, "for Goering was often, indeed almost always, the moving force, second only to his leader. . . . His guilt is unique in its enormity. The record discloses no excuse for this man. The Tribunal finds the defendant Goering guilty on all four counts. . . ."

The sentence was death by hanging, due to be carried out on 16th October, shortly after dawn. At 10.30 p.m. on 15th October a guard peered through the Judas hole in the door of Goering's cell, and saw him apparently asleep, his hands outside the blankets as the regulations demanded. At 10.45 p.m. the same guard again looked into the cell; Goering was silently writhing in agony on his bed. A doctor and chaplain rushed to the cell, but they were too late. Goering had cheated the hangman. The man Hitler had in 1941 named as his successor lay dead, a slight smile of triumph on his lips, the tiny metal potassium cyanide container he had retained on his person for eighteen months discarded on the floor at his side.

For Hermann Wilhelm Goering, the fighter pilot of the First World War whose amazing rise to power brought him many high honours, including the title of Marshal of the Greater German Reich, it can only be said that he possessed great physical courage and an intelligence not readily apparent to those who saw only the bemedalled façade. He was also a skilful hunter and could be an amusing and lively host. But Goering was frequently cunning, deceitful and vindictive, a man given to wild boasting—"My bombers will darken the sky over London!"—and fits of childish temper. He was blinded by the vanity that destroyed his career; his craving for riches became such an obsession that even personal ambition ceased to be of any importance. He sought a life of luxury, and having achieved untold wealth, loved it not wisely but too well, to the exclusion of responsibility, the Nazi Party and all else. He ransacked the art museums of Europe while German military aviation fell in flames. The organisation and administration of the Luftwaffe paid a bitter price for his indolence.

It was all over. The swastika flags had been torn down, the blood-red Nazi banners lay trampled in the dust. The crematorium chimneys of Dachau and Buchenwald would smoke no more; the shouts of "Sieg Heil!" had thundered from the great Nuremberg stadium for the last time. The Second World War had lasted five years, eight months and seven days, and in that time millions of people had been killed, including 60,000 British and at least 600,000 German civilians. The Allies had dropped 1,996,000 tons of bombs on Germany, destroying four million houses, crippling all communications and laying the whole country in ruins, at a cost of 22,000 British and 18,500 United States aircraft.

Between 1st September, 1939, and 8th May, 1945, the Luftwaffe lost about 94,500 aircraft of all types, including 38,900 fighters, 9,800 night fighters and 21,800 bombers. During the same period, 138,596 officers and men of the Luftwaffe were killed in action, and 156,132 posted as missing, believed killed. Their graves lay scattered from Norway to Greece, in Russia and the Western Desert, the final resting places of men who had fought well and often died with great courage, but in vain. They had trusted Adolf Hitler and the Nazi Party with their lives, and been granted an early death as their one reward.

The massive figure of Hermann Goering must inevitably dominate any study of the Luftwaffe, and it is not difficult to visualise him manipulating German air power with clumsy fingers while Udet, Jeschonnek and the other subordinates scurried hither and thither trying to circumvent or fulfil his instructions. This is not an untrue picture of the Luftwaffe at war, as we have seen. But it must be remembered that Goering was no magician. He could not conjure up an air force out of nothing; yet that is precisely what many Germans would have us believe happened in 1933. Goering waved his wand, and presto!—the mighty Luftwaffe appeared, already powerful and poised for the conquest of Europe.

In 1918, German air power had been totally destroyed; the Treaty of Versailles allowed the Reich only 140 aircraft, for commercial use. But long before Hitler became Chancellor of Germany, General von Seeckt of the Reichswehr was scheming to infuse the spark of life into another German Air Force, and the aircraft industrialists were seizing the opportunity to produce bombers and fighters again. Between 1930 and 1939 they willingly designed the modern aircraft Hitler needed to go to war, and allowed Goering to take the credit for their hard work behind the scenes. The Luftwaffe in defeat was another matter. Hitler was blamed for plunging Germany into war, and Goering was blamed for the disintegration of German air power; only the industrialists were apparently innocent and able to show unstained hands.

By September, 1939, the German aircraft industry had produced some 4,300 machines, the tools to be wielded, admittedly often with great crudity, by Goering and his subordinates. Udet, the playboy general who could not stand the pace; Jeschonnek, the inevitable yes-man; and Milch, with his burning ambition : these were the pawns moved by Goering to retain his throne. But it should never be forgotten that he became a powerful air leader only because Messerschmitt, Junkers, Heinkel and the other German aircraft industrialists created the weapons for him to use. The right of every aircraft designer and airman to the freedom of a peaceful sky was abused in Germany during that golden age of aviation before the Second World War, and the youth of Europe sacrificed in the vain attempt to prove that might is right.

The swift rise of Hitler's Luftwaffe is a lesson to the peace-loving, but so often apathetic, peoples of the modern world; the downfall of that Luftwaffe is a warning to any great power nurturing wings intent on future war. The contemplation of a nuclear war now seems so horrifying that the thought of another war restricted to so-called conventional weapons has become more bearable, almost acceptable. But this is an illusion. Total war in 1939 did not have the same meaning as total war in 1945; the razing of Warsaw and Rotterdam served the death sentence on Hamburg, Berlin and Dresden. When the first gun opens fire, and the first bomb begins to fall, human suffering extends its boundaries; agony finds endless possibilities; pain refuses to be administered by the spoonful, like a bitter medicine. "War," said the American General Sherman, "is hell." A simple statement of fact; but easily forgotten in time of peace.

The watchwords for peace remain : strength and determination. The strength to deter any potential aggressor; the determination that the carnage of two world wars must never be repeated again.

BIBLIOGRAPHY

BARTZ, Karl, *Swastika in the Air* (Kimber, 1956)

BAUMBACH, Werner, *Broken Swastika* (Robert Hale, 1949)

BULLOCK, Alan, *Hitler* (Odhams, 1952)

CAIDIN, Martin, *The Night Hamburg Died* (Ballantine, 1960)

CLOSTERMANN, PIERRE, *The Big Show* (Chatto & Windus, 1951)

COLLIER, Richard, *The Sands of Dunkirk* (Collins, 1961)

CONRADIS, Heinz, *Design for Flight* (Macdonald, 1960)

DORNBERGER, Walter, *V.2* (Hurst & Blackett, 1954)

FREIDEN AND RICHARDSON (Editors), *The Fatal Decisions* (Michael Joseph, 1956)

FRISCHAUER, Willi, *The Rise and Fall of Hermann Goering* (Odhams, 1950)

GALLAND, Adolf, *The First and the Last* (Methuen, 1955)

GREEN, William, *Famous Fighters of the Second World War* (Macdonald, 1957)

GREEN, William, *Famous Bombers of the Second World War* (Macdonald, 1959)

HARRIS, Arthur T., *Bomber Offensive* (Collins, 1947)

HEINKEL, Ernst, *He 1000* (Hutchinson, 1956)

HERLIN, Hans, *Udet* (Macdonald, 1960)

IMMELMANN, Franz, *Immelmann—The Eagle of Lille* (Hamilton, 1935)

IRVING, David, *The Destruction of Dresden* (Kimber, 1963)

MANVELL AND FRANKEL, *Goering* (Heinemann, 1962). -

McKEE, Alexander, *Strike from the Sky* (Souvenir Press, 1960)

McKEE, Alexander, *The Friendless Sky* (Souvenir Press, 1962)

NIELSEN, Thor, *The Zeppelin Story* (Wingate, 1955)

NOWARRA AND BROWN, *Richthofen and the Flying Circus* (Harleyford, 1958)

OUGHTON, Frederick, *The Aces* (Spearman, 1961)

REITSCH, Hanna, *The Sky My Kingdom* (Bodley Head, 1955)

REYNOLDS, Quentin, *They Fought for the Sky* (Cassell, 1958)

ROBERTSON, Terence, *Channel Dash* (Evans, 1957)

RUMPF, Hans, *The Bombing of Germany* (Muller, 1963)

RYAN, Cornelius, *The Longest Day* (Simon & Schuster, 1959)

SHIRER, William L., *The Rise and Fall of the Third Reich* (Secker & Warburg, 1962)

SPENCER, John H., *Battle for Crete* (Heinemann, 1962)

TAYLOR, Telford, *The March of Conquest* (Hulton, 1959)

THETFORD AND RIDING, *Aircraft of the 1914-1918 War* (Harleyford, 1954)

TREVOR-ROPER, H. R., *The Last Days of Hitler* (Macmillan, 1947)

VAETH, J. G., *Graf Zeppelin* (Muller, 1959)

WOOD AND DEMPSTER, *The Narrow Margin* (Hutchinson, 1961)

WYKEHAM, Peter, *Fighter Command* (Putnam, 1960)

YOUNG, Desmond, *Rommel* (Collins, 1950)

ZIEGLER, Mano, *Rocket Fighter* (Macdonald, 1963)

INDEX